The Cincinnati Arch

Learning from Nature in the City

The Cincinnati Arch

Learning from Nature in the City

JOHN TALLMADGE

The University of Georgia Press

Athens & London

Published by the University of Georgia Press
Athens, Georgia 30602
© 2004 by John Tallmadge
All rights reserved
Designed by Sandra Strother Hudson
Set in 10 on 14 Minion with Bickham display
Printed and bound by Maple-Vail
The paper in this book meets the guidelines for permanence
and durability of the Committee on Production Guidelines
for Book Longevity of the Council on Library Resources.

Printed in the United States of America
08 07 06 05 04 C 5 4 3 2 1
08 07 06 05 04 P 5 4 3 2 1

Library of Congress Cataloging-in-Publication Data
Tallmadge, John.
The Cincinnati Arch : learning from nature in the city /
John Tallmadge.
     p. cm.
Includes bibliographical references.
ISBN 0-8203-2676-3 (hardcover : alk. paper) — ISBN 0-8203-2690-9
(pbk. : alk. paper)
1. Urban ecology. 2. Human ecology. 3. Nature and civilization.
I. Title.
HT241.T35 2004
307.76—dc22
2004010510

British Library Cataloging-in-Publication Data available

FOR PAM AND ROSALIND AND ELIZABETH

CONTENTS

ACKNOWLEDGMENTS

This book is the fruit of a long journey, during which I have been blessed with many helpers and companions. A bow of thanks to my fellow pilgrims in the company of nature writers: to Alison Deming, Richard Nelson, Robert Michael Pyle, Scott Sanders, and Ann Zwinger for constant encouragement and vigorous testimonials; to John Elder for a lifetime of friendship, inspiration, and literary guidance; to Parker Huber for creating wonderful communities at Glen Brook and Crestone; to Mark Tredinnick for bringing my work to Australia. I am grateful to the Orion Society for providing opportunities for dialogue and inspiration at national conferences and John Hay Award colloquia, where honorees E. O. Wilson and Gary Snyder offered wisdom and encouragement at key points in the journey. Thanks to Mary Evelyn Tucker for the opportunity to share ideas at the Forum on Religion and Ecology at Harvard and to conduct a memorial for Thoreau at his cabin site on Walden Pond. Thanks also to Tom Butler and the staff of *Wild Earth* for inspiring conversations. I am grateful to Jonathan Cobb for his early support and editorial wisdom. Special thanks to my agent, Lynn Whittaker, who combined the virtues of editor, cheerleader, and business manager without losing her sense of humor, and to Christa Frangiamore and her colleagues at the University of Georgia Press, including the outside readers, for their help in the final stages of labor.

Many of these chapters grew out of talks, presentations, or articles. I am grateful to the Association for the Study of Literature and Environment for the opportunity to present at national conferences in Kalamazoo, Flagstaff, and Boston. Special thanks to ASLE colleagues Mike Branch, Ian Marshall, and Terrell Dixon for supporting this work. A bow of gratitude to Mary-Powel Thomas for bringing my writing to *Audubon*, and to Jennifer Sahn and Aina Barten for bringing it to *Orion*. Thanks to John Knott for publishing my "Resistance to Urban Nature" in the *Michigan Quarterly Review* 40 (1) (Winter 1991); to Parker Huber and Deb Mackey for publication opportunities in *Writing Nature* and *Whole*

Terrain respectively; and to Christian McEwen for commissioning an early version of chapter six for *The Alphabet of the Trees.* Thanks to everyone who invited me to speak or teach, particularly Mary Braun of the Wisconsin Academy of Arts and Sciences, Bob Burkholder of Penn State University, John Elder of Middlebury College, Joyce Gottron and Mike Moutoux of the Environmental Education Council of Ohio, Laurina Lyle of Austin Peay State University, Randall Roorda of the University of Kentucky, Trudelle Thomas of Xavier University, Jeff Thomson of Chatham College, and Jerry Waxman of Santa Rosa Junior College.

I am grateful to members of the Union Institute and University community for their support, especially to the faculty and administration of the Graduate College for a 1998 research sabbatical, during which I was able to begin composition. Thanks to learners and colleagues who lent their expertise and companionship, especially to Renée Roberts for her studies of time and the literary imagination; to Rick Van de Poll for expert forestry and natural history work; to John Miles, Susan Morgan, and Jim Kravitz for encouraging walks and talks; to Fred Taylor for inspiration and wisdom on the teacher's path; to Joe Meeker and the Dante seminar for keeping my heart in the comic mode and my eye fixed on paradise; to Ed Grumbine, Tom Fleischner, and members of the Escalante seminar for unforgettable adventures in the canyon country; and to members of the Urban Nature seminar for trying these ideas on for size.

I am especially grateful to friends and colleagues from Cincinnati who lent their wisdom and support to the project, particularly to Stan Hedeen of Xavier University and the Mill Creek Yacht Club for riparian, hydrological, limnological, ornithological, and industrial insights; to Robin Corathers and the Mill Creek Restoration Project for turning dreams into deeds; to Bill Stiver and Rick Sowash for inspiring hikes; and to members of the Langdon Club for keeping the lamp of natural history lighted.

But deepest and most profound thanks, with love, to my wife, Pam, and my daughters, Rosalind and Elizabeth. You made us a family. You showed me the way.

The Cincinnati Arch is the name geologists give to a huge fold in the earth's crust that stretches from central Kentucky across the Ohio River through Cincinnati and into southwestern Ohio. The city is located at its crest. Approaching from any quarter, you would not notice the arch. The layers of Ordovician limestone exposed along road cuts appear horizontal to the casual eye. But as you drive east or west, the surface rock grows younger, revealing the geometry of an invisible landscape.

The arch is also a classic architectural form that creates elevation by using the downward pull of gravity. The stones in the legs are kept from falling toward each other by the rigid wedge of the keystone. By holding space and weight in dynamic tension, arches create the feeling of aspiration and serenity in Gothic cathedrals.

A journey or pilgrimage also follows the parabolic curve of an arch: it swings out from a known point and returns symmetrically to a point on the same line or plane, but farther along. For this reason, ancient philosophers chose the arch as a symbol for the process of interpretation. That is why teaching stories, such as those of Jesus or Buddha, are known as parables.

Into the Pits

I never wanted to live in Cincinnati, Ohio. What wilderness lover would ever dream of settling deep in the Rust Belt astride polluted rivers? One might long for places like Bozeman or Spokane, hard by Yellowstone or the Bitterroots, but certainly not Cincinnati, a town known less for forests or lakes than for jet engines, floating soap, and indigestible chili. When Pam and I drove out of Minnesota, the corn was already head high and steaming, three hundred miles from the Boundary Waters and getting hotter by the minute. I was a fired assistant professor heading into administration. She was an ex-day-care director who had never lived outside her home state. Married less than two years, we had a baby on the way and no friends or family anywhere in Ohio. My career as a teacher of literature and wilderness lay in a smoking ruin. My new job would be associate dean of a graduate school with no campus, no courses, and no resident students.

They say life begins at forty. I had always thought that meant you arrived at a place from which you could finally deal. The powers and services of the world would be at your disposal, and you could actually run your life. Turning forty meant entry into the "dominant generation." I had never imagined that it could also mean starting a whole new life, and not by choice—as if you had come home one evening to find your house in flames.

Being fired concentrates the mind. You are discharged, like a shot from a gun. You are baked in a kiln until you become hard, impervious, and brittle. Your life is refined like metal. Your dreams are torched, like a forest struck by lightning. Choose any image; the feelings are always the same: shock and humiliation, followed by outrage and depression. But disaster also clarifies your relationships. Old friends suddenly turn away as if pain were contagious, while others unexpectedly come forward with full hands. Grief and grace break over you like waves. Meanwhile you claw your way back toward self-confidence through a grinding job search to which colleagues respond with a mixture of pity and envy.

3

But why complain? I had lost the position but still had the girl. I had found a new job that would pay the bills. I was still in the academic profession, albeit clinging by my fingertips. We were moving to a city that was said to be "livable." Indeed, from a rational viewpoint, we had done pretty well. The only things missing were teaching and wilderness. But they had been the foundations of my life.

Thoreau had declared that in wildness was the preservation of the world, and his words had never seemed more poignant or true than they did that day as we raced along under the hot, blue dome of the prairie sky. Thoreau had been thinking not only about the green world of nature but also about the corrupt and disappointing world of society, which his imagination could never escape. In the Maine woods, he had found a wildness that dazzled his mind and senses yet resisted quick formulations and easy love. On the burnt-over slopes of Mount Katahdin, even his own body had appeared monstrous and alien. Back in Concord, he had worked out a lifelong practice of walking and writing, feeding on the modest, local wildness like a fox and leaving his journals for a scent mark. It was his antidote to the quiet desperation of civilized life that enabled the larger evils of war, slavery, and rapacious trade.

For John Muir, another of my heroes, wildness and wilderness were matters of revelation. Reared by a Calvinist father who equated hard labor with virtue, Muir had turned to nature for relief and had found in Yosemite's meadows and peaks a landscape charged with divinity. He had practiced natural history like a sacrament, celebrating the crafts-manship that informed every outcrop and grove along all four hundred miles of the "Range of Light." Wilderness was a paradise where human beings could reclaim the original grace they had lost through civilized living. "This is true freedom," he had proclaimed, "a good practical sort of immortality."

For ecologist Aldo Leopold, who had taught me to love the prairie, wilderness came down to matters of history and citizenship. Trained as a Pinchot conservationist at Yale, he had first thought of wilderness as a hunter's paradise, but years of fieldwork convinced him that it was really a reservoir of genetic and ecological wisdom. At the University of

Wisconsin, Leopold had developed a practice of personal ecology, restoring the prairie flora on his worn-out farm while teaching his students how to read the landscape. He had come to believe that ethical principles should govern our relations with land as well as with people. The courts of evolution would judge us by our acts. To survive we would have to start treating land as a community rather than as a commodity to be exploited.

Ideas such as these had also inspired the Wilderness Act of 1964 and the entry of groups like the Sierra Club into the political mainstream, just as the 1960s arrived with their celebration of all things natural, wild, and free. Suddenly wilderness was hip. My friends and I had taken off to the woods with our foam pads and mummy bags, toting thin volumes of Edward Abbey or Gary Snyder to sniff under the trees for their tang of anarchic freedom. I especially liked Snyder's combination of wild adventure with natural history, politics, and religion. He had spent ten years in Japan studying Zen before settling in the Sierra foothills to raise a family and develop a style of life that he would eventually call "the practice of the wild." Into this paradoxical phrase were compressed the classic ideas of Thoreau, Muir, and Leopold, along with Zen notions of practice as an attentive performance of daily work combined with sitting and meditation. The goal was serenity, reconciliation, and insight achieved through harmony with land and community. Snyder's practice of the wild also drew on the "old ways" of North American tribes, whose relations with land were intimate, personal, intensely local, and deeply spiritualized. He envisioned a "future primitivism" that would combine the best wisdom of modern and native cultures.

Snyder's view of wildness had offered the most promise of all. I had relied on it for a bearing during many classes and journeys. But now, in the August heat, I felt it slipping out of my grasp. The interstate flung us toward city life through endless fields whose rich, healthy-looking green only affirmed our culture's addiction to oil and a cash economy. Snyder's view still shared the bedrock concept of wilderness as something apart from civilization, a place where humans were not in charge and their imagery did not dominate the scene. American environmental thought had projected this sense of apartness into the concept of pristine water-sheds preserved by law or visions of an Edenic North America that had endured for millennia before the incursion of Europeans. Nature was "other," and wilderness was "wholly other." Therein lay its sacred quality. To practice the wild meant cultivating a relationship to the Other. One could expect the same mystery and reciprocity that philosopher Martin Buber had described in I-Thou relationships, which he said were the foundations of our spiritual life.

All this had seemed fine enough when applied to places like the Wind River Range or the Boundary Waters, but how could it help me in Cincinnati? Every life needs a plan. Mine had been to combine class-room teaching with wilderness travel, thereby offering the students two kinds of adventure while satisfying my own craving for wildness, re-moteness, and freedom. That had worked for more than ten years. What now? During the interview, I had looked out the window over tar-roofed slums toward the rail yards, meat-packing plants, and chemical factories lining the Mill Creek valley. I had told myself that a dollar from Union Institute would buy as much beer and cheese as a dollar from Carleton College. With a baby on the way, that dollar was top priority. But my new boss had also told me a story about her father. When she announced that she was going into administration, he had drawn himself up and declared in a rich Mississippi voice, "Honey, I don't know why you would want to be a dean. Everyone knows there are only three reasons for the academic life, and they are June, July, and August!"

Day was departing as our road turned east, and the brown air over Peoria, Illinois, showed that people had left work and were driving home, released from their labors while I was still battling the journey and the self-pity of exile. We turned off the highway, found a motel, and pulled in under the glare of mercury-vapor lights. Along the yellow brick walls, shrubs were growing in beds of crushed rock. Cicadas rasped beneath throbbing air conditioners. We walked inside, feeling the still air part like curtains. The windows of our room were sealed. As we lay trying to sleep, the noise of machines and insects merged with the roar of the highway into a mindless, compulsive drone. It was the sound of pure appetite, of hunger run amok, of a fallen world from which there could be no escape.

All night I slept fitfully, tossing with city dreams. I was back in East Orange, New Jersey, where my family was moving out of our old Victorian house. We were driving through mazes of slums, down narrow streets strewn with glass and lined with dying trees. Dark, faceless people were crossing before and behind us. The roofs of tenements stood out in jagged silhouette before changing, inexplicably, into pointed firs that lined the long, straight, narrow road to the deep North.

I woke to the roar of semis on the interstate. Pam drove as the sun rose, a red eye burning through acrid haze. My dreams clung like damp silk, thick with childhood memories: abandoned cars rusting in backyards, vacant lots where we played baseball among piles of old paving, the nasty burrs that snagged our socks, my mother's nylons hanging in tatters from the clothesline after a shift in the wind brought clouds of sulfur dioxide, all on a day as blue as a Dutch girl's eyes.

No wonder the wilderness writers hated cities. Ever since the Neolithic, cities had been causing environmental problems. They fostered the growth of large populations dependent on external sources of food. They disrupted the water cycle, diverting streams, promoting irrigation that pickled the soil, and sending all their wastes downstream. They concentrated poverty and disease. The city where I grew up had gone on for miles, a dingy, haphazard growth of old brick, asphalt, clapboard, and glass that heaved and stirred under a smeared, anonymous sky. Its prevailing colors were rust and gray; its scent was a blend of dust, vinegar, and metallic sweat. You got used to these things and so failed to notice them, like the scent of your own clothes, until one day after a rain, when the sun came out on the hard corners of buildings and the washed streets breathed for a brief hour the purifying scent of distilled water. Then I knew that water always begins its earthly life by falling from heaven and yet persists in its clean, original grace only in wilderness, where it feeds and sustains all things.

The city, in contrast, seemed to be sizzling and frying with violent hungers. I saw violence against nature in the wanton disturbance of soils, whole acres scraped bare for construction, the bedrock shattered by dynamite blasts, hills cleft in two for highways, buildings and gardens razed and paved for supermarkets or shopping malls, the debris carted off to be dumped in a wetland as if history, whether human or natural, were only some kind of waste.

The city worked its violence on people, too, cramming them into apartments where they lived stacked like chickens in an egg factory, or forcing them into ghettoes out of fear or poverty, bludgeoning their self-esteem with racism, poor schooling, hard labor—or no labor at all!—while flaunting the impossible dream life of TV, movies, and slick magazines. No doubt some people were better off, with good-paying jobs and well-kept homes in respectable neighborhoods, but they had not really escaped the violence, only internalized it in the manner of slave masters or colonial overlords so that it ate at them from within, forcing them to compete ruthlessly for a "place in the sun" where they could lead lives of quiet desperation estranged from nature.

I remember sensing all this as a boy. The closest wild country was Eagle Rock, a county park you could reach by city bus. I went there once with my Boy Scout patrol, winding through industrial tenements past the Edison plant where electric lights and movies had been invented, until we stopped at the base of improbable basalt cliffs that rose far above the roofs of the houses. We got out and started climbing through tangled woods, past the rock quarry and picnic grounds to a bridle path that led into dry oak forest. The sounds and odors of traffic faded away. A half-mile in, we crossed a stream, hardly a trickle in early May yet still sweet enough to give us a whiff of wildness. Here was water flowing naturally over the ground, untrammeled by pipe or culvert, never treated or soiled by industry. We turned off the path and followed it through the leaf-strewn woods to a flat bend at the base of a small cliff hidden from view. There we constructed a lean-to of dead branches and broke out our lunch of oranges, Fig Newtons, and M&Ms. We felt like African explorers.

Later we walked up and down the stream, testing the steppingstones, looking for crayfish or caddis flies, and pocketing, like good Scouts, any stray bit of litter. Near camp I found a pale balloon with an odd pointy tip. It was wavering in the current, caught on a twig. I speared it with a stick and put it in the bag with the other trash. Years later, when I learned what it was, it seemed like a sort of sign, the white, snakelike tongue of the city itself, wagging in mockery as if to say, "I too am in Arcadia."

This fear and loathing of cities stayed with me for years, even when I was living in places like New Haven or Salt Lake. All across North America, it seemed, our civilization had sought to construe and manage land under the sign of the city, whereas I was always thinking in terms of nature. Once, for example, I came across a dead cat by the side of the road, its carcass half buried in sand. The cat looked completely relaxed, except for its mouth, which was wide open and swarming with maggots. I poked the carcass with a stick and it broke open like a piñata, spilling hundreds of pale, writhing worms. I backed off, overcome by the stench and horrified by the spectacle of unbridled fecundity and desire. Then it struck me that this is how we must appear to the animals! I staggered off thinking of crowds roaring in stadiums, swarming in rush-hour streets, or marching in huge formations—Red Square, Nuremberg, the National Mall—all those insatiable mouths, all that power and desire! They say that the scent of humans is nauseating to a bear.

Or think of maps. Take any state and look for the cities, those yellow, irregular lumps with black and red lines feeding into them. They contrast so vividly with the much larger expanses of white or green that make up the rest of the country. It's clear that everything feeds into cities, which grow outward along the roads that nourish them. Even in flat, schematic representation you can see the resemblance: no tumor wants or even knows how to check itself; it thinks only of present growth and meeting its own needs. How self-absorbed, how inward-looking the city is, infatuated with its own imagery and sure of its rightful place at the center, owning all things and using them as it will.

From inside the city, all this seemed perfectly natural and appropriate; from outside it felt creepy and horrible. Flying from coast to coast after nightfall, I would often look down at the cities gleaming far below. They shone with the same pale light as foxfire on rotting wood. From this angelic height, higher than Everest, they seemed to be smoldering in their own decay. And from still farther out, the eyes of satellites could capture the whole mosaic of pale fire stitched by cities and highways across all of North America, Europe, and Asia, as if the entire planet were slowly beginning to burn.

Cities were decomposers, releasers of energy and greenhouse gasses, consumers of land, soil, and fossil fuel, destroyers of habitat, and degraders of ecosystems. They were not interested in relating to nature on any terms but their own. I had grown to fear the cumulative effects of city life, with its obsessive focus on work, career, and the "good things in life." It was too much like living in a room of mirrors, cut off from any image but your own. Without wildness how could you avoid lapsing into a fatal narcissism? And how could you practice the wild in a place so dominated and bruised by human culture? How could you ever say "Thou" or learn from the Other? How could you ever reach down and touch the earth?

Yet here we were, rushing down the broad highway. *Facilis est descensus Averno:* what is called resignation is only confirmed desperation. And we had a baby on the way! Now "Cincinnati" began to appear on the highway signs east of Indianapolis. Eighty miles, sixty-eight, fifty-two. I expected soon enough to see the cornfields invaded by billboards and tract housing, the city's unmistakable feelers probing the landscape like fungus threads.

Forty-seven, thirty. And then, inexplicably, the land began to change. The taut highway began to pitch and veer. Suddenly woods closed in. We crossed rivers with promising names like "Whitewater," cut through hills of gray, stratified limestone that broke off in scree slopes, just like the Book Cliffs of Utah. Twenty miles. We crossed the Ohio border and turned north along the beltway, now clearly within the city's penumbra yet lacking all outward tokens except for the highway signs with their ironic, enameled green. Instead of losing the woods we seemed to be entering them. Not until we had bent far round to the north did we encounter the subdivisions and shopping malls that marked, unmistakably, the outer reach of the city. It was as if we were circling the rim of a deep well, dreading the plunge. Our point of entry was Interstate 71, which would take us toward the night's hotel and our rented house half-way between the center and the rim.

What would it mean to explore this dark wood and the city inside it? I had long since abandoned all hope of the old life with its luminous practice of teaching and wild journeys. The new life was as faceless to me as our unborn child. None of the nature writers had offered much wisdom for living in cities. Leopold had warned that an ecological education condemned one to live alone in a world of wounds. This would be a journey without a guide, yet not alone, for there was Pam. She had not been carried off by underworld gods but was entering freely, bearing our future. She looked across the seat and smiled, squeezing my hand. Perhaps it was no accident that our approach had been marked by hope's color, living green.

A Space of No Place

For someone used to a campus life with periodic migrations to the wild, working downtown was a weird, exotic prospect. I awoke before dawn, tense and disoriented on our first day in Cincinnati. The vice president had offered me a ride to the office, but faculty life had spoiled me for commuting. Stepping into his car felt like boarding a yacht.

We slid down a ramp into the pulse of interstate traffic and were soon streaming along with thousands of mechanized corpuscles toward the city's heart. The road descended toward the Ohio River in giant steps, cutting through steep limestone strata, then flattening out into residential and industrial neighborhoods on the terraces below. The landscape passed in a blur. I saw the living world as a green smear flecked with the rusty clutter of houses or the sooty buff of concrete walls. The city sucked us in like a great lung, emptying the suburbs. We would give up our work, exchanging time for money, and then be exhaled at day's end to stream back for rest and recharging like obedient cells.

As downtown approached, the world seemed to fade into gray. The road plunged through a final cut and spilled into a maze of skyscrapers and office buildings. We parked in a dingy garage, walked three blocks to an old bank building, and took an elevator to the tenth floor. The vice president showed me into a bare, windowed room with a steel desk, a Rolodex, a telephone, and a stack of documents two and a half feet high. He squeezed my shoulder and gave me a fatherly smile. "We're so glad you're here," he said.

For the next few hours I sat at the desk reading institutional literature and flipping through some of the documents, all program proposals, learning contracts, and dissertations awaiting the dean's review. But my gaze kept straying to the window and the world outside. Past the nearby office buildings, the view soared over tarpaper roofs toward the green, wooded bluffs that rimmed the downtown area. Cincinnati had been built in a natural amphitheater where Mill Creek joined the Ohio River, and the slopes of these bluffs, too steep and unstable for building, provided incongruous but refreshing corridors of wild green. To me on that first day they had as much enchantment and mystery as a prospect of distant mountains. I could see them bending north and west toward Mill Creek, the city's industrial gullet, then away west toward the restored woodlands of Mount Airy Forest, a fourteen-hundred-acre park that was reputed to harbor deer. Beyond rose a fair sky blooming with white cumulus clouds, icons of unassailable wildness, and above these I imagined the pure ultramontane heights of the stratosphere, the aurora borealis, and the deep heavens of starry, never-ending space.

So I drifted and daydreamed like a prisoner in a cell. I felt odd, and slightly giddy, to be sitting at a desk ten stories up in the air, like a climber bivouacked on a big wall. I realized that except for a ten-foot stretch of lawn, my feet had not touched the living earth all day.

Nevertheless, after a week on the job, commuting became routine: I would slip like a kayaker into the pitching flow, buck the jams, curves, and interchanges, haul out in a cheap parking lot on the edge of the slums, and hike a half mile to the office along streets that narrowed and deepened as the buildings rose. Growing up on the outskirts of New York had made "canyons of steel" a familiar sight, but after several years in Utah, that image seemed alien and perverse. This downtown environment struck me as an artificial desert that shared certain qualities with the canyon lands, including an abundance of bare rock and geometric landforms. But here there was no soil to be found, and the only plant life appeared to be thin shade trees and pots of annuals blazing on privileged corners. In Utah the desert had seemed a warm and colorful world of red sandstone enlivened by riparian greens and the blue of a depthless sky. But this man-made desert was overwhelmingly cast in gray: nothing but soot, concrete, asphalt, or dusty stone.

Walking on concrete felt like walking on slickrock, except for one key difference. Concrete was made of silica grains cemented by calcium carbonate, just like the sandstones of Utah. But it was a product of culture rather than nature. People had ground up and baked the local limestone to drive off its water of crystallization, mixed the anhydrous dust with sand and water, and then poured the heavy batter into molds, where it hardened once more into stone. Downtown was full of other mineral surfaces produced by equally strenuous arts: asphalt made by mixing the hot waste tar of oil refineries with pea gravel dredged from nearby rivers; glass made by fusing quartz sand with soda ash; steel wrung from iron ore, limestone, and coal in blast furnaces; aluminum wrenched from clay by potent electrodes. All these had been shaped and assembled into a landscape of hard plane surfaces and right angles designed to shed water, discourage growth, and facilitate the movement of people or machines. And why not? According to New Yorker Fran Lebowitz, the outdoors is what you must pass through to get from your apartment into a taxicab.

Yet to my eye the downtown environment actually blurred the line between inside and outside. People wore the same sleek clothes and thin-soled shoes in offices or out on the street. Potted plants were everywhere. I noticed the same right angles and plane surfaces, the same kinds of electric light. The real difference, if any, seemed to have more to do with elevation and movement. People drifted through the outside environment and came to rest in the air, inside, in the offices where work went on. Like the outdoor space defined by the grid of streets and the planar trajectories of sidewalk and pavement, this indoor space had a cellular regularity: it was made of stacked units as regular and replicable as a crystal lattice. The city itself seemed to have grown up like a coral reef, a rigid, skeletal structure that housed small animal droplets of blood and nerves. By day the great reef hummed and listened, feeding on messages. By night it grew quiet, emptied of life, a waiting husk. To me it seemed oddly placeless, at once frenzied and deracinated—solid, but somehow ephemeral and disconnected from the earth.

Walking to work each day, I passed buildings that were being constructed or demolished. Few of the great towers had stood for a human lifetime. Most, in fact, were not even as old as I was. Few could compare in age with mature forest trees, not even those in the city parks. The indoor spaces of offices seemed even less permanent, designed to be vacated and reoccupied quickly. Anonymity and transience ruled this inner space. People came, set up, and went. At times it felt like camping out—or camping in. People, like space itself, were construed as inter-changeable and replaceable.

This urban space was a cultural artifact that struck me as oddly par-allel to Newton's conception of space. Its most permanent feature ap-peared to be its geometry, which was enshrined in the city plat and recorded in the tax office. Everything else was subject to change—or *ex*change, to be more precise—for commerce was here the governing principle. This downtown space could be filled with anything, according to the vicissitudes of ownership, fashion, or the markets, because it was essentially no more than an empty geometric form. It was nothing more nor less than *lots*. The soaring towers looked grand and imposing, but they could be gone in a decade or a year, leaving no trace of the lives and works that had filled them. The location on which they had stood would be reoccupied, like a slate wiped clean and inscribed by some alien hand. So the gray world of downtown, for all its glitter and energy, began to seem more and more ghostly, a space of no place where history could evaporate in a moment.

In the wilderness, organisms and landscapes accumulate history, thereby acquiring a distinctiveness that impresses the beholder as char-acter. A gnarled tree is expressive because it wears its history: each forked branch denotes a winter storm, each annual ring measures warmth and rainfall. It's the same with a forest mosaic or a wrinkled face: each mark is earned, embodying a story revealed to the seeing eye. For growth re-quires that an organism be broken again and again in order to learn. And every wild creature and wilderness landscape bears the marks of its history. That is one reason, I think, that we seek them out. We admire wild creatures for their integrity, and we are drawn to places because of their character. For a place is a space with a story, and the feeling of power comes from this sense of veiled meaning, an intuition of how this place's story might intersect with our own.

In the wilderness, creatures inhabit their places—a home range, a niche in a canyon wall, a watershed, or a hillside. They grow into and out of their places. So wilderness space is profoundly historical, all place. But this urban space dissolves place into the liquid flow of exchange. There are no real places downtown, only addresses.

Living with Urban Time

Meanwhile, inside, the work went on. Ten stories up, in a small quadrangular cell, I spent the day reviewing documents and taking calls. I dealt with texts and voices, regulations, paper, and messages distilled from electromagnetic signals. The day went by in a stream of brief but intense encounters that demanded shrewd judgment and quick decisions. You never knew what was going to land on your desk or leap out of the phone and grab you by the throat. I dealt with people—for what was administration but "people problems"?—yet I met very few of these problems in person.

This absence gave rise to an odd sense of disembodied action, of relationships without scent that sprang up and blew away in the twinkling of an eye. It was the antithesis of the ecological complexity that I had come to appreciate while living on the prairies of Minnesota, with their old plant communities and deeply composted soils. These momentary and evanescent relations had little connection to the fertile, antientropic cycles of biological time, yet that was exactly what the organization desired. Its goal was to keep up the flow of business, and a quick solution meant one less thing to deal with. So the days passed in a blur, as indistinct as the scenery I drove past each morning. I kept my head down, learned the job, and pushed as much paper as possible, for I had a wife and incipient child to support. By 5:00 p.m. my brain had turned to oatmeal, and my eyes felt like two fried eggs.

After a few weeks, it began to bother me that I could not remember what had filled up my days. How could one work so hard and not remember the details? In the wilderness, each day had seemed chock-full of true and beautiful moments that still glowed in the mind after a decade or more. What was this urban time that ran through the memory like so much sand?

On the John Muir Trail, deep in the High Sierra, I had experienced a wilderness time marked by earth's diurnal rhythms and the body's cycles of hunger, exertion, and rest. This alert, interactive time was punctuated by moments of I-Thou encounter when the personhood of some other being in nature—a rock, a tree, an animal—stood forth in mind-arresting clarity. In the mountains and deserts of Utah, I had experienced geological time as a series of epic gestures inscribed on a canvas of rock and space. Sublime geometries marched through formations, landscapes, and eons, inspiring a tragic sense of life. In Minnesota, with its fire-dependent prairies and forests, its severe winters, and its rivers of migrating birds, I had discovered the cyclic richness and fertility of biological time.

In the natural world, time was concrete, attached to place, inscribed and embodied in organisms and in the land. It was cyclical, connected to growth and transformation. It accumulated in creatures and landscapes, which, as self-organizing systems, learned from their history. As such it conferred individuation and identity. Promoting survival, it proved comedic and redemptive.

But this urban time was altogether different. Superficially cyclical, at least in terms of the daily commute, it was, underneath, as abstract and fragmented as urban space. It was indoor time, cut off from the diurnal rhythms of sun, moon, and stars, not to mention the visceral experience of weather and season change. It was regulated by clocks and calendars rather than by the movements of constellations, the blooming of plants, or the passage of migrating birds.

This mechanical time was easy to measure and quantify; moreover, it could be broken into smaller and smaller units that could then be clustered and recombined to suit the business at hand. Urban time thus correlated perfectly with the fragmented and momentary relationships that I was experiencing as an administrator. It was time made for work, and no mistake. Before long I found myself looking at the clock more often than at the sky out the window.

Scholars believe that the mechanical clock was invented in Europe near the end of the twelfth century by monks of the Benedictine order, for whom time and salvation were closely linked. The Benedictine Rule prescribed a life of prayer, song, and work strictly organized according to nine daily periods in the hope that living with studied deliberation on earth would assure salvation in the life to come. Control time, and you controlled the soul's condition, thus assuring its final destination. A Benedictine monastery subjugated every aspect of a monk's life to the overriding goal of saving his soul according to the official program. It was thus a prototype for what philosopher Erving Goffman would call a "total institution," more secular examples of which include hospitals, prisons, and concentration camps.

The Benedictines' program of prayer and work combined with their aptitude for routine made their monasteries some of the most productive industrial enterprises of the High Middle Ages. At first they had used water clocks and hourglasses to mark the time, but these did not work well in the cold climates of northern Europe. Mechanical clocks, on the other hand, would not freeze and kept time with bracing regularity. It was not long before they escaped the cloister. Perhaps because the Benedictines were so deeply enmeshed in local economies, their invention spread quickly into the secular world.

By the end of the twelfth century, clock towers had sprung up in towns all over Europe. Business and government leaders were quick to recognize the clock's potential for organizing and controlling both people and work, thereby increasing productivity. The clock also allowed secular interests to siphon power away from the church. So the new device quickly became both ubiquitous and indispensable, extending its dominion into every aspect of life until, in our day, mechanical time seems altogether natural, more familiar even than the movements of the sun, the moon, or the stars.

I soon began to rely on the clock myself, in order to cope with the challenges of administration. The work poured into my office like a stream in flood, and I was soon, as they say, swimming up to my eyeballs, feeling swamped, or trying to sweep back the tide. Choose your metaphor; liquidity would soon make sense in terms of urban time's effects on both nature and the soul. Meanwhile I had to ration attention and develop a set of efficient, dependable moves, like someone working on an assembly line. Granted, this was headwork, a blend of analysis, judgment, and diplomacy, but it still felt like a race against the clock.

What was I chasing, and where was the finish line? Urban time, with its bland, Newtonian vistas, offered no vestige of a beginning, no prospect of an end. Its abstraction and divisibility allowed me to break work down into bite-sized tasks, but this efficiency came at a cost. The day became a sequence of events with no plot, no coherence, no truth coalescing from the stream of events. Appropriate for a space of no place, this was a time of no story.

Yet I embraced it for survival. In this gray world, it became clear that time was money. Like urban time, money appeared to be something abstract and divisible, made of interchangeable units capable of endless permutations. It was liquid, transferable, and portable, with no intrinsic identity apart from its capacity for attaching to anything as the market demanded. Such fluidity was exactly the point, of course; how else could it have served as a medium of exchange? Money appeared to possess a vague, unlocalized power and a magical ability to turn one thing into another: a tract of woods, for instance, into newsprint or real estate and thence into almost anything—opera tickets, say, a semester of college, food, clothing, a month of phone calls, a house in the suburbs. What was money but some kind of universal solvent, capable of reducing the most exotic differences to a common denominator of exchange, eroding all but the most stubborn identity with its promise of protean flexibility and endless opportunity. How ironic, then, that money, whose power lies in dissolution, should present itself in this downtown world as some kind of absolute, claiming to confer identity, power, autonomy, and freedom and thereby compelling worship and adoration. The Benedictines had sought to harness time and organize work in order to save souls, and their intuition was sound, for the only thing that confers true identity is the history that each sentient being accumulates and expresses. But money, which has no body, no history, and therefore no soul, can provide no real identity. It enables you to do things, of course, but what things will you do?

An identity rests in history, and soul grows out of what we learn from that history. In one sense, we all work for money, for life support and the wherewithal to do things. In doing, we act: we consume, we experience. But in this "vale of soul-making," as Keats called our world, life's story remains a mere diary unless we learn. It's learning that gives birth to story and to soul. Work, said Gibran, is your love made visible. Working for money draws our love toward a dream of action and possibility and the magical power to dissolve and transform all things. Working for work—and how many do!—substitutes action for experience and busyness for learning. In both cases, soul making is endlessly deferred. Both can go on forever, abetted by the sand-grain fragmentation and narrative anomie of urban time.

The Green Shadow

Perhaps I realized all this, deep down, but in those first days I was just glad to be working and solving what John Muir had called "the bread problem." I harnessed myself willingly to the clock and fed off the glamour and energy of downtown, with its soaring facades and crowds of smartly dressed young professionals cruising the sidewalks at noon. All this seemed very new after two decades of campus life, where students were always talking about the "real world" of bright lights, big cities, and good-paying jobs. Perhaps I had finally graduated. It seemed perfectly natural at the time to commence this new life with an explorer's eye, as if I had landed on some exotic shore, alert for life and the hidden links that sustained it.

But add the nostalgia and sensitivities of exile, and you have a formula for bitter dreams. It hardly seemed possible to imagine a practice of the wild for anyone living in the city, so far from places like Utah or Minnesota, where sublime wilderness flourished less than a day's drive away. This gray world of Cincinnati seemed barren of any life expression other than our own. I spent the day surrounded by human imagery, deluged with human concerns: "us and our stuff just covering the ground," as Gary Snyder had put it. But there were nobler ends in view—money, family, survival—so I put my head down and pushed the green world to the edges of the frame.

For a while it felt almost heroic, a kind of sacrifice. And deaning also brought an adrenaline rush as we managed one crisis after another, "putting out fires" as the vice president called it. This was risky, strenuous work, but fast and rewarding, like shooting rapids. It got you in shape. Every call, even a rabid complaint, felt curiously affirming. People needed decisions and solutions in order to move ahead. No matter that these contacts were brief and evanescent, mere blips on the screen, sand grains swept past by the flux of urban time. Their energy and intensity were intoxicating, even pleasurable at times. Eventually I felt myself beginning to acclimate, to accept perpetual crisis as normal. It meant not having to deal with anything else. Adrenaline became the drug of choice, and work a form of medication that helped me to ignore the heartache of separation from wilderness and the classroom.

Yet whenever the work let up, I felt let down, welcoming rest yet craving affirmation. At times I was seized by a sudden fear of everything I had shoved aside: the green world, my practice of teaching in the wild, the ongoing life's work of soul making. Human beings, I realized, were self-domesticating animals who managed themselves like crops or livestock to produce surpluses that somebody else could use. A barn, a factory, an office building all furnished environments controlled to optimize work, but American thinkers, by and large, had imagined wilderness as the antithesis of such domestication.

Thoreau, for instance, had celebrated wildness as something creative, original, and without bounds, something marginal, on the edge, outside the norm, and thus perceived as a threat to order, custom, and established interests. Wilderness came to embrace, in his eyes, the romantic virtues of self-reliance, artistic genius, and revolutionary action in service to an ideal. Projected onto the green world, this sense of wildness came to rest in two kinds of space: the marginal and discounted parts of Concord where he fished or walked or inspected snowstorms and the sublime fastnesses of the remote frontier west of the Mississippi or up north in the Maine Woods. Both kinds of space offered release from the quiet desperation that he had observed in village and city life. How, he wondered, could human nature grow its finer fruits if a person had no time to be anything but a machine?

I had begun to feel increasingly mechanized myself as days went by with my mind flipping back and forth from the telephone to the clock to the document on the desk. Sometimes my attention would skip, like a flung stone, and spin out toward the green hills beyond the next office building. All at once, I'd be dreaming of white light, clean stone, and thread cascades somewhere high in the Wind River Range or the Sierra Nevada, where deep purple *Polemonium* bloomed on rocky shelves and the air was so pure you almost felt it would ring if struck with a hammer.

I had been to places like that. I could go there again. Beyond Cincinnati's smudged horizons lived the dream of a wilderness preserved by its own remoteness. I could take comfort in just knowing it was there. Cities had been invented for trade and administration, but now they seemed only a vaster form of total institution. No wonder poets and philosophers from the time of the Greeks had celebrated life in a pastoral landscape poised between city and wilderness. Perhaps that's one reason our education pioneers established their work on a campus (Latin for "meadow" or "open field") as they sought to instill virtue and knowledge by means of literature. Certainly it had led me to imagine the academy as an ideal base camp for launching a practice of the wild.

And now, with the teaching life out of reach, these wilderness dreams took on a burning clarity. Their color and force seemed almost hormonal, oddly and even perversely akin to the adrenaline rush of deaning. Apparently both wilderness fantasy and fast-lane executive action could bolster one's sense of identity. One afternoon it occurred to me that these green dreams with their tang of wild remoteness were bound up inextricably with city life. The wilderness was the city's green shadow: without the soullessness of urban time and space, its virtue and meaning would evaporate.

I realized then how comforting it had always been to think of myself as a wilderness person. Projecting my loyalty out toward remote and beautiful places such as Yellowstone or Yosemite numbed the ache of placeless space and storyless time. It made the mad dash of commuting and the trek through artificial deserts seem bearable, even normal. Apparently wilderness could also become an addiction.

What could it really mean, then, to practice the wild? Was it merely the old American dodge of escapism, lighting out for the territory when things got rough or confused? The wilderness dream did have the effect of displacing attention from the near at hand, as if the solution to all our pain and desire could be found *out there*. And yet, even as I fed on these fantasies, especially while walking to work, I became aware of another sort of green shadow. Here and there, moss was growing in pavement cracks. In the chinks between curb and sidewalk, small parasols of ragweed or dandelion had opened from hidden roots. Grasses bristled among paving bricks in alleys. A fringe of algae scummed a rooftop pool. The gray world required continual maintenance of its sterile, Newtonian order, and whenever human control lapsed, other life forms rushed in to take advantage. They were not pure, perhaps, and certainly not pastoral, but they were real organisms. They were not a dream. They pursued their ultimate concerns in blithe disregard of our own. Something vital and wild persisted in the very heart of the city, where one would have least expected to find it.

Perhaps some wisdom lay hidden as well, though it seemed crazy to think of learning from nature in the city. To give up the cloying projections of pastoral would require a devotion altogether different from asceticism or adventure. I had no idea what such a practice would look like or how it could ever be reconciled with work. And I had no time to figure it out, for Pam had come to term and was about to give birth.

The Dead of Winter

When we arrived in Cincinnati, Pam was seven months pregnant. We had been married on the summer solstice a year before, exactly six months after the college had given me notice. I had spent the spring grinding through doomed appeals as our wedding plans germinated and blossomed. The night of our marriage was full of portents: a planetary conjunction, green tornado skies over Minnesota, a room full of friends feasting and dancing. We honeymooned in Glacier Bay. And eight months later, in the dead of winter, we stopped using birth control.

I admit, it was hardly a rational move. We knew many couples who had chosen not to have children for reasons they were very willing to share. Start with the environmental crisis, whose ultimate cause was overpopulation. Why create one more mouth to gnaw at the stricken earth? And in particular, why add another American, when we already consume far more than our share of energy, food, water, timber, and minerals? How can a capitalist culture fueled by greed and envy sustain itself, much less the living earth? Our environmental friends just smiled and shook their heads. Others wondered how we would support a family, since I had a terminal contract and no prospect of a job. My colleagues, most of whom had spent their whole lives on campus, could imagine only the bleakest scenarios, removal to some academic Siberia or, worse, having to quit the profession.

Nor did we get much encouragement from the outside world. In the farm country beyond campus, winter had settled in. The wind scythed down from Manitoba across nine thousand square miles of broken plains, driving before it a fierce, abrasive mixture of snow crystals and glacial soil. At dusk the shorn trees bristled like iron against the flaming sky. At night the stars burned with a dazzling, pitiless clarity that shed no warmth; it was hard to believe they were lit by thermonuclear fires. The natural world seemed to have regressed to a preanimate, mineral bleakness. Some days, when your breath froze in your nostrils and the snow squeaked underfoot, it was hard to believe in any form of life but your own. You just wanted to hunker down and dig in. You wanted to get away from that wind, that lethal sky.

The human world, too, seemed locked in a strange kind of depression. These were still days of Cold War, when scientists had begun to warn of a "nuclear winter" that would result from an all-out missile attack. Volcanic eruptions had shown that dust injected into the atmosphere could block out sunlight and lower temperatures. Imagine the same thing on a global scale: it would mean cessation of photosynthesis, massive die-offs, and, of course, the extinction of human beings. Against such a backdrop, wilderness ideals seemed trivial, even pathetic, and dreams of parenthood hopelessly self-indulgent.

That year, as winter deepened, Pam often caught me brooding about the arms race. Wasn't there enough to worry about, she asked, with a terminal contract and twenty below all week? But inner and outer life seemed naggingly caught up with the general state of the world. Thinkers like Kurt Vonnegut and Gregory Bateson had warned that the arms race was a form of addiction, a self-destructive spiral driven by pride. Like the alcoholic who thinks he can quit tomorrow and so keeps right on drinking, the great powers thought that they, rather than the weapons, were in control. The only way out would be to admit they were powerless and so open themselves to intervention and love, that is, to the future. But the great powers were willing to destroy each other, and everything else, in order to assert the primacy of their own way of life. It was sick. It was dangerous. No wonder so many people felt depressed.

I had read about the Inuit of Greenland, who are sometimes seized by a winter depression so acute that it sends them screaming into the night. Only the watchful compassion of family or neighbors can save them. They have to be brought back by hand, and the ice in their heart thawed by another warm body, gradually and tenderly, with concern for their dignity. It is a labor of love. That winter Pam held me, and I held her. It was the best we could do. But who would hold the great powers?

The philosopher Jonathan Schell had pondered that question in his book *The Fate of the Earth*. Extinction, he wrote, is the greatest evil that can befall us because it erases not only human life but the "common world" of past and future that ensures the survival of meaning. Belief in this common world allows us to face our own death or even the death of a group. But extinction would destroy the common world, as if the whole species had opted for suicide. A policy of mutually assured destruction, Schell argued, was tantamount to embracing extinction. It was a spiritual disease. The only alternative would be for all of us to embrace the future, even though we could not control or even imagine it. Schell likened this to the choice people make to become parents.

Now, years later, it is clear to me that Pam and I had chosen Schell's path of faith in the dead of winter that year. But we were not thinking philosophically or politically. We just wanted to have a child. It seemed the next step on the road of intimacy and commitment that we had chosen. Somehow the craziness of the world itself, hanging by a thread above the nuclear abyss, and the craziness of a professional life reduced to dust made it okay to do something crazy ourselves. We stopped using birth control, and the very first night, I knew that we had conceived.

I can feel the smile forming on your lips: "He writes as a man. How can he know?" Indeed, it was only six weeks later, after a missed period and a few good fights, that medical tests confirmed we had conceived. But that night I sensed an energy flowing through us that I had never felt before. It was not sex but something far more powerful, affirming yet oddly impersonal, like a current of molten light. Who can explain such things? I thought of Dante, who saw a river of light in Paradise and a rose full of souls who were drinking light. But this was something felt, not just imagined. I knew for certain that we had conceived. We had opened ourselves and received something holy and alive, borne into us on some sort of hot current originating God knows where. It was only much later that I realized how the choice to become parents, the choice itself, had broken the addictive hold of our old life and so made us, in a tiny little way, part of what was emerging to hold the human world. At that point, of course, Cincinnati was still far below the horizon.

Almost immediately we began to live in two worlds, as if life were governed by a sort of parallel time. Outside, the winter world seemed dark and full of doubt: our careers in eclipse, the state gripped by farm failures, the nation still grasping at wealth and power as it slipped down the slope of mutually assured destruction. But inside the warm folds of Pam's body, a new life was patiently growing, indifferent to anything but its own agenda. At first we felt its presence indirectly. After the bright intuitions of conception, Pam's body began to rebel: she suffered nausea, repelled by common smells and tastes. (Thank God for rice cakes, which have the texture of balsa wood with half the flavor!) One evening, sick with bronchitis, she broke out in hives from the antibiotic and had to spend the night in an oatmeal bath.

Experiences like these quickly dispelled any romantic notions of pregnancy. This was more like a seizure, except that a seizure runs its course, while this went on and on. We knew rationally that it was all perfectly natural, a process perfected by millions of years of mammalian evolution. The power now in control had been turned to a fine ferocity on the lathe of natural selection. It was ruthless, remorseless, and, as the world population showed, highly successful. It was big, very big, much bigger than the two of us, and yet at the same time, it was no big deal. Thousands of women went through it every day.

As we moved through the first three months into the relative calm of Pam's second trimester, the consistent, inexorable process of pregnancy brought an odd sense of order to our lives. Outside, our carefully nurtured world of work and community had begun to fray as the end of my teaching contract approached. The job hunt intensified, succeeded, then morphed into a search for housing. In Minnesota we began cutting ties, settling debts, and packing up to move. We drove to Cincinnati, began work, found a doctor, and started childbirth classes. While I learned to administrate and deal with urban time, Pam learned to cope with the isolation and dependency of expectant motherhood in a town where we had no family or friends. Meanwhile the pregnancy progressed with sublime assurance, as if following a drum or heartbeat of its own.

As term approached, I began to feel more and more marginalized, although Pam, too, had moments when the baby, and sometimes her whole body, seemed to be separate organisms and her mind nothing more than an appendage, like a video camera on a robot arm though which she could view the whole process with curious detachment. Her body was a vessel in which a potent reaction was occurring, a stage on which a drama had begun to unfold. My role was to support, facilitate, and assist—massaging her back, coaching her through breathing exercises, putting food on the table, administering gentle, reassuring hugs at any hour. We had decided against a home birth, wanting medical help nearby, but we asked for no anaesthetic or surgery unless absolutely necessary. Our mothers had given birth under anaesthetic and so had missed a good deal of the experience. In those days, pregnancy was considered a medical condition to be managed rather than a natural process that was wise and healthy in itself.

By November, two months into our Cincinnati life, Pam's belly was as round and hard as a basketball. Her skin glowed; her face looked soft and radiant. I thought her incredibly beautiful, even as she waddled around the house. We could feel the baby moving inside her. I would often lay my hands on her belly, feeling for the child and fancying, perhaps, an answering kick; or I would hum a tune or even talk a bit, so my voice might not seem strange to the newborn. Perhaps I was just trying to stay involved. Pam's body had no more use for me than yesterday's news; I had played my biological part eight months before. If anything, it was her mind that I nurtured as it tossed like a cork on the churning hormonal rapids that carried us closer and closer to term, that convergence of inner and outer time when our new life as parents would begin.

The birth night caught us by surprise. Two weeks short of term, Pam complained of pains early in the evening. We did some breathing, which helped, though they did not subside. We called the doctor at home. Over the fizz of dinner-party talk, he assured us they were Braxton Hicks contractions, nothing to worry about, take a warm bath and call again if they persist. We ran a tub, and Pam eased in while I packed our "labor bag" of sandwiches, books, and tapes, just in case. We went to bed; we breathed together; she says I drifted off. The next thing I knew, sharp nails were digging into my shoulder. Pam was gasping, trying to breathe. I glanced at the clock; it was after midnight. The pains were coming every two or three minutes, clenching her body like a fist. Whatever this was, it was not letting go. Between attacks she huddled, panting and shaking. "We have to go now," she gasped. "Call the doctor. Take me in!"

We staggered into the cold November night, starless with city haze. At 2:00 a.m. the deserted freeway glowed beneath rows of mercury lamps like a dream sequence out of a Bergman film. As we sped along, Pam clutched my arm, gasping with each contraction. I murmured comfort, chanted the breathing mantra as the city rushed by. We turned west toward the hospital, through the industrial zone, where huge factories rose in a forest of pipes and metal, stacks billowing smokes of many colors. To my dazed eyes, they looked weirdly exotic, beautiful as parasitic orchids. This was the world into which our child would be born; these were the realities with which he or she would have to deal. And yet not with these alone, but with all of North America in its vastness and woundedness, its beautiful wild places under siege, its sweeping farmlands, its soiled, energetic rivers, its cities and forests where wildness was always seeking to grow back in the green shadows cast by urban space and time.

Beside me Pam moaned and panted in her throes. I had no time to think about such things. She needed me, and I needed to focus on the road. Life was narrowing to a sharp, metallic point, piercing through every routine thought and action. I spun off the freeway and up the ramp to the hospital, ran into the emergency room, and dashed off forms while the nurses fetched Pam in a wheelchair. In the birthing room, homey with flowered wallpaper, the nurse told me to go park the car while she fitted Pam with a gown and an IV. "Take your time," she said. "We're not going anywhere."

So I went out, parked, and came back, my shoes squeaking on the waxed vinyl floors. The pastel halls were empty, except for an occasional nurse wafting by in sea green scrubs. I felt smudged and dirty in my rumpled clothes; I half expected to be seized and hosed down. The whole place glowed with sterility, a temple dedicated to the control of nature.

But in the birth room, nature was bursting forth. Orderlies wheeled in equipment, yanked open drawers, shouted into the intercom. Pam lay moaning, knees drawn up, her face knotted in concentration. A nurse tossed a wad of scrubs toward the restroom. "Change in there!" she ordered.

I changed and rushed to the bed. Pam looked up imploringly, clutched my arm, then gritted into another spasm. I looked across at the nurse. "She's dilated three centimeters since you arrived," she said. "This baby's coming."

"Where's the doctor?"

"Who knows? We've called an intern."

Now the pains came one on top of another, like breaking waves. Pam's body was seized and flung about; all the poor nurse and I could do was hold her down and speak words of encouragement, praising her bravery, helping her breathe. The doctor rushed in, a young, kind-faced man dressed all in green. He pulled on latex gloves, did a quick measurement, then began massaging her perineum in the ancient manner of midwives to stretch the tissue so the baby could come. He spoke soothingly, "You're fully dilated. When the next contraction comes, you can push."

Then Pam let out a yell that raised the hair on my neck. It was no scream but a full-throated karate yell. Again and again she yelled and pushed, and suddenly there was the baby's head bobbing between her legs, round as a softball and topped by a swirl of dark, wet hair. I was astonished, somehow, to see a real person emerge, a tiny face wrinkled and squished as a prune, yet at the same time perfectly formed. Pam yelled and pushed some more, but the baby seemed stuck in the birth canal. Finally the doctor took one snip with the scissors, and the baby squirted out into his hands, slippery and round as a sausage, bawling for life. It was a little girl. Later we named her Rosalind, after Shakespeare's resourceful heroine whose name means "pretty rose."

The doctor handed her to the nurse, who laid her on Pam's chest. Pam held her gingerly, stroking her wet forehead, murmuring, "Hi, baby." We all relaxed. A stillness fell on the room. Pam looked utterly spent, yet a glow lay about her, bright as a halo in a Renaissance painting.

The nurses wrapped Rosalind in a plastic sheet and took her away for

Apgar tests, eye drops, and other medical rites of the newborn. When I objected to the plastic, the nurses patiently explained that it kept the baby warm by preventing evaporation, much like a diver's wet suit. Meanwhile our regular OB breezed in, quipping, "Looks like I missed the birthday party!" How many times had he used that line? The intern slid off his stool and handed the surgical tools to our doctor, who began to sew up Pam's incision. As the intern backed toward the door, our eyes met; his looked large and moist above the surgical mask. For him, too, this had been an initiation.

Pam lay inert and oblivious while the doctor sewed and the head nurse cleaned up the bedclothes and afterbirth, which lay in a steel basin like a piece of raw liver. I looked at it with fascination, feeling a strange rush of sympathy. For nine months, the placenta had been our baby's lifeline, millions of cells working in matchless, intricate harmony to serve her developing life, yet now they were cast off like old clothes with never a thought. They had been sacrificed. Was it right? Was it cruel? Do cells have a soul? Life had left them and was rushing on. And what about us, whose lives would henceforth be devoted to nurturing this child? We, too, were being sacrificed. It was too much to deal with in this room that still throbbed with the energy of childbirth. The nurse asked me to step aside so that she could take the basin.

"This must all be routine for you," I said sheepishly.

She looked me in the eye. "Never," she said. Then, smiling, "Your wife had a very quick labor."

The doctor finished and, murmuring congratulations, swept out of the room. The nurses brought Rosalind back, wrapped in a soft flannel blanket, and laid her on Pam's chest. Then they, too, softly departed, leaving us alone with our child. I marveled at her exquisite features: tiny fingers curled like shrimp, real eyelashes, ten perfect little toes, skin smooth and rosy and silky soft. Pam held her close; as she latched on to nurse, an air of unutterable peace settled over them. I stood outside, as if on the edge of a campfire. Such perfect calm after such extraordinary violence! There was no doubt about it: moments before, something ancient and powerful had leapt into the room through the door of Pam's wracked body. A cosmic force had revealed itself, then quickly slipped back into hiding. It waited now deep in the body of our child, biding its time until, decades later, she too might conceive.

I had never imagined such wildness so close to home, so intimately linked with everyday life and with the body itself, this poor beast that bears us and that we take so much for granted. It was something older and deeper than the mind, an evolutionary wisdom that had unfolded in harmony with the planet's own history. We have all learned how gestating embryos recapitulate their phylogeny in the womb, beginning as proteric cells and progressing through more and more complex forms—coelenterates, fish, amphibians—to the point where they can survive in the world outside. It is as if each new baby carries the imagery of its species' past along with it, embedded as a prelude to its own story.

But the matter goes deeper than this. Even the chemical reactions in our cells have histories. Loren Eiseley remarks that our bones and teeth are formed by the same biochemical processes that mollusks use to construct their shells. Sometime in the Paleozoic, life discovered how to precipitate calcium carbonate from seawater, and it has never forgotten that art. Imagine the chlorophyll that made photosynthesis possible and thereby changed earth's atmosphere over millions of years. Imagine the hemoglobin that converts oxygen from a poison to a metabolic fuel. They share a basic chemical structure called a porphyrin ring that differs by a single atom at the center, iron for hemoglobin and magnesium for chlorophyll.

Even the elements in our chemistry have their stories. Except for hydrogen, they were all created by stellar explosions, supernovae prepared by billions of years of thermonuclear combustion. Iron, boron, carbon, and nitrogen all carry stardust memories into the core of each living cell. There are parts of us that go way, way back, and at the moment of birth, the cutting edge of time, they all come together to hurl new life into the world. The Zen masters tell us that no flower can bloom without the whole spring behind it. Just so, it takes the life of a star to make the life of a child.

Meanwhile Rosalind had fallen asleep. The nurses returned and carried her off to the nursery while I helped move Pam to her recovery room. Outside a pale November dawn had spread over Cincinnati. Far below I could hear traffic beginning to stir. I tucked Pam in and drove home to catch a few hours' sleep. The city looked abstract and unfamiliar, as if the buildings were cut out of paper. The sky was a wash of milk and water. The house felt as soulless as a motel. I drank a glass of orange juice and fell into bed like a hewn tree.

A Species of Eternity

Two days later, Pam and Rosalind came home. I took the week off to be with them, and in that brief interval discovered a new dimension of wildness in the heart of time. We had no schedule. All our attention focused on the baby, whose diurnal rhythms were not yet established. She was still living on womb time, responding to her body's inner promptings for food, warmth, touch, or sleep. And we lived with her, forgetting clocks, oblivious sometimes even to day and night.

Pam was healing, needing rest. We spent most of our time in bed. I got up to run errands or fix a meal but soon returned. It was a time of wonder, comfort, and "cocooning," a Yuppie term that bore, as I now saw, strange hints of metamorphosis. People had told us that childbirth would change our life, but I had imagined only mundane things like midnight colic or dirty diapers. Something far more profound and mysterious had happened. I had felt it first on the night of conception and then during the earthquake shocks of labor. But now, here at home, we were in the midst of it, submerged in a warm, irresistible flow. Exhausted, marveling, we had no will to resist. Besides, we now had a baby to care for. We were a family.

As for Rosalind, she slept, woke, and fed, casting her eyes about and flexing her tiny hands as if to get a feel for her body. She looked so small and fragile—she fit tidily in my two spread hands, no bigger than a loaf of bread—and yet she radiated a sense of tremendous power. What was it? I wondered. She absolutely compelled attention; we hung on her every movement, danced to her mood. Though she could not speak, she communicated with piercing clarity not only her needs but her delight in being fed and touched. I wondered how we must appear to her newborn eyes, huge beings with faces that filled her view, like smiling moons, a warm, salty, musky aroma, and always there, big as angels and instantly responsive. Of course, we gave to her, but she gave back. Indeed, it seemed that all she could do was give and receive love. But she did it with her whole being, her face lighting up to a touch, or nursing with blissful intensity. That was her power. She called forth our own capacity to love.

Pam's body began to flow with milk, which I tasted and found unutterably delicious. Creamy and sweet as honey, it thrilled me to the marrow. Truly this was the milk of paradise! And I was flowing too, not with milk but with warmth and affection, as caring and selfless as ever in my life. I was adrift in time, living totally in the present with all my senses focused and engaged. Only in moments of I-Thou encounter in the wilderness, when weeks of hiking had scraped my mind to a poised alertness and some animal or tree had stood forth in radiant personhood, had I ever felt the present as something so solid, so real. But those moments had passed; this went on and on. It felt like being awash in grace. I thought, again, of Dante's souls in the celestial rose, drinking the nectar of angels that was also light. For them truth, perception, and delight were one, and yet they never ceased caring for the world.

Childbirth showed me the essence of wildness at the very heart of the organism. Here was the growing tip of history, not just the story of two parents and their child, but of our species and of the planet from which we arose, and the universe story itself. With every birth, the world begins anew, returns to a state of grace so that its possibilities may begin once more to unfold. For every child is born without guile, in radical innocence. How, then, shall we respond? With love, embracing responsibility and transformation, or with fear, clinging to the old life with its secure and settled routines, denying wildness?

As for me, I had seen the wildness in the organism with my own eyes. Revealed for a moment in the violence of Pam's labor, it had now gone back into hiding. But I would never forget. My life seemed to have changed irrevocably. It felt as if I had come to a fork in the trail on a high plateau. The paths diverged gradually, and for a few miles I could still see the one not taken. It looked so close, yet in between a narrow canyon had opened; there was no way across without going all the way back. I had heard of men walking out on their wives during pregnancy or just after childbirth. Imagine them leaping across the chasm, spurred by incredible fear! Perhaps they preferred a life of desperate adventure to one of husbandry.

It seemed to me then that adulthood offered two basic choices: either to help life in its wildness and unfolding, or to resist life by choosing security and routine. To live for relationship or to live for autonomy, the path of labor or the path of addiction: choose one. And since so much of the outer world seemed bent on the latter, paralyzed by the arms race and the glitter of urban time, the way toward wildness seemed to open most promisingly within: within the organism, within the home, even within the city where I had never expected to find "nature" at all. There was more to this matter of wildness than I had ever imagined, and more to its practice than travel into remote and savage places. Before I had always gone out in search of it. Now, it seemed, I would have to start going in.

INVISIBLE LANDSCAPES

Resistance

After three days cocooned in the house, it was time for a walk. I remember standing in the open doorway, stupefied by the sight of oak trees and green grass, as if our suburban street were a new world rich with strange, undescribed species. If wildness was right here, right in the human body, it must be right there as well, right out there in the body of every organism that also lived in the neighborhood. For one dizzy moment, I felt the mixture of awe and excitement that Darwin reported after his first glimpse of the Brazilian forest.

But why here? The idea of nature in the city—let alone wilderness—had never occurred to me. Indeed, "urban nature" seemed a contradiction in terms. All my journeys had taken me out of the city toward remote and glamorous places: the lakes of Connecticut, New Hampshire's White Mountains, the sandstone deserts of Utah, the Boundary Waters of Minnesota. Now, in the stunned aftermath of childbirth, I felt the pull of discovery *here*, in a damaged landscape of lawns, planted trees, and modest suburban homes that epitomized everything I had once sought to escape.

So I hesitated, paralyzed by the very idea of learning from nature in the city. Perhaps every pilgrimage begins like this, with a moment of pure depression when the soul, immobilized by memory and desire, wavers on the edge of its future. Perhaps it was the red flash of a cardinal against a bare November tree that drew me across the threshold. But once across I kept on going.

Why such resistance to urban nature? As I sensed on that first walk—and have since learned in detail—a great deal is going on in cities apart from the human world. A glance at the edge of the sidewalk revealed that these lawns grew much more than grass: they were not mere vegetable carpeting but whole forests of diverse species, a dozen or more apparently. I did not know their names or pedigree at the time, but surely some had come over from Europe and traveled on flatboats down the Ohio with Cincinnati's first pioneers. The trees, too, seemed wonderfully expressive with their intricate, fissured bark and long, swaying limbs, lithe as the arms of dancers. Each twig seemed to be feeling its way into the future, recording the moment in its particular tuck and crook as if the whole tree were growing a complex, coherent story. Birds darted and perched: cardinals, juncos, house sparrows, tufted titmice, and one or two crows, black as judges, who stared down at this odd biped moving gingerly along. Squirrels chittered in the crotches of trees or raced along telephone wires above the sidewalk. Lichens, fine as embroidery, dotted the lower trunks of trees.

I recognized perhaps a half-dozen species in all and realized that my ignorance of their life ways was complete. It was as if I had been sleep-walking, blind and deaf to the other lives going on all around. Except for a few moments of intense encounter in the wilderness, I had lived this way all my life.

You may have heard that old American story about an Indian who went to visit a white friend in the city. As they were walking down the street, the Indian suddenly stopped and looked around. "I hear a cricket," he said. His friend laughed. "How can you hear a cricket with all this traffic?" The Indian took out a dime and dropped it on the sidewalk. Six people turned around. The Indian smiled as he pocketed the coin. "It all depends," he said, "on what you listen for."

If we listen for money more than for wildness, it should come as no surprise that we know more about bond prices than bird songs, more about the Dow than the Tao. But to be fair, most of us have little reason to pay close attention to urban nature. Consider how we get our food. In Cincinnati I start the day with a cup of Colombian coffee, a Florida orange, and a slice of bread made from Montana wheat. For lunch I have Georgia peanut butter and grapes imported from Chile. Dinner might include a slab of High Plains beef, an Idaho baked potato, and broccoli from California's Salinas Valley. Almost all I get locally are eggs, milk, and a few luxury items such as Amish chickens or Indiana cantaloupes, plus the obligatory air and water. In short, my ecological relations, though quite real and calculable, remain distant, indirect, and thus impersonal. I have more to do with a Montana wheat field than with the trees, plants, and animals in my watershed.

Such is not the case, of course, with tribal people, who depend very much on the local animals and plants. When all your food, clothing, and medicines come from the forest, the forest tends to concentrate your mind. Those who have spent time with hunting and gathering peoples have brought back admiring reports of their attentiveness, comprehension, and ecological insight. Barry Lopez writes that a native hunter might spend an hour glassing a slope that appears barren and empty to even a seasoned naturalist. Richard Nelson, who lived for years with the Koyukon of central Alaska, learned that for people who depend on animals every detail of appearance and behavior is significant. Hunting is their work, as worthy of time and practice to them as heart surgery, college administration, or the concert piano might be for us. What we would call wilderness is their workplace; they make no distinction between "nature" and "culture."

Suppose we lived thus intimately with the landscape? Nelson found that the Koyukon's pragmatic attentiveness had led them to a spiritual view of the forest as a community of sentient, intentional beings who spoke to one another in their own behavioral languages. The Koyukon insisted that every being must be treated with respect. Their hunting practices were predicated on both a sophisticated ecological understanding and a complementary system of ethics. Their lifework of hunting became a sacramental act, incorporating ritual practices that might appear superstitious to outsiders, for instance, offering a prayer of thanks to a slain deer and handling the carcass in a respectful and carefully prescribed manner. Such practices, we now know, arise not from childish ignorance or fancy but from centuries of intimate engagement with the landscape, of profound and sustained attention to its every detail.

From such attention, one learns to appreciate the connection between inner and outer life, as well as the unseen links among organisms and the fundamental, overarching fact that everything is connected to everything else. For the Koyukon, as Nelson discovered, there is no clear boundary between natural and spiritual worlds. They accord no special privilege to the human mind, which is only one among many intelligences and powers.

What do such findings mean for urban Americans sleepwalking over their home ground? Our impersonal ecology has removed the most powerful incentive humans have ever had to learn from the land: immediate, intimate dependence on it for life's necessities. Now food comes from the supermarket, medicine from the drugstore, and spirit from TV evangelists and New Age gurus. We must find other ways to connect with the wild green world if we are to have any hope of solving our environmental problems. But we hardly know where to begin.

Denial

My own education was hopelessly barren of natural history. In the late 1950s and early 1960s, schools were pushing hard sciences like chemistry, physics, or electrical engineering, no doubt because of the military-industrial mindset left over from World War II, the nuclear arms race, and the panic caused by Sputnik. The lab, not the ecosystem, was where things happened. Nature in vitro seemed more valuable and valid than nature in situ.

In fact, all the natural history I knew I had learned on my own, during childhood summers on Lake Waramaug in western Connecticut, where my grandfather had collected moths or butterflies, and after college on travels to the coast ranges, the High Sierra of California, and Utah's Colorado Plateau. I had gone there out of a young man's thirst for adventure, purity, and initiation. I was seeking identity through repudiation of the urban world in which I had grown up, rebelling against the parental mold. It was a kind of escapism, no doubt, this flinging of oneself toward remote and glamorous wilds. Nevertheless, these places moved and changed me; they were power places that compelled attention. I became an amateur naturalist out of devotion, inspired by a spirit of romance but sustained by a sense of empowerment and value that came from learning the land and exploring its intricacies. Still, my knowledge remained that of a hobbyist, far shallower than what one would expect from a trained ecologist or native hunter. And of course, I never paid any attention to the places I actually lived. For me natural history belonged to the wilderness as inevitably as a foam pad and a sleeping bag. It was not something to do at home, where nature was damaged, degraded, and confused.

But youth wants to see all things with a geometric clarity. It takes a middle-aged mind to taste the ambiguity and contradictions in such a model. I had no idea that my ignorance of local nature was a problem, nor that it might be abetted by my very devotion to the wilderness ideal. I accepted a priori the idea that wilderness could only be destroyed, never created, that wilderness and civilization were opposed, that nature and wilderness were essentially synonymous—landscapes where, to quote the Wilderness Act, "the earth and its community of life are untrammeled by man, where man is a visitor who does not remain." This sounded great to a fierce young adventurer. But when has North America ever been like this, except when covered with ice? Five hundred nations were living on this continent when the Puritans arrived and declared it a howling wilderness.

We know that those first Americans practiced agriculture, plant breeding, and wildlife management, often on a grand scale and with significant ecological effects. Many scholars attribute the extinction of the large Pleistocene mammals to Paleolithic hunters, who trapped mammoths in pits and killed them with spears. Corn, beans, squash, and potatoes were domesticated in Central and South America, then spread by trade as far as the Ohio Valley and southern New England. The Shawnees and the Miamis, who lived near Cincinnati, cultivated huge gardens and set fires in the woods to clear out the undergrowth for planting, berrying, and hunting. Burning was also common in New England and northern Minnesota. In the Escalante canyons of southern Utah, the Anasazis practiced intensive agriculture and irrigation. In short, this continent has been modified, influenced, and "trammeled" for as long as people have lived here.

No wonder native people find wilderness such a strange idea. Their relations with the land are informed by a deep sense of what the Buddhist philosopher Thich Nhat Hanh calls "interbeing." But we, it seems, must always be making distinctions, thinking of wilderness as opposed variously to Paradise (in the Old Testament), to civilization (in chivalric romances and Renaissance poems), to the city (in modern environmentalism), or in the most extreme cases, to any landscape that bears the faintest trace of human interference. I once heard a distinguished forest scientist assert that the Boundary Waters could not be considered wilderness because of the presence of white-pine blister rust, a disease introduced from Europe that constituted, to his mind, an indelible taint on the ecosystem. But his agenda—more logging—was easy to spot. More interesting is the question of why we would entertain such an absolutist view. To cling to a dream of nature's purity with holes in the ozone layer and radiation in snow six thousand miles from Chernobyl is surely to court despair. Why baste ourselves with Nietzschean dreams of the "death of nature"?

A view from the city may suggest one reason. Imagining wilderness as a distant, pure, and ahistorical landscape creates an ideal that is tailor made to receive our dreams. Worshiping wilderness from afar displaces our devotion from the here and now to the exotic and remote. Like romance it siphons off the affections in yearning after the unattainable. For desire trades in absence and incompleteness and the promise of fulfillment endlessly deferred. And what is wilderness to us if not a landscape of desire?

Of course, desire has its dark side. Enshrining wilderness in distant places allows us to justify our abuse, neglect, or exploitation of local nature, which appears less worthy and so less heinous to victimize. Loving Yosemite makes it easier to trash Cincinnati and to tolerate, on a daily basis, the consequent ugliness, impoverishment, and filth. No one should be surprised if the result is a general coarsening of life. How can we speak of stewardship, of caring for the earth, when our devotion gravitates toward places that supposedly take care of themselves?

History offers another reason. Scholars have shown that Edenic conceptions entered into our wilderness thinking thousands of years ago, not only in the Bible, where wilderness is created by the Fall and so forever after remains indissolubly linked to Paradise, as shadow is to body, but in classical myths of the Hesperides or the Fortunate Isles, where nature achieves perfection only in isolation and remoteness. For the romantic mind, wild nature came to stand in moral, aesthetic, and spiritual opposition to the depredations of an industrial age fueled by capitalism and utilitarian Protestant culture. The earliest ecological thinkers envisioned a self-sustaining state of nature modeled on utopian notions of human community that resembled, beneath their scientific skin, the Marxist ideal of "from each according to his ability, to each according to his need." Significantly, this state of nature was always imagined as wild, remote, and free of human beings, as *out there* rather than *right here*. Four thousand years of mythology, art, and poetry have taught us to value the remote and exotic as nature's one true home, that sustainable, beautiful, and venerable Paradise where we could all live in peace and joy if it were not for those two dismal realities, history and human nature.

The human desire to explore alternatives, to enter other realities, to be elsewhere is deeply innate, perhaps even genetic. The geographer Yi-fu Tuan avers that imagination allows us to escape from reality by creating a world of symbols. Language is one of our oldest tools, and through it the world, and the green world in particular, becomes something we "half create." Perception, expression, understanding—who can distinguish them? Emerson thought that words were signs of natural facts, but how can an experience or idea become a fact without words? The sense of resistance one feels in the phrase "urban nature"—indeed, the mere need for the qualifier "urban"—reveals the bonded layers of thought, expression, and belief that cement and uphold, like buried strata, the ideas of nature and wildness in which we trust.

But if imagination allows us to escape, it can also limit perception. Perhaps urban nature remains largely invisible because we lack an appropriate philosophy and vocabulary. Notice how many of our aesthetic and ethical notions depend on a sense of the green world *out there*. Urban nature is not sublime: it has no grand vistas, towering peaks, or imposing Euclidean forms created by some nonhuman force; it does not dwarf, awe, or terrify the beholder. Nor do urban landscapes fit the category of pastoral: there's too much built environment, not enough circumambient wilderness. (Indeed, the city and wilderness serve as pastoralism's defining poles, twin projections from an imaginary and idealized center.) Nor will the georgic mode suffice, because our wheat, lamb, and honey come from faraway. In places like Cincinnati, we live on the land, not off it, and certainly not by it in any ecological sense.

City landscapes resemble gardens in some respects, but horticulture proves only a partial fit. There's too much sterility in the form of roofs and pavement, and, oddly enough, there's also too much wildness, too many weeds and wooded borders and tangled banks, not to mention vacant lots going to brush. Of course, "wilderness" won't do to describe such landscapes either. Despite the degree of wildness, there's too much human impact, too many alien species, too few large animals to meet the legal and cultural criteria. The fact is that urban landscapes are just too mixed up, chaotic, and confused to fit our established notions of beauty and value in nature.

But there's another form of invisibility that's even more troubling because it trades in denial and is therefore partly willed. We may love wild nature, but we also want to own it and take what we want without feeling guilty the next morning. Dreaming of wilderness enshrined far away may medicate our bruised affections for a while, but urban landscapes serve as a constant reminder. Every time I walk past the unmowed lot with its blue chicory, dandelions, and thickets of Amur honeysuckle, I am reminded of how severely we humans have mauled the local ecology, driving away the animals, tearing up the ground, introducing all sorts of aggressive alien species.

Once you've started down this path, it's hard to stop, hard not to think of the extermination of the buffalo, the decimation of prairie flora, the shaving and burning of ancient forests from sea to sea. The landscape begins to look like a world of wounds, and its history begins to look like a pattern of war, enslavement, and genocide. These are not happy thoughts, nor are the feelings they evoke. It helps me repress them to think of this urban land as somehow less natural because it has been "impacted" or "spoiled." Maybe it's not really nature at all, not a real ecosystem, just a bunch of weeds and exotics mixed up with human junk. It doesn't count; it's not worth dealing with; I can ignore it. Such thinking makes urban nature invisible in a way that Ralph Ellison might have recognized. No wonder we turn away from the sight of these weeds and brownfields toward old-growth forests and shining mountains. We want to have our nature and eat it too.

Remembrance

My walk had brought me to the edge of a commercial district, where a large enclosed mall was haloed by restaurants, service stations, and office buildings. I turned back at the sight of a brushed-steel façade rising beyond a fringe of wiry trees. It looked like the prow of a ship bearing down on a coral reef. Which creation would prove more enduring: the live, expressive wood or the sublime but crystalline architecture? Somehow this stark contrast epitomized the challenge I felt in confronting the very idea of urban nature. Don't even think about it: you'll end up giving aid and comfort to the enemy. Wilderness is still under siege. Driven to bay in the last old-growth forests and alpine ranges of the Far West, it still needs defenders. And yet, we live here, in this mixed, confusing landscape, and most of our journeys begin in places like this whether they end in wisdom or plunder, addiction or transformation.

The path of my walk was now bending back toward the house. As it turned from the mall, the concrete sidewalk underfoot began to feel oddly natural, as if it were only a different sort of deposit. Quartz pebbles, rounded by long-lost currents, gleamed from its matrix of reconstituted limestone. In joints and depressions, algae, moss, and lichen had begun to grow, just as they do on rock ridges in the Boundary Waters. Lichens were colonizing the tree trunks as well, taking advantage of furrowed bark that channeled rainwater right to them. Husks of acorns and other seeds littered the ground, swept into crevices where soil was building up. Frost wedging had pitted the pavement, leaving tiny craters that caught sand and moisture, riddling the edges of joints with cracks that spidered inward as if they meant to deconstruct the whole slab. That was only a matter of time, but not urban time: these were the same processes at work on the Cretaceous granites of Yosemite and the Archean schists of the Boundary Waters.

Meanwhile all about grew trees and herbs and shrubs of many kinds, alive with birds and squirrels and who knows how many unseen invertebrates, from insects drowsing in the cool of late November to wiggling protozoans, fungi, and bacteria. The soil was full of larvae, pupae, tubers, roots, bulbs, and spores all waiting to burst forth as soon as the warm, moist weather returned. Life's numbed explosion would resume; I could feel it, like the heat of a sleeping body. This place, too, was governed by ecological relations extending in space and time, invisible in themselves yet revealed by the presence, persistence, and behavior of resident organisms. Some creatures stayed all year; others would return, like the warblers and goldfinches I had been told to expect, or the seventeen-year cicadas that our landlord said had emerged the previous spring and scarred the twigs of trees all over town. The neighborhood was full of wildness and secrets beneath the scouring ebb and flow of urban time.

But more than one kind of history governs these mixed, ambiguous landscapes. As I walked, I also became aware of human deliberation, in the regular spacing of trees, for instance, or the clipped uniformity of lawns, the rectilinear borders of the lots, and the garden plots that surrounded each house. Nature here was rich with the marks of human activity, both planned and haphazard. Every tree and shrub seemed to be making a statement. The ecologist Aldo Leopold was fond of comparing landscapes to books—old growth being classic, of course—and he often referred to his practice of tree planting and prairie restoration as a kind of writing. What stories, then, inhere in these urban landscapes? A true relation must take them into account. The origin and persistence of urban communities of life depend to no small degree on human activity. Why were these trees planted and by whom? It matters, and it cannot be explained in terms of food or timber—that is, in terms recognizable to classic ecology. I would learn more about this sort of thing in the years to come. All that was clear to me then was the importance of these unknown human stories that made the landscape appear, as John Stilgoe says, like a palimpsest, a complex and layered text rich with meaning and invitation. The stories were one more invisible dimension of urban nature, part and parcel of this "damaged" landscape on whose confusing stage I was now, for better or worse, a player.

The street curved down toward our house, which had been built just over the brow of a small hill. As I approached, I noticed that our neigh-

bor's driveway was edged by a retaining wall built from the local limestone. Perhaps it was only the angle of late afternoon sun, but the rock
looked curiously expressive, its surface knurled and bumpy as oak bark. I
bent down for a closer look and was astonished to see the bumps resolve
into the imprints of shells, some deeply grooved, others filigreed like
fine, spreading fans. I ran my fingers wonderingly over them, feeling a
strange, magnetic warmth despite their resistant, abrasive texture. These
were brachiopods, also called lamp shells because in cross section they
resemble the oil lamps sold in Arab bazaars.

As a boy, I had been fascinated by paleontology and the epic drama of
geologic time. I collected fossils from the sandstones and clays of New
Jersey, yearning for dinosaur bones but settling in the end for ferns and
mollusks. A family friend, majoring in botany somewhere in the Midwest, had sent me specimens from her field trips, and I had opened each
package with as much excitement as if it had come from Darwin himself
fresh out of the Andes. I remember unwrapping the elegant gray frag-
ments, mounting them on exhibit cards, and lettering their exotic, re-
sonant names in India ink: *Platystrophia, Rafinesquina.* Now it came to
me with a shiver that these were the very same shells. Long before I had
ever begun to travel, this landscape had reached out and touched me
unawares.

Now in the rich afternoon light I marveled at the hieroglyphic pre-
cision of the shells. They were signs, works, traces of vanished life. They
seemed to say: *Before the world changed we too lived here, struggling to
make a home. We too labored to create. This is what we learned, how to
make lime fall out of seawater into shell. We give it to you, this living process, in your teeth and bones. We made the rock on which your house is
built. We built the Cincinnati Arch, great unseen structure of innumerable
past works, bent heavenward. Remember us.*

So the past lives in many forms. There were other invisible landscapes
here, not just those of the geologic past—the Ordovician seas, the ice
sheets of the Pleistocene—but those of my own past, that layered history
of desire, adventure, and learning enacted in city and wilderness from
New Jersey to California and back again to this old Rust Belt city astride
the dark Ohio. The past itself was a kind of buried arch, supporting the

present's journey into light. And the arch itself—an architectural form renowned for efficiency and grace, but also the form a thrown ball makes as it flies up and returns to earth—seemed a fitting emblem for this dubious venture of learning from urban nature. Home is where it starts from, and to home we must return, but on the way the invisible landscapes light up, becoming real and present as they fluoresce under the black light of imagination. The task is to learn to embrace all these invisible landscapes in a single view, to reconnect the places we love and desire to the places where, for better or worse, we live, to marry *out there* with *right here* through some new kind of practice of the wild.

For me this would prove to be a different kind of adventure, not seeking a landscape that answered effortlessly to desire, but learning from a place not freely chosen, a place drawn out by fate like a hand of cards, unprepossessing yet curiously opportune. And more, it would be a journey bound up with others, not a solitary initiation or vision quest but a practice of heart, eye, and hand. I would start from home, but at the same time, I would also be making a home, moving less like a soaring hawk, perhaps, than a probing root.

I ran my fingers over the fossils again, shadowed now as the sun dropped behind the trees. They felt rough, resistant, yet also invitingly curved. I might have rubbed them between thumb and forefinger like a coin—that is, if I could ever have pried them intact from the bonded matrix. I stood up. There was the house, and inside were my wife and child, the new life waiting with its steep learning curve. I brushed off my hands and blinked. Then I opened the door and went in.

Exploring the Neighborhood

STARTING FROM HOME

Teakwood Acres

Two months later, our landlord told us we would have to move out. He wanted the place for his own retirement. So we began looking all over town for what the real-estate agent kept calling a home, as if home were something you could pull off the rack like a suit of clothes instead of having to grow it like a skin. I had always dreamed of home as a sort of cabin, spacious and rustic and set on the edge of the wilderness—a national forest, say, with views of snowy peaks or a lake framed by tall pines. My dream house was made of wood and stone with clean water nearby, still or flowing. But this was Cincinnati. Still, there had to be pockets of greenery near parks, bits of woods, older neighborhoods threaded with slopes and ravines where we might find a cheap but solid house with four bedrooms (since we meant to have one more child). But where? Cincinnati divided itself into fifty-two neighborhoods distinguished by income, topography, race, and local culture—though the real-estate people reduced these to the singular litany of location, location, location. It felt like hunting for a campsite, and indeed we were encouraged to take a nomadic view, to think about "resale values" and "moving up," as if this were only a first bivouac on a climb toward gleaming heights. Our agent reminded us that the average home tenure was a mere five years, which was about the amount of time we planned to stay anyway.

Nevertheless, we shied away from the sodded, upscale suburbs with their young trees, creaky floors, and soaring prices. We wanted a place to live, not an investment, a place where the trees had been given a chance to express themselves. Eventually we found some woods in a nondescript part of town called College Hill, though there were no colleges now. Our two-story brick and clapboard house had been built at the end of a cul-de-sac in 1960, part of a development called "Teakwood Acres." All the nearby streets had been named for woods real or imagined, hence "Birchwood" and "Palmwood" and even "Devonwood." Our subdivision bore the name of a tropical hardwood known to resist decay and therefore prized for making furniture and the decks of ships. I liked the sense it gave of something exotic near at hand, even though the nearest living teak was probably two thousand miles away in Costa Rica. Here the native beech and pin oak would have to do.

Behind the house lay a strip of woods a hundred meters deep that bordered the soccer field of a city park. In early May with the trees leafing out, the backyard looked like the edge of a rain forest. Green walls pressed in on two sides, hiding all but the adjoining houses, muting the sounds of traffic, and suggesting, in the dark prospect eastward, unexplored avenues of wildness reaching almost to the back door. It was not the edge of a national forest, but it had the right feel. There was even space for a garden plot in the modest lawn surrounding the house. As we moved in, I found myself thinking of germination, of new probing roots, uncurling leaves. Each box seemed ready to burst like a swollen seed. We were colonizing this house and would soon venture forth to colonize the yard, the neighborhood, these woods, this "place in space," as Gary Snyder might have called it. But what place was it exactly? At this point we only knew its location.

Cincinnati had been founded in 1787 by a group of Revolutionary War veterans who called themselves the Society of Cincinnati, after the legendary Roman general Cincinnatus. Like him they had been farmers with large estates before beating their plowshares into swords for the cause, and after the war, they had sought to create a civilization founded on Jeffersonian principles of civic virtue based on husbandry. Congress, being short of cash, had rewarded veterans with grants of land, and homesteaders had begun streaming down the Ohio from the fort at Pittsburgh, much to the dismay of resident tribes like the Shawnees. A long war ensued, with victories, massacres, and heroics on both sides until the Indians, weakened by epidemics and abandoned by the British, succumbed to the scorched-earth tactics of the American generals William Henry Harrison and Anthony ("Mad Anthony") Wayne.

Thereafter, Cincinnati began to grow, literally, like a weed. The site had also been favored by prehistoric people, whose mysterious earthen mounds dotted the flat, sandy amphitheater formed where Mill Creek and the Licking River joined the Ohio. The settlers found that the limestone bedrock under the surrounding hardwood forests decayed to a rich calcareous soil ideal for growing corn and fattening hogs. Situated on the major river leading west, Cincinnati soon became the center of food production and commerce west of the Alleghenies, shipping hundreds of barrels of pork each day along with dozens of secondary products, including the soap for which, a century later, it would become world famous. Cincinnati was known as the "Queen City of the West" until after the Civil War, when railroads stole its river traffic and shifted its luster to Chicago.

By then, of course, the city had grown far beyond its original sandy basin, spreading into the valley of Mill Creek and up its tributary ravines to the flat hilltops beyond. Outlying villages and farmlands were absorbed, including our own neighborhood, which had remained a separate town until the 1920s. Not three blocks from our house stood one of the old homesteads, a narrow, oblong structure of rough brick with ten-foot ceilings, a veranda, and a laid-stone foundation; it stood out in a row of squat brick cottages like a sycamore in a cabbage field. My secretary, who grew up less than two miles away, recalled how acres of tomato fields had been replaced by gas stations, churches, and chili franchises. Fortunately, the hillsides to the south were too steep and unstable for construction.

If you travel south from our house, you will feel the land rising beneath you until, a mile later, it plunges into the ravine of West Fork Creek, a tributary of Mill Creek, and thence slides gently toward the Ohio. Across the river, the land begins to rise again until, in about a hundred miles, it lifts into the foothills of the Appalachians that bend westward across southern Kentucky. In preglacial times the rivers all flowed north, incising meanders into the limestone bedrock. Some, like the Kentucky River, cut deep, straight-walled canyons as handsome as any in Utah, though in our moist climate their geometry is softened by dogwood, campanula, and ferns.

When the ice pushed down from the north, it filled river valleys all across Ohio, scouring their beds of sand and gravel and plugging the old drainages. Stymied, Kentucky's rivers pooled against the ice front, seeking new outlets and eventually cutting through the old ridges and divides. Today's Ohio River more or less follows the lobed front of these ancient glaciers. Paradoxically, it is much younger than its tributaries. Climatological charts show that the river's course coincides with the average path of the jet stream and the isotherm that marks the boundary between planting zones four and five. So the heavens inscribe their character on earth, and airy nothing creates, indelibly, a local habitation and a name. Here the Ohio makes a great bend up from the south and curves away again just west of town, so that Cincinnati itself appears balanced near the top of the river's arc, at a point where two great arches, bedrock and water, intersect.

Especially on winter days under damp, snow-laden skies, I like to imagine my neighborhood emerging from the Pleistocene. After ages of dark and grinding cold, an endless rain washes away the ice, leaving heaps of mud and gravel looming in chill fog. Great, lumbering beasts move in from the south as mats of dryas, fireweed, and reindeer moss spread over the stony ground. Spruce, aspen, willow, and white pine migrate west and north from their refuges in the Virginia mountains. Huge mastodons and ground sloths browse on saplings. Dire wolves roam the hillsides. Gray streams churn southward from the ice, cutting new valleys to feed the Ohio. Siberian hunters come, pursuing the great beasts with spears. The climate warms; the people change, leave, return. They come with new plants, put in gardens, erect strange earthen monuments shaped like snakes intent on swallowing the sun. The forest changes; the spruce and pine head north, following the spoor of ancient ice. Deciduous trees move in: American elm, pin oak, box elder, silver maple. For a while the Ohio Valley is abandoned. Then new people come, the Shawnees reaching an apogee in their long migration from the south, the Delawares and the Wyandottes fleeing European settlers in the east, and finally, from upriver, white people in flatboats bearing seeds, gifts, and guns. They clear the land, plant corn, cut roads; a village, then a city grows. This land turns into property: a hunter's woods at first, then wood lot, then a field, a nursery, and finally a tract of homes, in one of which, right now, a man sits writing in an upper room. He looks out at the bare trees laced with snow, rooted in glacial mud. They seem to be growing as they always have. A female cardinal, olive-colored, flies in and perches on a twig whose tip is red and swollen, alert for spring. It is the end of the millennium. He thinks, I have come here in the nick of time.

Call it a homestead, then, this small piece of city land—no more than half an acre belonging equally to nature and human beings. Shaped like a lopsided fan, it's hard to measure. One end abuts on pavement, the other in scraggly third-growth woods, where, even now, the nuthatches and tufted titmice forage for remnant seeds. It seems as good a place as any to begin, a place to start from, as they say home always is, but also a place to which one could return after a voyage of exploration and discovery. All journeys, after all, begin in the nick of time.

Etymologically, a home*stead* is a home *place*, the focus of a story. And the word "home" derives from the ancient root for bed or couch, the place where we lie down to rest. The journey begins, then, in repose, unconsciousness, or sleep. We go out to awaken, hoping to return both wiser and more refreshed. The path soars outward, then bends back, inscribing its parabolic arc. One might begin anywhere, but this place seems as good as any: a nondescript house in an aging suburb, a place altogether without glamour, virtually anonymous, certainly never to be noticed by nature photographers or glossy environmental magazines, a place lacking all sublimity, of no ecological distinction, void of endangered species, and yet for all these reasons, perhaps, more representative. The sorts of things learned here might apply almost anywhere. So many of us, after all, grow up in city places just like this, whose nature is, like it or not, our own.

A Semipermeable Membrane

They say a house is not a home, but just try thinking of home without one. I construe "house" in the broadest sense, as any dwelling built for lasting residence. A yurt, an igloo, a thatched hut, or a midtown apartment would all qualify. Climate affects the architecture but not, apparently, the need. The people of the South Sea Islands and tropical rain forests wear few clothes but still make houses, as if a modicum of indoor life were needful on some deep human level. Here in the North

Temperate Zone, a house provides protection, like a hard carapace or exoskeleton, defending soft flesh that evolved in African savannas.

But physical comfort is only part of the story. Starting from home means starting indoors, where so much of our life takes place. I mean not only our eight hours' sleep—a third of the day!—but most of our work, family, and recreational life as well. We love our cars, yet what are they but self-propelled capsules of our indoor environment, small chips of house on wheels that allow us to travel far without the sense of really leaving home. Think what a scant proportion of the day we actually spend in the open air. Small wonder we speak of "outdoor life" or "outdoor recreation," signaling indoor as the norm. The journey toward wildness begins with a single step across the threshold. Consider that boundary, then, and the two realms it divides.

Sitting at my desk on the prow of the house, gazing at winter woods, I enter a flat space. Contemplation opens. I look through Venetian blinds as if through the bars of a cell, imprisoned not by sentence but by choice, like a monk electing stillness and solitude. It is comfortable here; the room feels warm, dry, and familiar. I know this air, these smells, the feel of this chair. My body stills, my breathing slows, my heartbeat settles to a distant murmur. From outside, deep in the woods, come the clear, rasping calls of cardinals. Gray branches sway and click in a breeze I cannot feel. A clear glass veil intervenes between me and "nature."

At such moments the house feels like a spacesuit, a diver's mask, or a suit of armor, a fabricated refuge that keeps my body comfortable so that my mind can work on matters of its choosing. Without the house, the body's needs would always be clamoring for attention: "Feed me!" "Keep me warm!" But with those needs taken care of by the house, the mind can go its own way, attentive to ideas and dreams. So the house represents a kind of refuge or escape from nature, which is construed as whatever exists outside the organism and, ipso facto, forces it to pay attention. The house allows the mind to pay attention to itself.

Of course, there's nothing pathological in such an arrangement. All life forms develop some protection from the outer world. A seed's hull protects the delicate embryo from frost or desiccation. A mollusk's shell guards the soft, watery flesh from being torn, crushed, or chewed. Think of the dark, jagged front an oyster presents to the world in contrast to its sleek, pearlescent lining. Life's chemistry requires a vessel within which appropriate conditions can be maintained: pH, temperature, and concentration all balanced to preserve the pace and direction of key reactions. Significantly, however, these reactions (and the longer process in which they participate) must be not only protected and contained but also fed. So the vessel can't be sealed off altogether: things must be able to enter and escape. But only certain things, needful things, particular kinds of energy or matter. Everything else poses a danger to the process, a blink of chaos. What life requires, therefore, is a clear but porous boundary, a semipermeable membrane rather than a hard, impenetrable shell. This membrane draws the line between an organism and its environment, establishes a frontier between self and other like that between two countries engaged in trade.

Our life relies on membranes of all kinds, not just those of cells but also the larger membrane of our skin with its flaking epidermis, nerve endings, and pores, our clothes, which breathe while keeping us warm, the house with its doors and windows offering views and passage through the sheltering walls, and beyond these the bounds of property lines, the city edge, the watersheds that delimit ecosystems. Think, too, of Earth's very crust, which shields us from the heat and pressure of its molten core while allowing some of that chthonic richness to escape in volcanoes or thermal vents in the deep-sea floor (near which organisms of the most ancient lineage survive, living on sulfur, ammonia, and methane, enduring hot acids and temperatures close to boiling). Think of Earth's atmosphere, which guards us from searing ultraviolet rays and a hail of meteors, or the magnetosphere, which deflects the solar wind. Beyond these, too, our life is wrapped in the nested membranes of Earth's gravitational field, the solar system, our galaxy's own spiral arm, and finally, at the farthest reach of imagination, the deep structures of matter and energy, space and time that veil, even as they reveal, the face of God.

To be in the house, then, living within the membrane, is not to be cut off or sealed, but to be centered in a process of organic life that is reflected across the universe at every scale. This house, my home, appears from inside as the center of my visible universe. Its sense of comfort is not fixed or given, but constantly maintained, as if it were some kind of dance between inside and outside. Thus, it betokens not simply a building or location, but a state of bodily comfort and peace of mind. The house is no dead structure or mere address, but a living thing, a place where a story is always in production, where history accumulates and soul grows.

Meanwhile, of course, we must be warmed, informed, and fed. What feeds the house? In ecological terms, I am connected to the outer world by conduits of various kinds that bring in things I need and carry off the waste. This house is tied into a vast and intricate net of power cables, TV and telephone lines, water lines, gas mains, sewer lines, mail routes, and city streets, not to mention food-transport routes, rail lines, electronic banking, and the Internet. All these connect me to the outer world, and not just ecologically but culturally as well. This house, with me in it, is just a node or knot in this vast and intricate network that enables the impersonal ecology of city life while also transmitting views of the natural world.

In today's homes the net is most visible at points where it intersects directly with our consciousness, that is, in TV or computer screens. For many these form the real center of the house. In ancient times, the household was centered on the hearth, which provided both food and warmth. Perhaps because of this connection to our basic needs, the hearth also became a place of devotion, sacred to the household gods. A dancing flame, so soothing to mind and eye, easily suggests the dynamic processes of life itself, where chaos blends with form, and also, when contained in a frame, the comfort and equilibrium of home. In our time, this archetypal flame is usually enclosed or processed beyond recognition, in a furnace or water heater, for instance, or in the dancing phosphorescence of a TV screen. We gaze entranced at images of all kinds that seem to have dropped from the air. Indoor life, especially as we experience it in cities, is predominantly a life of the mind, where we engage with representations of things more readily than with things themselves.

Indeed, the artifacts with which we fill our homes present themselves as a blend of object and idea, part fact, part art. Consider the ballpoint pen with which I am writing this sentence. Its design and construction express principles of engineering, chemistry, and aesthetics that are rooted in Western science. But its ink and plastic hull were once crude oil derived from the cells of ancient plankton; its brass nib was once pyrite, malachite, and zinc blende deposited by superheated emanations from Earth's mantle. The pen's brisk, dazzling surface throws back culture like a mirror. I have to grasp it to feel the resistance of its hard matter, probe with imagination to sense its planetary origins. But the pen remains a composition of both art and nature, human and wild. Conformed to thought, it comforts, sets mind and hand at ease, and lets the writing flow. Meeting all expectations, it does not become an issue. Its otherness and history remain hidden though ever present. Some wildness, in a word, remains.

And because it is this way with all our artifacts and possessions, the mind is constantly going forth in search of the world outside the house, where things stand forth more vividly as themselves. We gather notions and images of this world from looking out of windows, reading books, contemplating photographs, or gazing enraptured at images flashing across the screen. They are so beautiful, gorgeous even, framed, edited, and exposed to perfection, so that the "world of nature" appears as a moving panorama or continuous painting, an ongoing work of art, as if the natural world itself were shaped intrinsically to the contours of human thought. What's more, the camera's omniscient eye can take us to even the most remote or private places, exposing animals we could never stalk, spying on rituals of mating, birth, or predation, magnifying unnoticed lives to heroic size, and dwelling only on the most beautiful, sublime, and vivid landscapes. Presented in this way, the world does seem to answer effortlessly to desire. It's not the world that I see through my study window.

Thus, the net works to keep us indoors, entranced by dreams, devoted to a vision of nature as remote, glorious, and Edenic. The glowing screen fosters impersonal ecology as much as food, water, gas, or power lines do. The writer Bill McKibben once taped and watched all the TV shows broadcast during a single day on the ninety-three cable channels serving Fairfax, Virginia. Then, for comparison, he spent a day on an

Adirondack mountain. Not surprisingly, he found the latter a richer, livelier, and more profound experience. McKibben concluded that a life ruled by TV was a life of "missing information" that could lead toward not only mental and physical impoverishment but also danger. Consider: TV provides much information, but only of certain kinds. It cannot convey touch, smell, taste, or texture. In a nature show, we can't feel the rain forest's sweaty heat, the flick or sting of insects, the smell of rotting fruit, the peaty soil creaking underfoot, the leathery slap of leaves against dripping legs, or the skin-crawling horror when that black branch suddenly looks just like a fer-de-lance. Whatever the risk, we crave only the solid earth, the actual world. We know there's no virtue in virtual reality. Missing information means missing interaction. And without contact, real encounter, and the learning to which they lead, how can we ever begin to establish honorable, dignified, and sustainable relations with the rest of life?

Our first step, it seems, must be across the threshold, through the membrane, and into the world outside. That world waits for us, not at some glorious remove, but right here on the other side of the window-pane, through the looking glass of culture, artifice, and received ideas. From inside the house, it appears somewhat forbidding, a green and shadowy world of many lives that flourish in the penumbra of our own remorseless and incessant activity. To step outside means entering the shadow, embracing uncertainty, stimulation, and the possibility of danger. It means confronting the new, the Other, opening oneself to be challenged, perhaps to learn. The step outside is therefore a fall from a kind of innocence, perhaps, but also an awakening. Stepping across, we begin to grow again.

The Circulation of Wildness

Outside the door, the first thing I feel is air moving against my face, fresh and tingling with strange scents. My skin shrinks against its coolness. I suck in breath, eyes widening; my nostrils flare. All this happens in a moment, as if I'd been slapped awake. Unthinkingly I take another step, as other senses waken. I hear the rustle of leaves, the creak and click of stems, the scratch and whir of insects, bird calls whistling, a whoosh of wings, a glimpse of darting shapes, even the distant, abrasive buzz of traffic. Outside there's nothing still. I'm enveloped by a sense of flow, of energy and movement no longer regulated by the membrane.

I take a deep breath, another step, and another. From the middle of the yard, I can turn back and regard the house, which now looks stolid, immovable, and opaque. It's no longer the center of the world, a globule of serenity from which the mind's eye can search the far ends of the visible universe. Now it's just another feature of the landscape, a dark, hulking object that seems to hunker down and draw in on itself, like a barnacle on a rock. It's hard to believe that one could ever have lived inside such a thing, so cramped, so swaddled, cut off from the pulsing currents of air and sound and myriad other lives that swirl incessantly and, even now, stimulate every one of my sluggish senses to a new alertness. Now the indoor life feels positively dead with its still air, stale odors, and addictive routines.

If this seems exaggerated, consider that when we step outside, we're usually going somewhere. That is, our bodies may be outside, but our minds remain indoors, focused on a destination that's usually some other part of the built environment or, if not, some locus of recreation. In any case, it's not *right here*. Nevertheless, a pause, a breath, and a moment to look around give a quick, overpowering sense of the essential wildness of the outdoors, whether it be in Montana or Cincinnati. The air is full of movement, moisture, and heat that we have not created—call it weather—and the landscape creaks, flaps, and shimmers with countless other lives. Even the pavements of Manhattan teem with algae, bacteria, and protozoans as fixated on their own peculiar work as those bond traders hurrying past in squeaky Italian shoes.

But here in my backyard, only a few steps from the house, the sense of wildness is nearly overpowering. So many lives! Imagine what it would be like to feel, for one brief moment, the thin-skinned pulsing life of a protozoan, the stridulating urgency of a cricket, the darting intensity of a warbler probing for sweet-gum seeds. Talk of life on other planets! There's enough strangeness here on earth, in the backyard, to stun the mind into gibbering wonder with a single glance. For what is wildness but that overpowering sense of otherness, of other life carrying on beside and in spite of us, pursuing its own incalculable business with an intensity that may seem honorable or demonic but always compels attention. And the feeling increases with each step away from the house. The woods, toward which I'm heading, seem its proper abode.

By now it's easier to look back and see the house as part of a landscape formed by the neighborhood as a whole, where wildness seems to gather and flow in dynamic tension with more domesticated zones. Human control seems most severe indoors—though even there it's hardly absolute—and it seems to extend outward in a halo of diminishing intensity through the gardens, across the lawn, and into the woods, where the balance momentarily shifts toward wildness until I step through onto my neighbor's lawn. The landscape consists of zones of graded domesticity all interfused and edged with wildness where they meet. It's a mixed and complex scene, hardly amenable, as I've said, to categories like the sublime or the picturesque, yet not without its own distinctive features.

First and foremost is the present abundance of wildness itself: uncultivated, unkempt areas rich in wildlife of all shapes and sizes. We take it so for granted, but spend a day in any European city and you'll be struck by how much wilder and greener American cities are. Each yard, it seems, abuts its own tangled bank, flaunting our abundance of open space. I remember crossing Belgium once by train and glancing out the window at a highway overpass: in the triangle where two ramps met, someone had planted cabbages, as if no bit of arable land could be spared. In Europe one has the sense that every square inch of ground has been worked over. In Switzerland I saw neat bundles of twigs stacked beneath every forest tree, leaving the ground as smooth and grassy as a park. In England I heard about an American suburbanite who was impressed by the rich, perfect lawns of the Oxford colleges. He saw a gardener pushing a roller and asked him for the secret. "It's quite simple," the man replied. "Just water, mow, and roll it like this every week—for five hundred years." Such economies of scale and discipline seem hardly conceivable to us, who were born in a young society with ample space. My backyard is still wilder than most of Europe.

Next is the complex array of wild edges and corridors that run between the yards. In this respect, the neighborhood seems less like a landscape than a growth. Sometimes it reminds me of a tissue whose cells touch edges, bathed in plasmatic fluids. At other times, I think it's like a foam, whose contiguous bubbles are held in place by the pressure of air inside pushing against the surface tension of the surrounding water. Both structures are sustained by the inside pushing against the outside, only here it's not fluid but wildness that circulates. The green shadow percolates through chinks and crannies into larger pools, trickling from yard to yard, or sometimes opening out into a steady flow, as on our steep, wooded hillsides where the deer move easily from one side of town to the other, while pileated woodpeckers forage for dead old growth. It's not hard to mark the circulation of wildness in squirrels racing along the power lines or rabbits moving down the hedgerows, nor in the possums and raccoons venturing out of the woods to raid my tomato patch. A casual upward glance may spot a great blue heron or a red-tailed hawk. Crows visit, too, sometimes in clacking throngs. In fall or spring, great flocks of geese may pass, crying encouragement from two thousand feet. I always rejoice, too, as the white-throated sparrows arrive in March with their sweet, flutelike songs, heading north to the Boundary Waters.

But there is more to the circulation of wildness than grand displays like these. Outside the house, right now, the morning breeze carries an unseen cloud of pollen, spores, and winged seeds of all kinds, plus crumbs of lichen, algae, bacteria, encysted protozoans, molds, or insects, some homing on pheromones, intent to mate, or gravid with eggs and seeking a place to lay. No wonder each spot of bare ground, including my garden, soon bristles with weedy shoots. Even a rain pool left on a downtown roof will, in a few days, sport a green halo and a wriggling population. Closer to home, observe how seedling maples sprout in the uncleaned gutter as last autumn's leaves, composting furiously, dissolve into a wet, black earthly paradise for roots and microbes.

Nor is the indoor world immune. My bread dough, left on the counter overnight, begins to ferment with the action of yeast that simply falls from the air. My sourdough may not achieve a San Francisco tang (for each place grows its own peculiar strains of yeast), but its flavor is as rich and strange as that of any wild food. Each bite reminds me how much unexpected life surrounds and permeates the house. My cat, too, goes in and out on her own errands, hunting and patrolling to the peril of rabbits, birds, and squirrels. It's an open question who has domesticated whom. Certainly she marches to the beat of a different drum.

I find it exhilarating, even dizzying, to contemplate this rich, pervasive flux of wildness that pulsates over, under, around, and through the barriers we so thoughtlessly erect. Like air and water, life seeks out every crevice. It will find a way. The proverbial camel's nose under the tent is nothing to it. I find that wildness circulates on every scale, from the grand seasonal migrations to the weekly rounds of deer and coyotes to the swirling tides of aerial plankton ebbing and flowing through the reefs of downtown office buildings or suburban homes. Even my body feels wildness entering with every breath: rich atmospheric gases, fragrances benign or noxious, bacteria, yeasts, mold spores, dust, or pollen, some of which trigger immune responses while others, like aliens with green cards, settle in and get to work. We now know that many small things colonize our bodies. Some, like the skin mites in our eyebrows, do neither good nor harm, while others, such as acidophilus bacteria, materially assist in processes like digestion. It is amazing what lives, what societies we carry around with us.

By now I'm a hundred feet from the back door, deep in the woods. The house has all but disappeared in a sea of leaves. Each breath draws in rich scents of tree, bark, and foliage, blossom and decay, occasionally edged with a whiff of mold or even the faint, metallic odor of exhaust. It's harder now to say where the human world ends and the wild begins. I'm deep in the green shadow, breathing hard yet curiously calm, like a fish swimming in some immense tide. Everything seems caught up in the rhythm of breathing, in and out, here and there, ceaselessly exchanging places, nutrients, energy, and information. Even my organism with its mind and motions, this little journey with its thoughts, participates. The circulation of wildness includes me, body and soul. I breathe now as part of the landscape.

The ancients recognized the primal significance of the breath, not only to our organism but to the spiritual life as well, and so made it the foundation of meditative disciplines such as yoga. For the reciprocal exchange of breath between the body and the atmosphere mirrors the dialogue of self and other through which we learn and grow. No one can live a solely inner or outer life without corruption. We need the living world, and it needs us. Breathing in, we embrace the other; learning, we feel our self enlarged to include the other. Soul deepens, wisdom ripens. Our life is larger now. And breathing out, we give back something to the world, a part or parcel of nature transformed by our own organic life— or, in more spiritual terms, a bit of experience transmuted into wisdom. Pursued deliberately, this simple autonomic act becomes a practice and thence, on reflection, a kind of sacrament. For to breathe in this way is simply to be here now, centered on the process of life itself and consciously attuned to the circulation of wildness that interfuses and connects the human and natural worlds.

Without wildness, then, there is no growth, neither in the kitchen, nor in the yard, in the woods, or in the soul. There can be no dynamic tension across the membrane, no spur toward adventure or comfort in reflection. Standing still in these woods, I sense how intensely other beings pursue their ultimate concerns, heedless of my human power to interfere. Their wildness, I realize, manifests in their own distinct processes of self-actualization. And yet the differences are by no means absolute. We all need air, water, food, a mate, a place to live, a home range in which to pursue our happiness and raise our young. We also share this landscape. Wild things, then, may be other, but they are not wholly other, and in that open space, along that edge, we find the common ground where learning can occur. That other beings learn from us has long been known: we call it adaptation, a virtue in the abstract but often treated as a crime when it manifests in varmints, weeds, or pathogens. But the real question is how much we, as "dominant species" in these urban wilds, can learn from the other beings that surround us.

Fortunately, the wild always draws us, provocative and enticing. We're wired for learning, tuned for observation and encounter despite the soporific effects of TV, indoor life, and even the written word. We sense on a deep, somatic level how important it is to keep up the exchange between inner and outer, self and other. Perhaps that is one reason, apart from sheer laziness or neglect, that American cities contain so much more green edge and tangled bank than those of Europe. For wildness is not a luxury but a necessity, a requisite of culture as vital as churches or universities. How fortunate that we have so much left and so near at hand. All we have to do is reach out and open our eyes.

According to E. O. Wilson, the love of other life forms is a deeply in-grained human trait, perhaps even a survival adaptation. He calls it "biophilia." If this be true—and I think it is—perhaps we should also recognize a deep human need and affection for wildness as manifested in other creatures, persons, or places. Call it "therophilia," something we discover by starting from home.

A MATTER OF SCALE

"Life," wrote Thoreau, "consists with wildness. The most alive is the wildest." So he departed singing, moved by therophilia. But he was a man awake. Reading his books, I often feel admonished to get up and head outdoors, or at least to throw open the windows. He knew the deep, instinctive love of wildness that surges within us like the pull of subterranean rivers. Even with all the comforts and blandishments of the city, its latté and oratorios, one feels the tug of remoteness, freedom, and the splendor of wild things. This life of work and homesteading, bent to the notched wheel, forces us always into a coping mode. Especially with young children at home, life seems to come on too fast. You feel the harness chafing as you lean into the future, bent like a backpacker straining toward a pass.

At such times therophilia chews at the soul. Dreams come: arctic coastlines, firs pointed against a pewter sky, the sudden taste of ice, the ache of stretching for a hold. You wake up restless, resenting the life you've chosen with all its responsibilities and routines. The morning mirror throws back an image of pale indoor skin, starved for vitamin D. Behind it you feel a drooping back and sagging limbs. A sort of winter depression can set in. Even imagination atrophies amid dreams of past adventure, for therophilia dancing in the brain can feed nostalgia with its own euphoric recall.

Better get outside then. It's early spring, after a thaw, with ice still lingering in the gutters and the trees beginning to bud. The sweet air carries a scent of liquid water. The trees are full of sky, the lawns moist and earthy, smelling of damp straw. Overhead cumulus clouds ride east on a wind that must have started out high in the Rockies before sweeping across the plains of Kansas, Missouri, and Indiana. My outspread fingers tingle at its touch, as if they could almost feel bare granite and sublimating snow. That's all it takes. For the next block, I move as mechanically as a sleepwalker. My body may be in Cincinnati, but my mind has fled to high peaks and wide-open spaces.

On days like this, the city feels hopelessly degraded. What difference does it make that wildness abounds in its green shadow? I can't connect with it. I don't want it. I want moments of pure adventure far from the human world. In the throes of the ascent, when every instinct and sensation are focused on the next move, the mind feels as clean and hard as flint. A week on the trail tones body and soul to a calm alertness. You feel equally prepared to scale a peak or bed down with the animals, who do not lie awake in the dark and weep for their sins. I love this place. I really do. But on days like this, balancing home and wildness feels too much like work. Sometimes it's all I can do to drag myself back to the house.

My children fed this mood, of course, with all their needs and messes. But, interestingly enough, they also showed me how to fight it. From our earliest walks, they brought attentiveness and wonder to even the most common things. Rosalind discovered feathers—blue jay, cardinal, mourning dove. In her tiny hands they looked as big as fans, beautiful talismans of airy life. Elizabeth loved "treasure walks" where we gathered acorns, sweet-gum balls, or dried grass stems as stiff and precise as wands. No discarded husk ever seemed less precious to her than a golden slipper dropped by a passing goddess.

As the girls grew, so did the grass in the park beyond our woods. One year the city failed to mow, and the soccer field became a tossing prairie. On a June day when Rosalind was eight and Elizabeth almost six, we went out there to escape the house, threading our way through poison ivy and honeysuckle until we were able to stand up straight at the meadow's edge. The sight of all that glowing, rippling grass washed over us like pure delight. Did our ancestors feel like this when they first stepped out of the forest onto African savannas a million years ago? We waded through calf-deep timothy, English plantain, and oxeye daisies, heading for the far side where unmowed grass rose up in a green wave shoulder high. With a shout, the girls plunged in like swimmers breasting surf, then reappeared leaping and burrowing as I thrashed along behind. When I caught up with Rosalind, she was down on her hands and knees. "Look!" she cried, "a slug!" Then, nose to the ground, "Daddy! Look!" I dropped beside her, staring into a patch of moss that grew on the damp, shaded floor of the meadow. Tiny mushrooms had sprouted there, stems thin as horsehair, ribbed caps delicate as Chinese parasols. Over them towered smooth, straight stalks of grass, their ink black shadows slanting across the moss. A beetle lumbered into view, as big and shiny as a pickup truck. What lives, what emotions, what battles or discoveries were being played out here while I sat indoors dreaming of distant, glamorous wilds? "It's a grass forest!" I murmured. But Rosalind had already bounded off toward Elizabeth, who was chasing white and orange butterflies. "Let's be naturalists!" she cried.

It occurred to me then how grownups, who have become adept at living, so often miss the wildness at the heart of life itself. That's why we hanker after the strong drink of wilderness; we need such tonics to take us out of ourselves. To find the wildness near at hand we need, somehow, to regain that beginner's mind before which the world still appears fresh and luminous and unbounded. But how? On those early walks my children taught me that wildness is not just a state of nature but a state of mind. Where do you suppose the horizon lies for the small denizens of the grass forest, which grows up today and tomorrow is mown down? We humans bring all things to the text of ourselves. But the world is larger than our conceptions of it.

Gauged by average human dimensions—a body five and a half feet tall, weighing a hundred and thirty pounds and lasting seventy years—the Cincinnati landscape manifests little wildness. Few trees in my neighborhood are more than fifty years old, and the only animal approaching human size might be a stray deer or coyote wandering through. Move down the scale, however, and the living world becomes more prolific and diverse. Although our woods no longer hold black bear, elk, wolves, or buffalo, we do have possums and raccoons plus smaller mammals such as squirrels, chipmunks, rabbits, moles, or mice. More than two dozen species of birds have passed within a block of the house, from great blue herons and pileated woodpeckers to juncos, warblers, and house sparrows. Insects abound, especially in summer, when fireflies glow on hot June nights and crickets rasp outside the windows all through July.

At smaller scales, it becomes even harder to distinguish our woods from wilderness, particularly when you reach the teeming metropolis of the soil. Turn over any rotting log or clump of decaying leaves, and you'll expose a host of wriggling invertebrates, some barely visible without a lens: thrips, centipedes, grubs, springtails, roundworms, annelid worms, and nematodes. A microscope would reveal even more, tiny crustaceans, mites and spiders, transparent rotifers bulging frantically into view, plus all kinds of protozoans, ciliates bumping along like barrels, flagellates whipping around, clots of blue green algae, delicate meshworks of mycelia destined to fruit eventually as yellow honey mushrooms or red-capped boletes, perhaps even the gloppy plasmodium of a slime mold programmed—who knows how?—to gather one day into a bright, chrome yellow dollop, soft as mayonnaise, on the surface of some damp, unassuming log. Not to mention, of course, the myriads of bacteria, many unknown to science, whose job it is to perforate, ferment, digest, and otherwise transform all the vast residuum and waste of "higher" life into the nutrients those very forms can use. Without them the planet would be no more than a gigantic landfill, clogged with junk.

Time offers a similar venue for thought experiments with the sense of scale. The Cincinnati landscape bears dramatic testimony to the Ice Age: moraines, changed drainages, canyons cut by meltwater, even the present course of the Ohio River itself. The ice stopped here before retreating north, and a glance at the weather map shows that Cincinnati still rests on the isotherm between two climate zones: our winters seesaw between ice and thaw, wreaking havoc on city streets and concrete bridge abutments. Walk outside a few days after a snow, and you'll find water running in the gutters, cutting small canyons in slabs of remnant ice. Up close the ice resembles that found at the snouts of glaciers, congealed to a waxen uniformity by freeze-thaw cycles and studded with relics of the surrounding landscape—in this case, bits of sand and concrete lifted from the pavement, woodchips, bark, seed husks, broken glass, perhaps a bottle cap or twist tie (not to neglect the human world), or even a feather dropped by some passing bird. All these are first embedded, frozen in and then released by scouring water, washed downstream, and eventually deposited in the elbow of a curve against the ice or else in a small delta at the lip of a storm-sewer grate. One can see the same processes at work that created the vaster landscape over tens of thousands of years. All at once, time begins to lengthen out. It becomes harder to distinguish the present and the future from the past. The landscape begins to shimmer, seems less permanent; its present damaged and domesticated state appears as little more than an eddy in the larger flow of climate, ecosystems, and advancing or declining species.

But one does not need geological epochs to appreciate how wildness depends on the sense of time. Imagine a smooth granite surface in Yosemite's High Sierra—specifically, the top of Sentinel Dome. A crack has formed, and over the years, it begins to fill with sand weathered out of the bedrock. Soil forms, and one day a blown seed catches in the crack and sprouts. A tree begins to grow—specifically, a Jeffrey pine. It hangs on for a hundred years, buffeted by prevailing winds, until its trunk extends like a twisted arm far out above the bare rock surface, while its twigs and needles bristle upward, stiff as a comb. One day a photographer—Ansel Adams—frames it at high noon against a dark horizon. In the remorseless light the tree looks totally exposed, no cover anywhere between it and the churning clouds. The awed viewer sees it as an icon of rugged individualism and endurance, like a climber achieving some first ascent by "fair means" alone. Its splendid isolation and tortured form seem an expression of character, as if its entire history were bodied forth. We think, this is what it means to be wild, to be in the wilderness and survive.

Now imagine another smooth rock surface—specifically, a concrete sidewalk in downtown Cincinnati. Soil has accumulated along a joint, and one day a ragweed seed lodges and sprouts. It grows for a hundred days, buffeted by wind and sun, gnawed by insects, beaten and bruised by passers-by. It is small, dusty looking, of no more account to the casual eye than any of hundreds of other vigorous, opportunistic, and street-tough weeds that flourish like some green stain at the edge of the human world. By summer's end it too has attained an eloquence of form that testifies to a lifelong spirit of survival. Both plants are dead now, yet who can say that one was more wild than the other? Both lived out their allotted time, accumulating a history expressed in their very shape and so achieving character. The only difference is that the pine lived longer than a human life and grew in a place removed from human work. It therefore acquired an air of sublimity that Adams, with his art, transformed into the radiance of an icon.

It is easier, I admit, to dream of remote and glorious places than to exercise the imagination on the humble and near at hand. An icy gutter or a spoonful of garden soil cannot match the glamour of an Alaskan fjord or a tropical rain forest—unless you are willing to shift your perspective dramatically. For children this comes naturally. For adults it takes commitment and concentration, especially in middle age, when there's so much else to attend to. I still need the wild with its tonics and challenges as much as I ever did when young; it still refreshes my spirit, startles me, helps me to learn and grow. But now my children teach me how to perceive it close to home. They show me how the wildness of modest, unassuming landscapes, even in the midst of cities, connects with that of remote, untrammeled places. Deliberate imagination can expand the eye to see them all as part of a larger landscape in which people might learn to live sustainably, even for centuries. To connect the places we inhabit with those we admire, the lands of heart's rest with the lands of heart's desire, such is the challenge and hope of an urban practice of the wild.

Now, at midlife, I seek a beginner's mind that floats on history like the water lilies of Quetico. I find its traces in the footsteps of my children, even after they have run far ahead, disappearing into the grass forest. Out there, beyond the trees, it's quiet now. I emerge gingerly, stand for a moment, and bend down. There is a certain slant of light at the base of smooth, translucent stems that stirs both memory and desire. I think of Minnesota prairies tossed by a wind out of the Rockies. I think of the sandy-colored grass that grows in western Kansas and high on the tableland of Mount Katahdin. I wonder what adventures lie in wait for my daughters as they leap toward adolescence. Standing, awash in light, I watch them bound away, cavorting like young lions.

HUSBANDRY

Dancing with Wildness

Meanwhile, back at home, there's work to do. The vegetables have finally sprouted in our garden: beans, basil, carrots, cucumbers, dill, and parsley, plus volunteer tomatoes and a random, unrecognizable squash that erupted from last year's compost. I'll let it grow, interested to observe, come August, just what manner of beast it is. Midway between the house and the woods, my garden sits like an open book, its pages neatly inscribed with seedlings. Here the earth says beans instead of grass, but that's not all. It also teaches me about wildness and human action.

Aldo Leopold famously declared that there were two spiritual dangers in not owning a farm: one was to assume that heat comes from the furnace, the other, that food comes from the grocery. For spiritual health, he suggested heating with wood and planting a garden. As to the former, my yard supplies enough deadwood for a dozen fires each winter. A box elder limb torn off by a February storm might burn for two evenings in our fireplace; a silver maple gnawed by carpenter ants and felled for safety might last a whole season. By now we've lived here long enough to be sure that the firelight dancing in the hearth was culled from sunlight that fell on this small piece of land when our kids were young. Come spring, I clean out the fireplace and spread the ashes over the naked garden, warmed by the thought that they will come back as herbs and greens. This simple act reminds me that, despite the impersonal ecology of natural gas that heats our home, piped in from places like Wyoming and Alberta, the living world nearby still ceaselessly pursues its work of binding sunlight, retarding the flow of energy by bending it into loops, and so making space in time for life. The heat we use all comes as a legacy from past to present organisms. It's a gift we would be wise to remember.

As for the garden, it does supply a small but tasty crop, hardly enough to offset the impersonal ecology of the supermarket (sustained by agribusiness and global transportation), but more than sufficient to relax the mind and exercise the imagination. Especially in early spring, with new light falling freely through the trees, I can stand in the garden and look toward both woods and house while feeling the springy, fragrant earth beneath my feet. The woods always beckon with the allure of wildness, the promise of exploration and discovery, while the house promises comfort and intimacy. Midway between them, the garden invites me to dig in, get dirty, and engage directly with the processes of birth, growth, and decay. It offers a venue for year-round practice that yields an instant and immeasurable crop.

Admittedly, one does not automatically connect husbandry with wildness, just as nature and the city seldom occur in the same mental frame. They're more often thought of as opposites. Husbandry refers most commonly to the practice of raising crops and livestock, to agriculture in the broadest sense. Figuratively, it also means prudent management or conservation of resources, connoting thrift, stewardship, and sustainability. To a man steering close to the wind through middle age in order to keep family and home together (not to mention body and soul), husbandry also suggests the art of living generatively amid complex relationships. Etymologically both senses seem appropriate. "Husband" derives from the Middle English *housbonde* (meaning "farmer" as well as "the spouse of a woman"), which descends from the Old English *husbonda* ("master of a house"), which derives from the Germanic *husam* ("house") and *bondi* ("dwelling in"). So a husband is one who dwells in and maintains a house—a householder, one who practices an economy (from Greek *oikonomos*, "manager of a house-hold") that also includes other forms of life. For the earth is also a household, as Gary Snyder reminds us, "economy" sharing the root *oikos* ("house") with "ecology" (*oikos* + *logos*, "speech or reason"). Thus husbandry is not only a practice but an art, akin to poetry perhaps. In its deepest and most inclusive sense, it refers to the conduct of our relation-ships with all the living things we cherish and care for, human or wild. It is the practice of human ecology, the way we maintain our life in the living world.

According to Scripture, husbandry began as part of the original creation. God made the world and planted a garden in Eden, placing therein the man and the woman he had made "to till it and keep it." He planted the garden for pleasure amid the world of good things he had created; we hear of him walking there in the cool of the day like a tired administrator. It's a comforting thought that he got as much enjoyment from a good walk as we do. Meanwhile our first parents were charged to preserve and nurture this green world, in which all creatures, including themselves, had been told to be fruitful and multiply.

Stewardship and husbandry, then, were first established as forms of service to God, that is, as forms of worship. Husbandry was a divine calling, a devotional practice, a mode of celebration and praise. In this light, it seems fully compatible with unfallen nature and the original grace of creation. In Paradise humans lived, and were meant to live, in an intimate, engaged, and interdependent relationship with nature.

But a second view of husbandry enters with the myth of the Fall. Humans, curious and headstrong—some would say creative—conduct a dangerous bit of psychopharmacological research and discover a fruit that not only expands consciousness but alters human ecology. The Tree of Knowledge in this respect seems to work much like a domesticated plant; indeed, the knowledge it conferred might well have been the fact that some plants *could* be domesticated and thereby gain favor with humans, thus introducing a class system into the garden. In any event, God responds not by killing Adam and Eve, as he had threatened (and what exasperated parent has not made such threats, which kids know will never be carried out), but by changing ecological and social relations forever. Women are cursed by the pain of labor and the abuses of patriarchy. Animals are cursed by being estranged from humans. And men are punished by having to till the ground, which is now cursed because of their behavior. No longer will the earth produce food plants spontaneously, but thorns, thistles, and other noxious weeds. "In the sweat of your face," God warns, "you shall eat bread." The Fall affects not just people but all of nature, creating wilderness (in contrast to both Paradise and tilled land) and converting husbandry from a devotional practice to an adversarial struggle. It's no longer a matter of worship but of survival.

One can read the myth of the Fall, then, as an explanation for the origin of agriculture—and also of wilderness, human history, the battle of the sexes, and even, by extension, capitalism, impersonal ecology, and urban time. Not bad for the fourth millennium BC. No wonder the act of gardening resonates so deeply. Every gesture of turning earth, planting, pruning, or cultivating carries a trace of the ancient hope that through deliberate, devoted practice we might somehow grow our way back to that original state of grace, where we spoke with animals, addressed all things by name, and walked with God through the garden in the cool of the day.

Especially in spring, with pale sunlight falling through open woods on the newly cleared earth, I feel close to this prelapsarian husbandry, devout, trusting, and full of faith. How easy it is to dream of a garden rich and vibrant, like some vision out of the seed catalogs that have been piling up since February. I imagine a smooth, exuberant growth process unfurling just as programmed, void of pests, diseases, drought, or competing weeds, and eventuating in a textbook harvest: dewy tomatoes swollen like balloons, lustrous basil, squash as elegantly curved as Brancusi sculptures. For a brief moment, life and art would fuse under my ministrations. History would vanish; Paradise would return. All it would take would be good soil, good intentions, practice, and faith in a seed.

Just such sentiments drove me outdoors that first spring looking for the sunniest patch of backyard lawn. In Minnesota the best soil was found in town, which grew houses instead of corn. There my tomatoes had surged up from two feet of soft black earth. But here, under an inch of turf, the soil was yellow clay, hard as concrete when dry, adhesive and glutinous when wet. It was better for making bricks than growing beans. My amused neighbor, who had watched the house being built thirty years before, recalled how the builders had excavated the cellar and graded the spoil back from the foundation, burying the original topsoil under two feet of clay. They had trucked in enough new topsoil to hold the grass (a mere inch or two), scattered their seed, and left. In the end, I had to use a pickax, followed by three bales of peat moss, a dozen barrow loads of compost, and a stuttering rototiller, all to massage a plot no more than ten by fifteen feet into some semblance of tilth. With only four hours of full sun a day, my vegetable patch is hardly a good business proposition. And yet it provides, besides a tasty meal, invaluable lessons in the georgic mode.

For us the garden year begins in March. I turn the soil and dig in last winter's compost, disturbing the fat, lively earthworms that have spent the wet months tunneling, digesting, and excreting all manner of plant debris. The neighborhood kids gather round, delighted by creatures so icky and exuberant, actually *living* in the dirt that parents so despise. How wonderful to see life taking slimy advantage of something the adult world hates. Such resourcefulness and wildness, such unexpectedness, gives many city kids—the lucky ones, that is—their first glimpse of life's mysterious power of transformation. You won't see this sort of thing in perfect yards, of course, where the chemicals that police the turf drive off the worms as well.

But in untreated yards it's a pleasure to smell the earth. Hold it up close, sniff out its odors of damp leaves, straw, clay, mold, water, ground-up rock, sap, bark, or leafy green. Rub it between your fingertips and feel its gritty velvet. Moist, crumbly, and warm, it drinks the sun. Your very nerves sense the compressed fertility that will feed, come June, explosive growth. The soil, you realize, is the place where wildness lurks, not only in the wilderness out there, but right here underfoot, in the green shadow that begins where the sidewalk ends. It doesn't take much space to discover this.

Next comes putting in the seed. For this aesthetic distance will not do. Lay out and mark the rows by hand; poke holes for beans or cucumbers with your finger, then pat down the dark earth over them: it feels like tucking children into bed. Look at your hands, smudged with soil; feel the cleansing astringence as it dries. If you like, clap them together; raise a little dust. Even Buddha drew strength and enlightenment from touching the earth. "Humus," "humility," and "human" all share a common root. We are all made of the same clay and will eventually return to dust, but what sort of harvest will we leave?

Husbandry begins with faith in a seed, which contains the substance of things hoped for and the evidence of things not seen. The decision to plant a garden is like the decision to become a parent. You resolve to embrace the future, no matter what it may hold. You commit to this small piece of land and to these plants. You cast your lot with them.

And here they come, tiny green elbows puncturing the crust of freshly turned earth baked dry by the April sun. They look smooth, immaculate, tender and innocent as a baby's fingers. I want to kneel down and admire them at nose length. Everything stirs at this time of year, swells with the urge to open, stretch, push up, and thrust into the light. Therophilia dances in the blood; the old itch to travel prickles beneath the skin. But you are fascinated and committed now, so you stay put. As the days lengthen, basting the woods and streets with generous radiance, the green world emerges once more into view. Each leaf opens like a spreading hand to claim its small piece of sky. Young rabbits chew at the lawn's dewy edge. Warblers and whitethroats return, filling the dawn with praise.

Early on you visit the garden every day, dreaming of photogenic harvests and perhaps a bit impatient at how slowly the young plants grow. You keep an eye out for pests, which soon appear like eager editors: cutworms, slugs, even those cute rabbits with a taste for tender greens. You need to help your plants grow big and tough enough to survive. Fortunately the cucumbers soon grow spines; the beans spiral up their poles, lifting succulent growth tips out of reach. At ground level, the weeds soon appear, jostling for rights to water, land, and light. For there are many species that love disturbed ground: purslane, violet, bindweed, amaranth, ragweed, and dandelion. They'll run amok if you don't intervene, making invidious distinctions with your hoe, just like Thoreau. Now comes the true test of character, requiring not merely discipline and resolve but a certain attentiveness to the ways of beans. You snip, you cultivate, you aerate, mulch, and hoe, all to foster some forms of growth while hindering others. It takes work, and the days are getting hot. Spring's tenderness has shaded by degrees into the robust tropical green of early summer. Growth has become routine. Boredom can set in. But the plants still need you, for each week brings some new and more insidious plague: cucumber beetles, cabbage moths, even the thirsty squirrels that chew on your tomatoes. The world is full of mouths with teeth. Your plants grow furiously, trying to escape the fatal chomp just long enough to set their seed. All you can do is buy them time, holding the enemy at bay until they send their last transmission to the future. In return they leave you part of their estate. That's the deal.

In this transaction you can succeed only by learning the ways of other living things—not only the crops but the weeds and pests as well. The garden summer unfolds as a play of cultivation, growth, predation, and decay in which you serve by turns as dramaturge, protagonist, or foil, an actor sometimes ad-libbing desperately to save a scene. You're always learning, nurturing, responding. Your hands are always dirty. You are continually judging, pardoning, condemning. Your hands mete out life and death. The outcome of these acts is never certain. To garden is to grope like a blind person feeling for the future. You are immersed in a process you can't really control but only nudge or hinder by small degrees. It's not unlike teaching, whose harvest lies far off and is rarely visible. But here, in summer, is where you learn the ways of the world. You must engage these creatures on their terms, accept their character and nature—that is, their wildness—and decide how to deal with it. Now husbandry shifts from dreamy devotion to active, sometimes desperate struggle. It feels at times like a kind of martial art.

Especially in summer, when I'm down on hands and knees thinning carrots, pulling violets, or crushing cucumber beetles, I sense the tingling wildness of the garden. Everything grows fast and furious, following implacable passion in pursuit of its own ultimate concerns. At such times, I feel ridiculous talking about "domesticated" plants as if we owned or controlled them in any but the most superficial ways. What do we presume to mean by "raising" crops? It would be more accurate to say that they raise us, considering how much attentiveness, discipline, and commitment they require. Such practice elevates the soul, responding to therophilia in ways up close and personal. Thoreau was determined to know beans, but to do so he also had to know weeds and woodchucks, not to mention his own troubled heart.

By late August the garden begins to flag. Under the dog-day sun, when the air clings to your face like silk, who wants to go out and weed the garden? Better to sit indoors with a good book and a tall iced tea, lulled by a purring air conditioner. It's so much more comforting to read about wildness than to go out and face it. But theory, for all its charm, won't help your vegetables get through August. By now the garden is fully grown, a roiling mass of foliage that covers all but a few square inches of bare soil. It looks more like a jungle than an open book, a tangled bank whose beauty stems from sheer exuberance. The plants have made it past a gauntlet of diseases, insect pests, and hostile weather, including drought, wind, hail, and pelting rains. They have a brave but ragged look, broad leaves drooping in the heat, spotted with mold or wilt, tattered and torn, chewed by slugs or beetles. Among them a few over-looked weeds have grown up stiff and straight as spruce trees, bristling with clumps of spiny, impudent seeds. They seem to strut: we made it too, they say. Why bother to hoe them out when it's so hot, and besides, it's time to pick the beans. For, if the plants are tattered, their fruit is ripe and swollen, recipient of their parents' every hope and blessing. All the plant's beauty, wisdom, and mature energy go into its seeds and the fruit that wraps them like a receiving blanket. A seed is the plant's miniature, its nature in time and space fully encoded, sealed, and launched into the future. Fragrant, nutritious fruit evolved to help the seeds disperse: consumed by wandering animals and then dropped somewhere in a tidy lump of dung, fertilized and ready to sprout. Gardening has simply revised an ancient contract: they feed us, we perpetuate their genes. Call it a symbiosis, or, if that seems too strict, a form of mutual aid.

Harvest time always brings mixed feelings. The fruits never look as voluptuous as in the catalogs, nor do they come in as abundantly as you'd hoped. Who, except Robert Frost, ever tired of the great harvest of extravagant desire? Sometimes the beans are bent, the tomatoes bulbous or lopsided, the pears and apples dimpled by insect bites, the basil nicked by slugs. No leaf is perfect, no fruit without a blemish. It's enough to make you look twice at the supermarket displays, where the apples and tomatoes look as uniform and symmetrical as if they were turned on a lathe. After all that work, you'd think the vegetables would come out perfect, as full and regular as a well-wrought sonnet. But guess again, for gardening is not an art, though it takes skill and work: it's a practice, a relationship that unfolds in time and therefore bears the gnarled impress of history. You cannot take the wildness out of it, for the very medium is alive.

Nevertheless, we do eat the vegetables, which gives its own particular pleasure. My daughters now sneer at frozen beans and supermarket tomatoes, claiming they taste like cardboard. They love to go out with baskets to cull carrots or pick basil for grinding into pesto. None of this makes much difference to our budget, but the special feeling that comes from eating homegrown foods cannot be bought at any price. It feels like a green communion, connecting us bodily with the chemistry of our soil and the flow of energy and information through the actual landscape where we live. We touch the earth, and it touches us. We get a taste of personal ecology.

It's sweet to enjoy so viscerally the fruit of one's labors, even on such a modest scale, though, of course, it's not just your labor, but the plant's as well. You don't grow squash; it grows itself. You merely lend a hand by planting, nourishing, or wading in to its defense. The reward for such efforts, vegetable and human, is a full expression of the plant's inner nature, its true, essential squashness. A rounded utterance, sublime in its own way, it's utterly convincing, and tasty too. Even that mysterious volunteer, which turned out to be a Hubbard squash, now lies warty, blue, and seemingly content on a bed of crushed weeds. Only now, when gathering its fruits amid their obsolete and drooping greens, does it occur to me that I've been tending wildness all along. The plants spring up, exfoliate, flower, and set seed to their own clock. If I want to help, I've got to get in step. I have to learn the moves and listen for the beat. So husbandry, for all its pretense to dominion, is no more than a dance with wildness. Entering on it, I gain strength and grace while learning the secret ways of things. I stumble a lot but get back on my feet. I learn how to follow as well as how to lead. I learn to hope and pray and judge and accept defeat. I sweat a lot, but if I persevere, I eat.

By late October the crops are all but done, except for the carrots and parsley, which can survive a frost. The garden's a tangled wreck of bleached and twisted stalks, littered with leaves blown from the nearby trees. Odors of mud, mold, and rotting straw pervade the breeze. The woods smell like a leaky attic; the kids want to sleep in and watch TV. At this time of year the garden offers no refreshment to the eye, nothing but dirt and litter and mementos of failed enterprise. It makes one want to wash one's hands and walk away. But there's still composting to be done.

All summer long, we've been carrying table scraps and grass clippings to a shallow bin just inside the woods, where they've been left to rot. Now comes the produce of our backyard trees, tupelo leaves red as agate, pale yellow silver maple, orange hickory, and the shoe brown leaves of oaks. On top of these, we heap the garden refuse: the bean stalks dry as pasta yet enriched with nitrogen, tomato vines still green and robust, frost-blackened basil, the Swiss chard no one would eat, the turnip greens broad as your hand yet chewed into lace by slugs. All this gets heaped indiscriminately with coffee grounds, banana peels, apple cores, potato skins, burnt rice, broccoli stems, the heels of celery or carrots, leftover succotash, tea bags, and half-eaten bowls of oatmeal from the house. The late rains hose it all down, awakening the molds, yeasts, and bacteria that, blown in with aerial plankton, have lodged on the surface of every leaf or stem. The pile begins to smolder gently with Frost's "slow, smokeless burning of decay." Thrust in your pitchfork and you might even see a wisp of steam curl up, especially in late December when a three-night frost has hardened the surface. Outside everything seems dead or dormant, but inside and underground a rich, unimaginable life goes on. Attracted by the warmth, earthworms converge and tunnel in. Their probing aerates the soil; their castings leave it rich and friable. For them a compost heap must feel like some kind of paradise, and a good thing too. Without their humble but persistent work, this Cincinnati clay would stay as hard and obdurate as concrete, fit to grow nothing more than smartweed or English plantain. But who would know? It took years of patient research for Darwin to conclude that earthworms turned the entire topsoil layer of England once every several years.

Especially in late fall or early winter, standing with fork in hand at the wood's edge, I am reminded that the method of nature is to recover, recycle, and transform everything. Nothing is produced that can't somehow be used. Particularly in wild systems, which have achieved the wisdom of sustainability through years of practice, each growing season not only increases biomass but also builds the soil. In the economy of nature, each citizen is both a producer and a consumer, and the year always ends in the black.

You would think that such returns would immediately appeal to a culture fixated on compound interest and the bottom line. But guess again. A glance into the woods reveals the glint of pop cans or beer bottles casually tossed into the green swamp at the height of summer. Nearby a plastic grocery bag waves gently, snarled on a honeysuckle twig. A foam cup, white as a mushroom, peeks from the leaf litter. Pieces of old carpet, left by some transient, mimic moss. Mylar snack bags glitter among the leaves. I am often tempted to admire these triumphs of American packaging, so impervious to every form of decay. They keep our food fresh, which is a blessing, but once their job is done, they refuse to retire. They go on resisting transformation, sitting out the dance of biological time.

On most days, this resistance is simply annoying, marring the beauty of the woods like a child's dirty shoes dropped in the living room. At times it can even be comical. Once in the High Sierra, I passed a trail crew whose camp had been raided by a bear. A short while later, seeking a place to defecate, I found a sunny glade that the bear himself had used. There on the pine duff lay a perfect scat, distinctively shaped like a rope of sausage—except that instead of the usual brown, fibrous mass of seed hulls, chaff, and bits of roots, this scat was composed entirely of a Wonder Bread wrapper, its red, yellow, and blue balloons undimmed by their tortuous passage through the toughest guts in the Sierra.

Like other animals, we humans are accustomed to thinking that nature—bears and all—will somehow absorb our messes and clean up after us. But it's not so. Only geological time can suffice to absorb and transform much of our culture's waste, from Mylar packaging and glass bottles to heavy metal and radioactive waste. Much of this will simply be entombed, locked into rock like the refuse of Ordovician seas. A beer bottle is certainly as durable as a brachiopod. What tales will it tell in 450 million years, and to whom?

That's why, standing on the compost heap in midwinter, I often pick up a bag and head into the woods. Having created litter impervious to bacteria, we humans must now take over their job of recycling. It feels good to police the woods, especially now, when winter light has hardened the edge between the wild and the human worlds. As a householder in this place and time, I take anonymous responsibility for cleaning up the woods, working as best I can to follow the method of nature. Recycling and composting both ensure that my household rests on healthy land, that our modest economy feeds into the circle of biological time. It comforts me to realize that my compost heap receives the products of many distant lands, transforming them into good American earth. It's one way to make the world your home.

Thus composting completes the garden year. Standing with fork in hand in this frosty January light, I can almost feel the deep bacterial warmth seeping up through my boot soles. It reminds me how important it is to keep faith with the unconscious, to honor the darkness as well as the light, to remember the vital role played by humble and invisible things. As an image of human life, the garden teaches me how to dance with wildness, how to embrace transformation, how to build the good earth of the future one season at a time. It reminds me that digging in is as important as going out, that husbandry demands as much attentiveness and perseverance as any vision quest, as much aspiration and endurance as any adventure or initiation. Viewed from the garden, the path of practice leads to generativity and increased consciousness. It connects the woods and the house, the wild and the human worlds, in a single dance.

Wounds into Springs

Meanwhile, back in the house, another sort of husbandry goes on. I mean, of course, the practice of marriage and parenthood. What is the meaning of this small Herculean labor construed under the sign of wildness? At times I wonder what could be more wild than teenage daughters. Nevertheless, we do seem at first to be dealing with incompatible notions. The house with its taxes, utilities, and appliances, the marriage with its life term and struggle for intimacy, the daily grind of parenting with its snotty noses, hurt feelings, sibling conflict, and endless laundry all carried on indoors like some kind of slow explosion—all this seems antithetical to wild nature with its purity, integrity, and freedom. Backpacking in the mountains, I used to meet husbands on furlough from lives of quiet desperation, pale legs pumping under big packs, bonding at altitude with their buddies while sweating off one or two pounds of office fat. The initiatory gleam still smoldered in their eyes, as they hiked the John Muir Trail for time or bagged just one more four-teen thousand footer. What did they come here to endure? Tanned and hard from weeks on the trail, I swore condescendingly never to live in the suburbs with wife, house, children, everything that Zorba the Greek had called "the full catastrophe." In those days, the homelessness of endless voyaging had an epic attraction. It felt heroic and Odyssean, fed by an insatiable desire to know the vices and the worth of landscapes as well as men. In the wilderness, I always felt powerful and free. But now? There's always one more bill to pay, one more bruised feeling to massage, a lunch to pack, a room to vacuum, or a weed to pull. What sort of manhood is this anyway? How can it be the end of all our exploring?

When godlike Odysseus returned to Ithaca after two decades of war and wandering, the first thing he did was to slaughter the competition. Penelope's suitors had moved in like a suite of noxious weeds. You'll recall that before Odysseus went to war, he was a farmer who sought to beat the draft by feigning madness, hitching a donkey to his plow and sowing salt along the beach. Only when Palamedes set his infant son in front of the plow and Odysseus swerved aside was the ruse exposed. In Homer, Odysseus survives the thousand perils of war and voyaging through a combination of shrewdness, bravery, hardihood, and devotion to home and family. His slaughter of the suitors is his final act as a warrior, a violent yet noble rite of passage back to the life of husbandry where, presumably, he will find his ultimate purpose and fulfillment.

But while husbandry gives meaning to Odysseus's trials, it contributes little to Homer's poem, which dwells on war, adventure, and exotic perils. We don't remember Odysseus as a husband but as a warrior and a voyager. Perhaps that's why his myth feels incomplete, inspiring poets through the ages to invent some other ending. Dante, for instance, imagined Odysseus setting off again, in old age with only a few trusty companions. His thirst for experience proves insatiable. He exhorts his men to drive beyond the Pillars of Hercules so that, by penetrating forbidden regions, they will prove their superiority to the beasts and realize their destiny as followers of virtue and knowledge. But Odysseus is too old for this sort of ambition. His inspiring speech proves fatal as the ship founders off the shores of Purgatory, struck by a divine wind. He tells his story from deep in Hell, walking wrapped in flame in the pit reserved for false counselors. Yet we are still moved by his courage and resolve. He has struggled against the infirmity of age, the temptation to rest on his laurels and retire quietly from the epic scene. Like Zorba he's passionate and romantic, acting far younger than his years. How many of us secretly hope to do as well—or look as good—once we reach fifty? Odysseus's story and its avatars suggest the hidden links between warfare, voyaging, and husbandry. This is treacherous ground that every man must navigate in his passage from youth's aspiration to the generativity of middle age. The journey begins with initiatory ordeals that tear you out of youthful security and comfort while, at the same time, teaching techniques of suffering. You learn to manage the process of being broken and remade that underlies all growth. You need it not only to begin but also to move on. For adult life really consists of a series of deaths and resurrections. The path to generativity and healing lies through a world of wounds.

In our urban, industrial culture, war and military service have been the most common paths of male initiation. If you think of America as a peace-loving country, consider how few decades have passed without a war since the first English settlers landed at Jamestown in 1607. Our history is a thick red line. For a century and more, New England was a battleground: King Philip's War, the raids of Metacomet, the French and Indian War, the American Revolution, the Whiskey Rebellion, Shay's Rebellion. War spread inward with the frontier, that "burning edge" as Gary Snyder called it. Tecumseh, "Mad Anthony" Wayne, and the War of 1812 left Ohio charred and smoldering. Then came the Cherokee Removal, the Mexican War, the Civil War, the Indian Wars, the Spanish American War, and World Wars I and II, followed in our time by the Cold War, Korea, Vietnam, the Gulf War, Afghanistan, Iraq. America is in love with war. Why should anyone be surprised that the costliest, deadliest army on earth belongs to us? We're a warrior culture. We believe in regeneration through violence.

During the Vietnam era, when I came of age, young men were still required by law to report for two years of active duty. Every able-bodied man between eighteen and twenty-six was handed over to the Pentagon. If America was a melting pot, the military was its crucible. All manner of ethnic, racial, and familial differences were subsumed in the creation of this society-within-a-society whose purpose was not only to reinforce the power of the state but to project it toward the uttermost parts of the earth.

The young men I met in basic training were plucked from the tossed salad of U.S. society: blacks and whites, Anglos and Latinos, Protestants, Catholics, Muslims, and Jews, sons of the first, fifth, or seventh generation at all levels of education or skill. Nerd or macho, fat or thin, the army took us all. We had almost nothing in common at first, yet after eight weeks we all knew how to shoot and salute, make our beds, dress a wound, read a map, toss a hand grenade, call in an air strike, and spit shine our boots.

As a teacher, I took a professional interest in the army's methods, which played to every aspect of a young man's reality: surging hormones, burgeoning intelligence, the quest for identity and power, the love-hate relation to parents, family, and society at large. Drill sergeants projected a pumped, steroidal manhood with their barrel chests, booming voices, and starched fatigues. Even the skinny ones with pimples and bad teeth strutted and swaggered like B-grade action heroes. All training was highly sexualized. I still have the M-16 manual with its comic-book images of a juicy blonde in a beret and microfatigues caressing the rifle in stiff, black silhouette. The actual weapon felt light and futuristic with its gray alloys, pistol grip, and fiberglass stock with spring-backed firing chamber designed to absorb the recoil. To prove it, the drill sergeant shoved the butt of an M-16 against his groin and fired off a twenty-round clip. "Lieutenant!" he bawled. "I just had an orgasm!" One week later we were nailing targets at three hundred yards, and the M-16 seemed as familiar as a baseball bat. The targets were human silhouettes that popped up to resemble charging soldiers. Drawing a bead and squeezing off a round became almost a reflex. The burnt metal aroma of spent cartridges lingered like aftershave. I was proud of my expert rifleman's badge.

Meanwhile they whipped our bodies into shape with calisthenics, laps, pushups, and endless sessions on the monkey bars, where small but wiry guys like me did better than the beefy jocks we'd hated all through high school. The army found ways for everyone to be a man and worked them ruthlessly. They pumped up our esprit de corps at every level; we were the best and meant to prove it, not only on the PT course but over there in the jungles and rice paddies of Vietnam. Clear-eyed immigrants in my platoon wanted to repay the debt they owed this land of opportunity. Ghetto kids grasped at the chance to make it anywhere but back on the block. Middle-class college grads found it exhilarating to team up with men who'd worked in factories. My best buddy in basic was a guy from a motorcycle gang with a sweet disposition and several missing teeth.

Where else but in a conscript army would you find so much mixing of class, race, and character? On weary nights after a day of drill or shooting, we heard each other's brief life stories floating from one narrow bunk to the next. Though obviously contrived, the shared ordeal of basic training fostered a kind of intimacy hard to find among men in normal life, where competition rules. We depended on one another to make it through, the alternative being to start all over again. Some of us helped by tutoring, others by listening. We knew that in actual combat we would need these buddies and these skills. That was the dark side of boot camp's Boy Scout exuberance. Many drill cadre had served in Vietnam; you could recognize them by the purple shadows under their eyes, which someone called "death rings." On night-duty watch, there was always someone in the orderly room, pacing back and forth under the fluorescent lights from one cinderblock wall to the other. A brief greeting, or even a face at the door, was all it took to unleash the stories. In the hospital-like sterility of the orderly room, the trainee became a kind of confessor, his naive curiosity seeming to offer a prospect of release, forgiveness, perhaps redemption. We had all seen combat footage on TV—the grainy black-and-white of World War II seemed tougher and more heroic than the lurid reds and greens of Vietnam—but what was it really like over there? These cadre, most no older than ourselves, had been there and survived. They had come back. We clung to their stories in fascinated horror. As they spoke, their eyes glazed and their words came faster, as if they weren't being spoken but exhaled. You could tell that Fort Dix and the orderly room had disappeared: they were back in Nam crawling through rice and mud under machine-gun fire. The war had possessed them, conferring a strange power of speech. And when we left, as we had to, they started pacing again. The story had brought no relief, as if the words and memories themselves were a kind of wound.

By day we learned to use unimaginable weapons. The M-60 machine gun required three men, an ammo bearer, a gunner, and an assistant gunner to change the barrel, using a big asbestos glove. The rounds were as big as cigars, and at three hundred rounds per minute, the M-60 put out a lot of heat, enough to melt the barrel, so you best not drop that glove, troop. The sergeant bragged, "When the M-60 talks, nobody walks!" then opened up on a Jeep carcass downrange, slicing it in half. He also demonstrated the claymore mine, an "antipersonnel device" the size of a cheap novel. Inside its curved plastic case were a couple of hundred steel bearings backed by C-4 explosive. You set up the claymore on a tiny tripod, curved side out, and then backed away into cover while unreeling the detonator wire. To fire, you just squeezed the battery pack. The blast sent a phalanx of hot steel flying outward; at fifty yards it was wide enough to shred a platoon.

Day after day, we practiced firing, disassembling, cleaning, and re-assembling our weapons until we could do it all without thinking, even in the dark. It was thrilling to feel the violence exploding outward toward the target, potent and lethal yet fully controlled, by us! The army put incredible power into our young hands. We felt omnipotent and invulnerable, even more so than in the usual teenage fantasy. We were real men, armed and dangerous. I still have a postcard with a painting of the statue at the entrance to Fort Dix, a charging infantry soldier backed by swirling clouds. "Welcome to Fort Dix," it reads, "Home of the Ultimate Weapon!"

By day we felt like men, but by night, in the solitude of the barracks, we felt like boys again as the fears and memories returned—the TV images, the cadre's stories. Many did not want to own their fear and so clung to the macho attitudes of the day. Testosterone seemed to foster its own kind of magical thinking. For those of us who were not going to Vietnam, because we had enlisted either for noncombat training or for the National Guard, the stresses of basic training often caused an odd dissociation like that reported by rape victims. Time and again, I found myself watching, distant and abstracted, as my mind and body went through incredible motions—crawling through barbed wire under screaming tracers or yelling "Kill!" as I bayoneted a torso of old tires (remembering always to stab, twist, and pull). I could not imagine actually doing any of these things, and yet the creeping horror of it was, I could. I could kill. In a tight place, I would kill. I would kill without thinking. And the weapons, which delivered incredible violence at a safe distance, would make it all so much easier. Anonymous flesh did not stand a chance against them. At some point, it occurred to me that the weapons themselves were the enemy.

And therefore survival became the goal, not just in the simulated ordeal of basic training but in the manufactured hell of actual combat that many of us would face. Once you arrived "in country," the magical thinking of youth and hormones would quickly evaporate. The thing was to come out alive: the cadre were living proof. These weapons created by the state at tremendous cost, requiring untold hours of imagination and labor to produce, had one purpose only: to turn young men into dead meat. This was the human sacrifice that states required to maintain the power and mystique that secured their own existence. Think of the mothers and fathers who'd spent years conceiving, bearing, raising, and cherishing these sons, only to hand them over like some sort of tax. As I left for basic, my mother had remarked that in a just world—run by women, say—she'd at least have been paid. I had laughed then and rolled my eyes, but I was not laughing now.

When godlike Odysseus was drafted into the Greek army and shipped off to Troy, his mode of being shifted from husbandry to survival. The army cared nothing for him as an individual, as a husband and father and steward of the land. It just wanted his strong body and supple mind. Despite the fact that his strategies led to victory after a nine-year stalemate, there's no evidence that victory brought him any reward at all, other than release from Troy and the army. And what then? Only years of peril on the open sea or in strange lands, followed by the challenge of armed and dangerous usurpers. Odysseus won through, not because of any goodwill or aid on the military's part, but because surviving the perils of war, voyaging, and the enmity of the gods had made him tough, wise, and resolute. I imagine him leaving home in his early twenties and returning at midlife, after two decades of initiation. The remainder of his life is not written, but I believe we are meant to imagine it in the only terms that give meaning to the rest. For all his trials and exploits would appear tragic or pathetic if he had perished before reaching home or, worse, had clung to them into old age, fetishizing war and the heroics of exploration.

Odysseus's story teaches that husbandry is the chief end of male initiation. It also lays out the two archetypal paths, warfare and wilderness travel, that American sons have traditionally followed on their journeys toward manhood. In warfare young men find themselves thrust into deadly peril far from home and family, in environments of chaotic violence where all normal social relations are overthrown, where everything, even nature itself, must be sacrificed for the ultimate goal of victory. Survival calls forth every resource of body, intellect, and will; suffering and loss create deep bonds with one's companions, for whom self-sacrifice becomes not an option but a given. No wonder that in the end it is often so difficult to return to a world that has no experience of such things. And yet the alternative is to remain trapped in the war story, like Coleridge's Ancient Mariner, Dante's Ulysses, or the young Fort Dix cadre who saw reality only through dark death rings.

Returning was also the ultimate challenge for those who took the wilderness path. Like soldiers they faced epic perils far from home in strange landscapes surrounded by wild beasts and alien peoples, often without maps or guides, sometimes alone, or even naked, like the mountain man John Colter, who ran two hundred miles to escape the Blackfeet. Their stories endure as paradigms of survival by strength, intelligence, and will. Scouts, explorers, and naturalists hold as commanding a place in our national mythology as war heroes. Kit Carson,

Lewis and Clark, William Bartram, John Wesley Powell, all provide models of resolute manhood that even today inform initiatory programs such as Outward Bound. We commonly think of the wilderness traveler as a solitary on a quest, sometimes a quest for riches or healing but often a vision quest in search of power or identity. The wilderness, remote and uncompromising, imposes an ascetic discipline, engaging all resources for survival. You forego all civilized comforts, harden up, learn fast and deep because you have to. Extreme environments produce extreme consciousness, such as Black Elk's vision or the godlike views John Muir and Clarence King received on the peaks of the High Sierra. This visionary clarity confers the first thrill of ecological identity, a bond with earth itself that overcomes the youthful rush of hormones and magical thinking. It confers intimacy, not invulnerability—though, indeed, when standing on a summit with the world radiating from your feet, you do often feel as if you could go on forever. At such times you feel a wonderful power, especially if you are young and rebellious with few possessions and no career, sick of the adult world dinning in your ears about service to God and country while it wallows in consumerism, mass culture, industrialized lusts, and the worship of money. Why not give your devotion to the earth and its untrammeled communities of life?

The wilderness path, then, provides many of the same initiatory challenges as war, but without the horrific violence, organized murder, psychic trauma, or environmental destruction. Both paths produce the wounds and stories that distinguish men from boys. And both can be dangerously corrupted to thwart rather than foster a life of husbandry. The problem comes when adult life is defined in terms of initiation rather than the other way around. Then initiation is fetishized; its heroics of suffering and extreme consciousness become ends in themselves. Hence we have Sparta, fascism, gun-worship, and people speed-hiking the John Muir Trail. The men I met so many years ago on furlough from office life were chafing at the demands of husbandry. They were not yet reconciled to a generative life. Therophilia drove them into the mountains, abetted by the spirit of romance, that perpetual sense of unfulfilledness so dear to adventurers and capitalist entrepreneurs. How can you nurture the future and uplift the young when your own identity remains restless and uncertain? But initiation is something you are meant to pass through, not repeat endlessly in some romantic dream.

From both war and wilderness, the ultimate challenge, after survival, is to return so that you can adventure on life now. In politics this is peace, the pursuit of sustainable social relations. In ecological terms, it is husbandry, a dance with the wildness of other species for mutual aid and comfort. In interpersonal terms, it is marriage and parenthood, a dance with the wildness of other persons that feeds the spirit and grows the human future. To move from warriorhood into husbandry, a man must learn how to love and heal as well as to fight, and this means somehow turning his wounds into springs, his blood into living water. How can this be done except through the winter chemistry of the unconscious, which is fed, like my compost, with practice and deliberate imagination?

When I contemplate the house, the garden, and the woods from these lofty perspectives of epic and adventure, it sometimes amazes me to realize how deeply the thread of wildness runs through all the stages of manhood, linking them in a pattern as significant and productive as the garden year. Generative manhood requires all the skills of the warrior, the explorer, and the husbandman drawn from the compost of experience into a diligent life practice. I think of Darwin returning from the uttermost reaches of South America to a life of marriage and scholarship, of John Muir coming down from the mountains to raise grapes and daughters while writing books. I think of godlike Odysseus, who had built his house around a great olive tree, returning to devote every mature strength to household, land, and kingdom. But above all I think of Cincinnatus, the Roman hero for whom this city is named. He answered the call to war, persevered to victory, and then refused the gift of dictatorship so that he could return to his farm. How well he knew that the life of husbandry requires one sometimes to fight for the intimacy and time one needs to dance with the wildness of others.

ALIEN SPECIES

Toward Spiritual Ecology

But what about the weeds? In cities, where people of all races and nationalities live side by side with organisms from every continent, the question of alien species is always pushing to the fore. You can't walk two steps from the house without running into them, whether your path leads through the garden, across the lawn, through the neighborhood, or into the woods. As a wilderness lover, I tend to view exotics with suspicion, fear, or outright hatred, particularly in cases where they threaten a cherished landscape. If some genie offered to eradicate white-pine blister rust from the Boundary Waters or European water millfoil from Connecticut's lakes, I would not hesitate to accept. I am unfailingly drawn to whatever is native and aboriginal.

It's a prejudice, of course, one that I never questioned before moving here.

When Odysseus returned to Ithaca, he brought more than experience and strength. He brought knowledge of exotic landscapes along with actual remnants in the form of foods and seeds. These, we may be sure, found their way into the circumambient hills, where some became established. Plant transport by humans is as old as exploration. Indeed, the great voyagers of the Renaissance often went seeking useful plants as much as gold or slaves. Geographers agree that the spread of human cultures across the globe has been made possible by the discovery and domestication of less than two dozen key animals and plants, most of which are alien to the countries in which they now flourish.

My garden is a showcase of such useful aliens, as are the vast midwestern farmlands through which I drive to reach the mountains. Corn arose in Central America, potatoes in South America, and wheat in southwestern Eurasia, along with apples and pears. After millennia of selective breeding, they may be said to have coevolved with human culture. The geographer Jared Diamond has shown that cultures possessing a broad array of useful domesticates achieve considerable social, technical, and military advantage over the course of history. Indeed, the spread of European culture into North America and the flourishing of Cincinnati itself, which make my own life possible (including this page that you are now reading), could not have occurred without the energy and time released by the surplus proteins and carbohydrates of alien domesticated plants.

In short, the human ecology of urban cultures rests on an alien foundation. But there is more to it than the mere exchange of energy and nutrients. As I walk out the front door on the way to the market (which carries an astounding variety of produce), the first things I notice are the trees. An eastern hemlock grows at the corner of my neighbor's house; in her front lawn is a river birch, and a pin oak towers beside the street, tall and robust as a ship's mast. All are native to southwestern Ohio, and all appear to have been planted.

Down the block, I find more local natives: silver maple, sweet gum, green ash, sugar maple. However, I also encounter some that are native to North America but not to this area: red pine, white pine, Alberta and Colorado spruce, southern magnolia, paper birch, even a jack pine looking even more scraggly and forlorn than it does in the Boundary Waters. And scattered promiscuously throughout are many exotic trees: Siberian elm and European linden, both of which tolerate dust and smog; the Callery pear of Asian origin; the Chinese gingko with its archaic, fan-shaped leaves; the Scotch pine with its thin red bark and prickly needles, now distributed worldwide; the shaggy Norway spruce wrapped in Wagnerian gloom.

These are the trees in my forest. And beneath them flourishes an equally diverse, complex, and mixed array of flowers and ornamental shrubs: the native violets, coral bells, rhododendron, and oak-leaf hydrangea; the alien hosta, daylily, lilac, and rose of Sharon. All have been planted and nurtured by human beings, and many have been bred for desirable qualities, such as shape or color, that have nothing to do with food. They fill the eye, mind, and heart rather than the belly.

Viewed from a certain distance, this assemblage of plants appears characteristic of human cities in this part of the country. It has a consistency as distinct as that of any plant community described by ecologists in the wild. The difference is that geography alone cannot account for their presence and distribution; we must factor in human activity and needs. And what do people need besides food, clothing, and shelter? They need to be close to other living things; they need to be growing and learning, in touch with the wildness in others of all kinds; they need beauty and truth and a sense of meaning. They need stories and tokens of stories to feed their spirits.

As I walk through the neighborhood, I'm struck not only by the overall consistency of the biota but also by the distinctiveness of each neighbor's plantings. One house will have spruce, another magnolias, still another red maples or pin oaks. What accounts for the differences? Are they merely accidents of history, reflecting no more, for instance, than what the landscaper happened to have in his truck that day, or is there some hidden pattern?

Not far from my home, a sixty-year-old Tudor house sits on a corner lot surrounded by big white pines. Every time I walk past, I smell their pungent resin. I hear the whisper of their needles in the breeze, I feel the coolness gathering beneath them, and suddenly it feels as if I'm no longer in Cincinnati but somewhere far to the north, along the shores of Lake Huron or Basswood Lake, or deep in the hills of Connecticut, New Hampshire, or even Maine, perhaps with a view of Katahdin. It's enough to stop me in midstride. There, sure enough, is the familiar carpet of dead needles, cinnamon brown and brittle to the touch, that Aldo Leopold likened to accumulated wisdom. There is the green stain of *Gloeocapsa* algae on every exposed surface from the smooth bark of young branches to the rough-sawn picket fence. For a moment, it's as if I have fallen down a rabbit hole and come out in another part of the universe.

What accounts for the presence of these pines, which are not native to Cincinnati? All I can say for sure is that they were planted. But who planted them, and why? I may never know, but I strongly suspect it was someone with a particular fondness for white pines and the landscapes from which they come, someone who loved the North Woods, with their rockbound lakes and glaciated hills, someone who loved clean water and sun-dried mornings with the smell of winter lurking in every shadow.

Someone who left all that behind and moved to Cincinnati for love or work or anything called conscience once, and yet could not forget and so, as a gesture of homage, planted pines. It's a hidden story, then, that informs the ecology of this place, something immune to science and perhaps unknowable, but no less real on that account.

Loren Eiseley called humans the "dream animal," to suggest how much of our life is lived through an inner world of memory, imagination, and desire. If we see the green world through such dreamy eyes, it's no wonder that our husbandry weaves dreams into it over time. The trees in my forest are all woven round with secret stories, and the neighborhood as a whole, with its landscaped yards and vegetable gardens, expresses some of our culture's deepest longings. Walk down the street, and you will feel a sense of order rising like fragrance from these tidy homes, where all the plants seem comfortable, healthy, and well proportioned. There's no sense of conflict between the wild and the human world, only sweet companionship and mutual aid. Here plants from all over the earth grow side by side in a harmony created and sustained by human beings. It brings to mind the earthly paradise that Dante found on the summit of Purgatory, where archetypes of every species grew blissful and perfect, in tune with God's perfect husbandry and expressing, in their diversity, the plenitude of his own infinite nature. It should come as no surprise that this neighborhood strives for order and diversity in its plantings. For the dream of Eden is one of our oldest dreams, and if we aspire to it in our husbandry, we might find the way back to heaven. On this path, classic material ecology will no longer serve. We need a spiritual ecology as well.

Violets and Honeysuckle

So much for the useful species that we depend on for food or love for the beauty and meaning they provide. What about the weeds, which crop up everywhere unannounced and uninvited? Before spring is over, they have squatted in the garden, sprawling among the beans with street-punk insolence. I go after them with the hoe, but by July the heat has done me in. I'd rather stay indoors with a cool drink, contemplating nature through the study windows.

Out front the situation is no better. You can easily tell where my lawn ends and that of my neighbor, the ex-Marine, begins. His is a lush, springy carpet; mine is a shaggy mat where grass contends with Indian strawberry, white clover, purple violets, and dandelions. He shakes his head at this unruly polyculture, relying on chemical sprays to achieve the golf-course look, while I, stubbornly, continue to weed by hand. I enjoy abundant earthworms and lovely spring flowers but never the satisfaction of a uniform and perfect green nor, for that matter, a painless back. My only hope, he says, is to hose down the yard with Roundup, scrape it clean, plow, and reseed—in other words, start from scratch, as if the place had no history.

Michael Pollan, my best authority on things horticultural, takes a wry view of the American lawn. How could a form of gardening so unimaginative and wasteful have come to dominate our settled landscapes? Why should it be the most pervasive expression of our dance with wildness? The dance itself, in this form, is hardly graceful, a plodding two-step between drench and mow.

Some historians believe that the American taste for lawns arrived with English settlers, who associated them with estates and landed gentry. Others see the lawn as a vestige of pioneer concerns about security: open space around the house meant less chance of a surprise attack by robbers or hostile Indians. Still others find hidden ideology. For Pollan the lawn betokens an extreme but simple-minded lust for order. Whereas a garden is nature guided and shaped by culture, a lawn is "nature under culture's boot." Pollan's phrase sounded paranoid to me, until I saw workmen arrive to spray my neighbor's yard wearing uniforms, black boots, and rubber gloves.

The fact is that weeds flourish in our yards and gardens because of conditions that we create. By chopping off the grass before it heads up and goes to seed, we encourage the wood violet and Indian strawberry, which spread along the ground. Our prairies never have a chance to mature; the grass forest remains only a vague dream of possibility latent in soil and genes. Our mowing gives the edge to broad-leafed weeds that shade out tender grass and disrupt the pleasing uniformity of height and texture. Most Cincinnatians resort to chemicals to preserve the illusion of grass as the master race. After spraying and mowing, all that remain are ranks of thin blades standing at attention. They make a lush, springy carpet for the victor's godlike feet, a comforting view of absolute discipline for his approving eye.

And yet, weeds always keep coming back. Indeed, as Pollan notes, they're more successful than my grass or vegetables at growing under the disturbed conditions that I create. Whenever I try to impose control, I make the earth say weeds along with beans or grass. Weeds are the dark side of husbandry, the gardener's shadow.

This becomes even clearer when I step from the lawn or garden into the woods. It's there that the problem of alien species looms largest to ecologists, backpackers, and other pilgrims to the wild. Beyond my compost heap, the ground is laced with garlic mustard, bittersweet, and English ivy. Two steps more, and the way is barred by nodding fronds of Amur honeysuckle. It was this handsome and ubiquitous shrub that first made me realize how much our Cincinnati woods abound in exotic plants. Its story can stand as a figure for the problem of alien species in general.

Amur honeysuckle (*Lonicera maackii*) evolved in eastern Siberia and flourishes on floodplains and hillsides along the northern Chinese border in the watersheds of the Amur and Ussuri Rivers. It was discovered in 1855 by the Russian botanist and explorer Richard Karlovich Maack (1825–86) and cultivated in Russia and Europe before being brought to America in 1897 as part of the U.S. Department of Agriculture's plant introduction experiment program. By 1931 Amur honeysuckle was being marketed by commercial nurseries. From the 1960s to 1984 the Soil and Conservation Service worked to develop improved varieties for wildlife habitat and soil stabilization, and many introductions were made.

By the late 1950s, the plant had reached the Cincinnati area, where landscape gardeners admired its elegant, vaselike shape and graceful, abundant foliage. It makes a handsome ornamental, whether planted singly or as a hedge. It leafs out early and stays green until the first hard frost, sometimes right up to New Year's. In the spring, its creamy blossoms spread a cloying sweetness; in the fall, its bright red berries feed

both the wild birds and the gardener's eye. It grows vigorously—often
as much as three feet in a year—yet responds well to pruning, requires
little maintenance, and seems immune to local insects and diseases.
No doubt its importers considered it a blessing.

Unfortunately, these same qualities also suited Amur honeysuckle
for life in the woods. Because of our odd topography, crisscrossed by
hillsides and ravines, Cincinnati abounds in curvy, narrow strips of
greenbelt too steep or unstable to build on. Ecologically this means lots
of "edge" that is perfect for species that thrive on disturbed ground.
Amur honeysuckle loves poor, calcareous soils. It moves in quickly to
colonize vacant lots, road cuts, schoolyards, old playing fields, or abandoned factory sites. Old-growth woods, with their thick duff layer, slow
it down, but not for long. The plant sends up many long, flexible shoots
from a single rootstock, and these arc outward, bending down as they
mature and thicken. New shoots sprout vertically from nodes along
these branches, so that older plants seem to be leapfrogging over the
ground. A ten-year-old honeysuckle looks like a green fountain. Its thick,
persistent foliage casts such deep shade that the ground beneath is often
completely bare. Research suggests that the plant may also produce alle-
lopathic chemicals that inhibit the growth of nearby seedlings, in the
manner of black walnut or American beech.

A forest colonized by Amur honeysuckle looks green, lush, and
healthy from a distance, but troubling symptoms appear as you approach. Few native wildflowers or perennial herbs will grow on the bare
soil beneath, nor will you find many other shrubs or vines. Although
the trees and upper canopy seem perfectly intact, few seedlings are
growing up to take their place. Normal succession has been interrupted,
with results that no one can foresee. Under such conditions, it's doubtful
that the present mix of oak, hickory, beech, and sassafras will persist
for more than thirty or forty years.

A walk by the wood's edge reveals how the honeysuckle spreads.
Young plants occur in two locations: in rings around older plants, or
scattered among the trees. Apparently the seeds either fall directly to
earth or get dispersed by birds or squirrels. The rate of germination

must be high, to judge by the number of seedlings in my yard. It's a spring ritual to pull them up while the roots are shallow. Honeysuckle is okay in small doses; it can be decorative, even handsome, and, of course, I appreciate the way it hides the neighbors' yard. But I'm haunted by thoughts of a friend whose woods are now clogged with mature honeysuckle, an impenetrable rat's nest of stiff, bristly limbs as big around as my arm, with the ground beneath as barren as a desert. At this point, his only recourse would be to saw each plant off at the base and drag it to the chipper, a small herculean labor to be sure, even if he could untangle one bush from another. And then he'd still have to police the stumps repeatedly, clippers in hand, or paint them all with Roundup. Not to mention pulling up each year's crop of seedlings, for experts estimate that a seven- to nine-year seed bank remains in the soil.

I think of him each spring when pulling honeysuckle. It feels like a life sentence to hard labor that should belong to nature. The woods are supposed to take care of themselves. But the honeysuckle is no respecter of persons or property. Given an opportunity, it will put down roots; it will increase and multiply. What matter that it complicates my life? It tasks me; it heaps me. I see in it outrageous biological strength. And after spring weeding, sweating and scratched, I'm tempted to see inscrutable malice too.

It's maddening to realize that the honeysuckle is here because of gardeners and homeowners like me. We fell in love with its beauty and strength. We brought it home and expected it to stay put. We expected it to do its job. But we were seduced. For no sooner had it set roots than it began grabbing habitat from species we love, such as trout lily or Dutchman's breeches. We hate it not only because it does its thing regardless, exposing our shortsightedness, but also because it is winning. It thrives here, because conditions are perfect, and it is following its bliss. The fact is, we really hate it for its wildness.

Perhaps that's why Amur honeysuckle is called an "ecological monster" in park brochures and garden bulletins. Its history carries the scent of horror: desire turned to revulsion as the houseguest morphs into a thug, the lover into a vampire. Suddenly the household becomes a place of mortal danger. Intimacy invites not fulfillment but destruction. Worst of all, there seems to be no escape. For the danger and death arise from our own susceptibility and desire.

Once loved, Amur honeysuckle is now feared and loathed. Our stories have changed it from a valued cultivar to a noxious weed. That shift has much to tell us about how we use ideas of nature to perpetuate beliefs, enshrine values, and justify our acts. For Amur honeysuckle has never stopped being itself (unlike humans, plants cannot dissemble). It is only our stories about it that have changed.

Alien Artifacts

In relation to wildness, then, alien species present us with a mass of thorny and conflicting facts. We may make better headway if we look at them not just as creatures but as constructs.

Ecologists define aliens as species that did not evolve along with the landscape but were imported, deliberately or accidentally, by humans. This definition excludes species that arrived on their own, using "natural" means of dispersal, for example, burrs clinging to animal fur, seeds dropped in scat, or insects blown by the wind. The experiments in island biogeography conducted by E. O. Wilson demonstrate how rapidly a sterilized landscape can be colonized and repopulated by immigrants from nearby ecosystems, despite barriers as formidable as miles of open sea. Two decades after an eruption that erased many square miles of old-growth forest, the slopes of Mount Saint Helens are teeming with life. And fifteen thousand years ago, when the last ice sheets were melting back toward the Great Lakes, Cincinnati had no plants at all. Everything that sprouted here—the dryas mats, the fireweed, the aspen seedlings—represented alien species. Paleoecologists peering at smears of mud from pond core samples read their microscopic footprints in fossil pollen. The white pine, now at the southern limit of its range, arrived here six thousand years ago from a refuge in the mountains of Virginia. White and black spruce, once native, have long since retreated far to the north. Hemlocks remain only in cool, shaded canyons of the Hocking Hills a hundred miles east of Cincinnati.

The idea of an alien species is thus more complex than it first appears. One must enfold a time horizon that can range from centuries to millennia. In many cases, ecologists aren't even sure if a species was imported—a case in point is Kentucky bluegrass—so they just say it's "of cryptic origin." If a plant was reported by white explorers or early settlers, it is considered aboriginal, unless we can trace its progress archaeologically, as in the case of corn, which had reached eastern North America by AD 200. But how can we know, except from a sparse and imperfect fossil record, which of our "native" plants developed before humans crossed the Bering land bridge and which were carried by those earliest explorers as berries in pemmican, for instance, or seeds embedded in their skin garments?

When a newly arrived species begins to reproduce on its own, ecologists say that it has "naturalized" or "escaped from cultivation," suggesting that our care, like that of selfish parents, comes at a price. We expect these plants to know their place, but wildness sneers at such conditional love. There is no use complaining. As my teenage daughter says, "Just deal with it." But that's the problem.

And in fairness, things could be a whole lot worse. Ecologists recognize that, for all the species we import, only a very few escape to run amok. A numerical approximation called the "tens rule" describes this relationship. For every thousand species introduced into an area, one hundred will escape into the wild, ten will become naturalized, and one will become invasive. In other words, the vast majority of imported species actually do stay put or at least cause no harm. Some, as we've seen, are vital to the culture. And yet, our rhetoric makes no distinction. Why should we want to stigmatize them all?

In social terms, an alien is someone living in a foreign country, a resident with limited civil rights. Native birth is often the essential criterion for citizenship, but any field mark can be stigmatized, be it religion, ethnicity, color, or ideology. Wildness is viewed as deviant, criminal, or subversive. Suppressing or exterminating the alien becomes a heroic act, embodied in myths and celebrated in poetry and art. History shows that the group in power can define an alien any way it wants, with the ultimate goal of securing its own existence. As Aristotle, ever succinct, once wrote, "It is meet that Greeks should rule over bar-barians."

The movies carry this self-serving logic to new heights of ingenuity, presenting creatures that are alien in both the social and the ecological sense. Another planet or a galaxy far, far away represents the ultimate exotic landscape. And space aliens behave just like terrestrial exotics: they invade and wreak havoc, except that now they have spaceships and high-tech weapons. For the first hour, humans are hopelessly outgunned; the plot turns on heroic efforts to "save" the planet. Things are made easier, emotionally, by the creatures' hideous appearance, which consists of nasty bits of earthly nature cut up and reassembled. Insects and parasites dominate this iconography of the grotesque, contributing body armor and slime. The fact that such creatures also possess technology and intelligence—hitherto our exclusive property—makes their invasion not only threatening but scandalous. How dare they do unto us what we have been doing unto others for centuries?

The fact that space aliens are constructed from bits of nature that we loathe or despise suggests a scapegoating process. Cosmologists agree on the high probability of extraterrestrial life, given the size and age of the universe. But if we ever discover such life, it will bear little resemblance to our own. Too much chance and history have gone into us. Our very proteins go back more than a billion years. These movie aliens may be Other, but they are not Wholly Other. They belong to Earth, and they belong to us. In fact, they represent our own behavior stripped of all pre-tense to grace or virtue. You might almost say they're a caricature of how we must appear to other species.

Of course, it is horrifying to be confronted with our own capacity for violence or evil. But it is worse to realize that nature might not be bound to keeping us on top, might in fact be willing to sweep us away to make room for new experiments. Evolution, says Annie Dillard, loves death more than it loves you or me.

No wonder we need the movies! As a product of nature *out there*, space aliens embody the horrible creativity of a nature indifferent to hu-man desire. By defeating them in battle, we human beings regain our dominance. The movies glorify our virtue and power by scapegoating constructed organisms. In these fantastic projections, victory naturalizes the status quo; the monster becomes an aberration blasted into the outer darkness. Humans win; nature loses; the world is saved.

It is hardly surprising, therefore, to find metaphors of war, disease, or purity cropping up in the rhetoric we apply to alien species. They are construed as "invasive," stealing territory from other species by "outcompeting" them (the natives become "displaced," like refugees). As "noxious weeds," aliens disrupt our husbandry and challenge our dominion, not only in the cornfield but in the forest. They do their own thing, which costs us plenty. A wilderness boundary means as little to them as a barbed-wire fence. No wonder the federal government has stepped in with an Interagency Council on Invasive Alien Species, complete with mission statement, action plans, and Web site. A click of the mouse calls up an "arsenal" of "control measures" for "infestations," a library of articles and bulletins covering "target species" that "pollute" or "degrade" "natural environments," "endangered ecosystems," and "pristine wilderness." Such metaphors convey a sense that aliens have upset the order established by both nature and culture, traditional antagonists who now make common cause. Apparently it's all about control.

If you think we can escape from this Machiavellian calculus by aligning ourselves with nature, consider the idea of a *native* species. The word springs from the same root as "nature" and "nation": the Latin *nascitur*, "to be born." In social terms, a native is someone who was born here and therefore enjoys certain rights that others have to earn. "Native" embodies claims of primogeniture and tradition. But it can also be a term of abuse. In colonialist rhetoric, to "go native" means to sympathize with those you were meant to rule, to adopt their viewpoint and toy dangerously with their customs; it means to go over to the other side, to become a renegade, a traitor to your own kind, to reject civilization for nature, which is construed (in Conrad, for example) as a heart of darkness.

This sort of talk carries over into ecological thinking. A "native" species means one that evolved as part of the "original" ecosystem that flourished before European incursions. In other words, the aboriginal horizon ends with Europe: history begins with us. It would be hard to imagine a more self-serving idea. Far nobler to view native species as a living link with prehistoric time, with the world as it was before we arrived to mess things up. Contemplating, preserving, and nurturing native species might offer a tangible link with that unfallen Nature. It might take us back to a time before sin and error, when we could, if we chose, grasp at a second chance.

Some Kind of Paradise

Beneath every other value ascribed to native species and ecosystems lurks this cherished concept of Edenic wilderness. It has inspired generations of ecological activists to campaign for the extermination of aliens and the restoration of aboriginal flora. But aspirations like these soon fall into contradiction. At Fernald, just west of Cincinnati, a huge uranium plant is being decommissioned, and an ecologist I know was asked to restore an old pasture on the site to its former wetland condition as a demonstration project. Work began by scraping and grading the entire area, which was then stabilized with coconut-fiber mats and covered with topsoil. Native plants were sown or transplanted, organic fertilizers were added, and the soil was inoculated with mycorrhizal spores. The plants came up in a textbook mosaic of indigenous flora, but problems arose almost at once. White-tailed deer browsed off the tender shoots; Canada geese uprooted aquatic plants and fouled the pond with their droppings; cattails muscled into the shallows. My friend spoke of fencing the area, stringing monofilament fishline over the pond to keep out the geese, and stroking individual cattails with a gloved hand dipped in Roundup. The alternative, he said, was to keep replanting, which was unthinkable in time or cost. And the problem species were not exotics but natives!

I don't wish to impugn restoration. Certainly it is honorable to make amends by undertaking a sort of reverse incursion. It is good to side with the forces of healing and nurturing rather than those of exploitation and degradation. It is noble to preserve and protect the habitats of endangered species. And it is wise to establish sanctuaries for biological and genetic diversity. Nevertheless, by seeking to replicate wilderness in the compressed span of a human generation or less, restoration struggles against history and the actual, stubborn wildness of resident organisms. As a form of gardening, it still creates weeds, and they reveal the flaw in its aspirations. For restoration, in its eagerness to achieve the order and grace of the wild, also seeks to get the better of biological time.

But it is not only restorationists who cling to the idea of Edenic wilderness. Our most notable environmental prophets, from Muir to Leopold, have extolled wilderness as a biotic community in equilibrium, vital and self-sustaining. Evolution has guaranteed that periodic catastrophes such as fire or storm will be weathered and absorbed. Over the centuries, all niches have been explored and filled. Resident species have adapted to one another, forming unconscious but highly successful patterns of mutual aid. Wilderness, therefore, is conceived as a base datum of ecological normality, exemplifying what the land would produce if left to its own devices. Moreover, because its relationships have proven survival value, wilderness can be used as a metaphorical standard against which to judge human values and behavior. The right way is, quite simply, nature's way.

How tempting it is to imagine some kind of paradise at the end of biological time! But doing so casts human life and work in a very negative light. Humans are conceived primarily as usurpers, degraders, or despoilers of ecosystems, driven by greed or appetite and abetted by pride, folly, or ignorance. People, to paraphrase Dickens, are "naturally vicious." There is no room here for husbandry, responsible or otherwise, no account of the myriad intimacies and symbioses in which we engage, no acknowledgment of the success that some cultures have had in enhancing the diversity and productivity of ecosystems.

But there are deeper, more troubling reasons why we cling to Edenic visions. Underlying the idealization of wilderness lurks another ancient concept, that of a "state of nature" in which things grow and develop with no interference from civilized humans. The qualifier "civilized" is important, for the state of nature often included people who were deemed primitive or barbaric. Both the Smithsonian Institution and the American Museum of Natural History include extensive exhibits of indigenous North American cultures, as if native people were somehow part of nature in contrast to the urbanized, modern world outside. Dioramas depict their lives as enmeshed in the landscape yet curiously static and routinized, as if they had no history before we arrived on the scene.

Until the late eighteenth century, European thought regarded the state of nature as a baseline of potential development. Nature could be improved by art, cultivation, or education, but it could not be degraded. That changed with the Romantic revolution, when nature came to be seen as a repository of truth, beauty, or inspiration that could suffer damage at vicious or ignorant hands. But either way the state of nature was thought to persist in its wildness until acted on by civilization. And that placed it in a curious position with respect to time.

On the one hand, beings in nature lay outside history (defined by civilization as a progression of unique moments). But on the other hand, because they participated in time via birth, growth, and decay, they also lay outside eternity (that is, the realm of the gods). They were neither mortal nor immortal, because for them time moved but never progressed. To speak of "natural history," therefore, was to speak paradoxically. Organisms were depicted as types rather than individuals, and their stories resembled myths more than biographies. It is easy to see how such organisms could populate the idealized landscape of Paradise, which inhabits the same curious ahistorical time. And it is easy to see why we would be so attracted to them. For a myth is easier to grasp than an actual life. The process of individuation, the story that reveals the character and meaning of each mortal life, does not exist in the state of nature.

And if such idealized beings are easier to grasp, they are also easier to deal with. If culture is considered superior to nature, as it was during the Renaissance, then we can do what we like to other creatures in the name of improvement or civilization. We can domesticate, enslave, or exterminate them, all for some greater good. The agenda of the conquistador is naturalized and made to seem honorable and just. On the other hand, if nature is seen as superior to culture, then it can be used as a convenient standard against which to measure societies, institutions, or individuals. In benign forms, this leads to an ethic of wilderness preservation or restoration. In extreme cases, it can lead to an idolatry of nativism and a dream of reducing the population by any means necessary.

But neither view is just or humane. The real scandal of alien species is that they expose such self-serving ideas. For alien species are living proof that human and natural history cannot be disentangled. There is no such thing as an Edenic state of nature, no such thing as pristine wilderness. Indeed, these concepts betray a seductive nostalgia for Paradise that is rooted in our age-old desire to escape from history. For history reveals how willing we are to enslave, prey on, or destroy other beings to serve our ends. And none are exempt, not even members of our own species. What difference is there, except in degree, between ethnic cleansing and pulling weeds?

When I am oppressed by such thoughts, I find it reassuring to step into the backyard, where natives and aliens flourish in a dense, intricate mosaic. When I see daisy fleabane growing next to Indian strawberry or purple violet, I am reminded of how tenaciously indigenous life ways persist amid the oppressions and blandishments of aliens. When their nation was overwhelmed by industrial culture, the Mohawks of upstate New York did not cease to be warriors. They became high-rise steelworkers and wrote new stories across the Manhattan sky.

For all of us who live here now—in North America, on the cusp of the millennium—the old nativist constructs will no longer serve. There is no going back to island biogeography in the wild or the human world. A global economy means a global ecology. There was a time, not long ago, when every species in Cincinnati was alien, for the land had just emerged from beneath the ice. Since then the history of this place has been a series of incursions by one species after another, including *Homo sapiens*. For we are the preeminent alien species, restlessly colonizing foreign ground ever since we came out of Africa.

How, then, does one become native to a place? It requires time and attention, with the long horizons necessary for succession, coadaptation, and the evolution of mutual aid. It is a life's work and more than a life. Better begin at once, then, on the ground beneath our feet, which is the only ground we know. Even this unprepossessing urban soil with its grit, litter, and ragged weeds, its microbes and earthworms and layered dreams, can shine with promise in its becoming. It's a place in process—no paradise, but full of lessons—and it can bring us together. For the nature we have in common is not sublime and remote but modest and near at hand. It's where we live and work. In fact, it's home.

OLD GROWTH

A Walk with Saint Thomas Aquinas

Growing up in New York's gritty penumbra, my friends and I were always climbing trees. My yard had a beech, a pignut hickory, and a Norway maple that hugged the cinder-block wall of the garages next door. We'd shinny up to get on the roof, escaping from bandits or enemy commandos, or just to get a view over the houses and streets where grownups hurried along in their sensible shoes and Republican cloth coats. On clear days, we might catch a lucky glimpse of the Watchung Mountains, beyond which, so far as we knew, there was only the wild, wild West.

Because I was little, the trees all felt mighty big, even the young maple by the garage. The pignut hickory could not have been more than twelve or fourteen inches in diameter, yet it grew straight as a telephone pole, forcing me to hug it like a bear cub as I squirmed toward the first branch eight feet up. Beech trees were more inviting, with their short, thick limbs and gray, warty bark that seemed to hang in folds like the skin of an elephant. The sinewy branches grew straight out from the trunk, so that three or four boys could sit side by side, trading boasts or M&Ms while spying on the little kids below.

These were not forest trees, of course, but isolated specimens. Like potted plants, they represented an absent world of life, variety, and meaning. I loved them because they provided escape and elevation, be-tokening wildness farther and wider than the narrow frame of our city yard. The true forest lay up north in Connecticut, where second growth had colonized the hillside around our summer cottage. My grandfather had chased butterflies through fields of wildflowers, but in their place I found galleries of maple, birch, and ash, thick as bamboo and perfect for teepee poles. Underneath, the ground was a tangle of jewel weed, Virginia creeper, cleavers, ajuga, and poison ivy. I had never heard of succession and thought the whole place fabulously wild.

Not until arriving in California as a young GI did I encounter genuine old growth, first in the redwood preserve of Muir Woods, just north of San Francisco, and then in the coniferous forests of the middle Sierra Nevada. Entering the deep ravine of Muir Woods felt like diving to the bottom of the sea. All sound was muted; the light was a filtered algal green. The peaty ground was strewn with fallen fronds that cushioned every step. Few plants grew on the ground except for large ferns that seemed to erupt like dark green fountains. Everywhere you felt the pressure of immense, slow-moving life. I found myself crouching slightly, taking quick shallow breaths. It was easy to imagine dinosaurs lumbering through groves such as this, built to the same scale with their leathery skin and monstrous, demonic faces. Of course, they had owned the earth far longer than mammals or human beings. Muir Woods was a remnant of that lost epoch, a flowerless, gargantuan world of brown and green.

The ancient forests of the Sierra Nevada felt very different when I first encountered them eight months later. Perhaps it was the season—early spring, with patches of snow still glistening on the duff—or perhaps it was just a yearning for sweetness and light after a dull winter of army routine. Maybe it was the climate and the topography, high glaciated ridges and air so clean and dry that it carried light like a crystal. Whatever the cause, I found these Sierra forests of sugar pine, red fir, and incense cedar wonderfully refreshing. Each tree stood forth in sculptural clarity, set off against brown heathery duff or some Zen assemblage of erratic boulders. They were immense trees, reaching a hundred feet or more and branchless for several stories. But they did not look big until you stood next to them or tried to estimate their height by squinting across an outstretched thumb. Unlike the coastal redwoods, these Sierra trees never oppressed your vision but lifted it skyward like the pillars of a cathedral. No wonder John Muir had felt like dancing; no wonder he had pressed Emerson, that sunset intellectual, to camp out in a sequoia grove instead of spending his last Yosemite night in a hotel. To walk here was to breathe sacredness like air, to sense in living nature the bracing paradox of revealed religion itself, that something so old could yet feel so fresh and vital—in a word, so young. And this feeling did not emanate just from the trees, but from the landscape itself. Everything appeared to have been arranged—the plants, the stones, the contour of a slope, the crease of a stream, even the angle of the light itself, all placed with the deft assurance of a Vermeer interior. The calligraphic silver of fallen branches played off handsomely against the gray of exposed granite or the pewter bellies of noonday clouds. There was profound, implicate order in both the presence and the process of this landscape. I could not get enough of it, even after many trips.

Nor did these feelings abate when I returned to graduate school in the city, back on the East Coast, where big wilderness and ancient forests were both in short supply. After brooding on the Sierra for two years, I got a chance to teach wilderness literature in the Adirondacks, and it was there that I experienced eastern old growth for the first time. We started hiking near Cranberry Lake, a region that, while technically part of New York's Adirondack Park and thus defined as "forever wild" by the state constitution, was still riddled with old logging roads and parcels of private land. The program director said that we would encounter virgin forest, but he could not tell us exactly where it was. For two days we hiked through thick, dark woods along a path edged with jewel weed and enchanter's nightshade. It felt as comfortably wild and familiar as Connecticut. But on the morning of the third day, we came to a place where the forest suddenly brightened, as if someone had thrown open the shutters. Great trees—white pines!—towered eighty feet or more above thickets of blueberry and mountain laurel. The ground was a quilt of lichen, star moss, wild sarsaparilla, and bigleaf aster. With each step, I felt the springy crunch of pine duff, the sharp, minty fragrance of bruised sweet fern. Truly, this was a clean, well-lighted place that glowed with the same angelic vitality as John Muir's Sierra forests. We had to stop, and days later, back in cool second growth, we were still talking about it. Imagine what it must have been like when the whole range was like this!

I have never been back to that place in the Adirondacks, but I've met old growth in many other places—in the Wind River Range and the North Cascades, on Alaska's southeast coast, in the mountains of Costa Rica or Michoacán, in the Boundary Waters or Quetico—and every time I have felt the same things: a sudden, unmistakable buoyancy or lightness, the way you feel when you shed your pack after a long day's journey, a palpable freshness, an almost electric tingle in the air, a pervasive sense of order and coherence that goes deeper than visual composition. Everything feels clean and healthy. The whole landscape seems to glow. No wonder I always come back feeling cleansed and rejuvenated—"detoxified," as one of my backpacking friends would say—but also reconstituted and enhanced, as if something had been added to my organism: not food, which gives up energy as it passes through, but something more vital and permanent, a new capability or way of seeing, perhaps a deeper capacity for empathy or faith, like a new chamber in the heart.

Barry Lopez writes of the manifest yet inexplicable coherence of wilderness landscapes and their power to heal by extending that coherence, through experience, into the inner landscape of our memory, imagination, and desire. We live in both landscapes at once, and stories give us a way to bring them into phase. This accounts, Lopez explains, for the feelings of lightness and refreshment that people feel in the presence of a story that is told with due respect for the land and the listener and the integrity of the relation between them. I believe that it also explains how authentic stories, stories that bear witness to lived truth, inspire people to undertake journeys of pilgrimage to good, wild, and sacred places. Therophilia, our innate love of the wild, moves them to seek insight and transformation, leads them by still or moving water for the restoration of their souls, and stories make maps for them to follow.

That's why the stories of our wilderness prophets continue to move us in an age of high technology, global economics, and a market capitalism infused with urban time. More than a hundred years ago, John Muir founded the Sierra Club to get people into the mountains so that they could experience old growth directly, as if the line of words on his page could lead directly into a line of footprints on the trail. Story for him was only the beginning of the journey, essential as inspiration or preparation but finding its fulfillment only in action of the whole body, which would be *moved* to take up its bed and walk. And pilgrimage itself, this journey that flows from a story, would find its fulfillment not merely in the completion of the trek but also in the creation and telling of the pilgrim's own story, the new story that adds to one's ecological identity as it disseminates the land's wisdom and truth into the human world.

Muir, of course, was not the only one to perceive old growth in this way, as a landscape "beaming with consciousness like the face of a god." Robert Marshall, who craved the purity and remoteness of the Arctic, wrote that "wilderness stimulates every one of the senses" in contrast to the edited comforts of domestic life. Aldo Leopold, poking around on his abandoned farm, discovered beauty and richness in modest things, in sound, movement, and change as well as the unseen dimensions of land: human history, ecological relations, the struggles of a single chickadee to survive the winter. For Leopold the land's beauty manifested as music, a pattern of form, movement, and delight played out over the cycle of a year. Each season's "abundance of distractions" flourished and settled in the observer's memory to enrich imagination just as each summer's pine needles accumulated to enrich "the wisdom of the stand." That's why for Leopold each veteran burr oak or remnant *Silphium* was a history book, albeit written in characters few could read. Each organism embodied a story of ecological coherence that was no less real for being unseen.

But it was Saint Thomas Aquinas, greatest contemplative of an age that sought coherence in all things, who came closest to capturing my own sense of old-growth forest when he wrote that beauty was the experience of "wholeness, harmony, and radiance." Remembering him after years of urban life made me realize how deep and complex are the ways in which wilderness connects with the spiritual part of our life. For we also experience wholeness, harmony, and radiance in the best of human relationships. Could there be more to it, I wondered, than therophilia alone, which after all is only a form of desire? Perhaps wilderness was consonant with some deeper, more universal aspiration.

The Arrow of Biological Time

Driving around Cincinnati, you can't help noticing our abundant woods. One moment you'll be cruising an old working-class street packed with stout brick homes; the next you'll plunge into a ravine so dark and shady you'd expect to meet a bear as soon as a beer truck. Thanks to the Ice Age, we enjoy a steep, complex topography that favors wildlife and confounds the builders. Yet few of our wooded tracts present more than a glimmer of old growth's wholeness, harmony, or radiance. They resemble instead the forests of my youth, dense, leggy second growth with an understory of weeds and brush. Our urban forests come in all shapes and sizes from large preserves like Mount Airy Forest (1,400 acres) or Spring Grove Cemetery (733 acres, half of them wild) to neighborhood parks and backyard borders. Many of these are connected by corridors of varying width, from a single hedgerow to hillsides a quarter mile across. Individually they're as crooked and edgy as jigsaw puzzle pieces. From the air, they make Cincinnati look like a Persian rug, with the colorful, miniaturized forms of buildings and roads woven into an intricate green background. That aerial view has a kind of beauty; there's a complex interest in the balance of rectilinear construction with irregular, fractal forms of watercourse, hillside, and vegetation. But up close one feels more struggle than harmony, more chaos than wholeness, more "hideous ruin and combustion" than vital radiance.

No doubt part of the reason lies in the abundant and pervasive disturbance inflicted on city landscapes, where each change of ownership brings new priorities for maintenance and use. In our fifteen years on Teakwood Court, eight out of fifteen houses have changed hands, some as much as two or three times, and each new owner has mowed, pruned, thinned, dug, or planted in his or her own peculiar way. Is it any wonder the land sometimes feels a bit dizzy underfoot? Things around here are dancing as fast as they can.

Nevertheless, as I wander the neighborhood and its environs, I notice that our woods vary in age as well as shape. Some places appear recently disturbed, while others seem to have been let alone for months, years, or even decades. On almost any walk, one can observe the process of ecological succession that so intrigued Thoreau. He described how portions of Concord had progressed from fallow to brush to woods where, over time, one tree species after another would predominate until a diverse maturity was achieved. Subsequent generations of ecologists observed and codified the successional process for forests all over North America.

They noted recognizable and predictable stages, and for a long time, they believed in a "climax" state that was biologically diverse and self-perpetuating unless upset by natural disaster or human intervention. Succession was conceived as a finite, linear process that culminated in wilderness. It moved in a direction opposite to that of "progress," which America had always measured by how much society had domesticated or exploited the land. Succession was therefore a counterhistorical process that tended to subsume and obliterate the marks of enterprise as it reestablished the original state of nature. From the viewpoint of a farmer who'd spent his youth clearing the land of trees and stones, succession signified laziness or defeat. But from the viewpoint of wilderness lovers and restorationists, succession meant healing and redemption. Against the utopian ideal of progress, they set the Edenic vision of climax forests shining from sea to sea. Left to its own devices, the land would recover. History and its depredations would disappear. The best thing for people to do was just let the green world alone.

By the middle of the twentieth century, these ideas had percolated into the deep aquifers of the wilderness movement, providing faith and refreshment for generations of activists. But ecologists had already begun to have doubts. For one thing, detailed studies of plant distribution in similar climates, latitudes, and elevations began to show that the features of climax forest held true only at very large scales, as a kind of statistical average. Conditions in a particular watershed, on a particular mountainside, or in a particular valley might cause dramatic variations from the type. Moreover, the actual composition of old growth in a given area seemed to depend on the conditions when succession began—for example, on the type and distribution of seed sources, the state of the soil, or the nature of the initial disturbance itself. Local succession did not always lead to the same final state. Instead of obliterating the past, it contained and embodied it. Succession was therefore a historical, not a teleological, process.

In addition to these unsettling discoveries, forest scientists working in northern Minnesota had begun to realize that the so-called climax state was not inherently stable. Studies of forest-fire history showed that a given area was likely to burn about once every hundred years under natural conditions. The entire ecosystem, it turned out, had adapted to periodic fires that destroyed sick or elderly trees while returning light and nutrients to the soil. Subsequent thick growths of raspberries, blueberries, and aspen saplings provided abundant food for deer, bear, and moose, who found only slim pickings in the old-growth stands of white and red pine. To a fire ecologist mapping the Boundary Waters, succession appeared as a circular rather than a linear process. Instead of a stable, Edenic climax, old growth was a forest waiting to be burned. Catastrophic disruption merely punctuated the life cycle of this community. Fire was neither a beginning nor an end, but a catalyst. If there was stability here, it lay in the cyclical repetition of a pattern. The forest's character had emerged from its history as a complexion of overlaid cycles—the sort of form that chaos mathematicians would call a "strange attractor"—and the resident species had responded by evolving their signature adaptations. The aspen, for instance, had learned to send up clones from subsurface roots, while the jack pine had developed serotinous cones that would open only when heated, thus ensuring that its frail, winged seeds would fall onto clean, well-lighted mineral soil. Thus, while the landscape might suffer mass death periodically, it had learned how to absorb such changes over the long term. Evolution could be thought of as a way of extending the time horizon across many generations. The jack-pine cone and the aspen-root clone represented the system's ability to learn and remember. You could think of them, in short, as marks of wisdom.

After many years of traveling in the Boundary Waters and considering these unseen dimensions of its ecology, I had begun to think of wilderness in terms of time rather than space. Remoteness, vividness, purity, and sublimity were all qualities predicated on removal from the civilized and the familiar, and thus appropriate foci for the dreams of alienated youth. No wonder the wilderness challenge promised identity through initiatory ordeals laced with escapism and romance. It fed the soul by splitting the world in two. But the Boundary Waters showed wilderness as a system that grew in place, the coherent articulation of a dynamic and self-organizing process. Seen in this light, the most salient feature of wilderness is its history. Wild systems are old systems. Constituent species and resident individuals have long-standing relationships that support one another, even as each single-mindedly pursues its own ultimate concerns. Proximity and interdependency characterize these relationships—call it intimacy if you like, a quality that manifests across spatial and temporal scales from the eukaryotic cell to the conversation of death between wolf and moose, or from the momentary opportunism of an alien species such as garlic mustard to the ancient symbiosis between tree roots and mycorrhizal fungi.

Wild systems also manifest endurance, which appears as sustainability under a human time horizon and as resilience under a time horizon of centuries or millennia. The older the system, the greater its capacity to absorb disruption on larger and larger scales. The system accumulates and embodies its history through self-organization, achieving both a distinct character and a repertoire of long- and short-term coping strategies. Some of these, such as biodiversity, manifest at the system level, while others, such as immunities or serotinous cones, manifest at the species level as products of evolution. Diversity and complexity, therefore, also emerge as aspects of old growth. And all these add up to an overall sense of vitality. As Tolkien said, "The old that is strong does not wither." Wilderness systems are old, but they feel young.

Seen in this light, succession appears as a process of sorting out relationships. A once-dominant species does not disappear from the system but settles down, like some chastened colonial power, as the biota grows more complex and interdependent. Succession is a process of addition and integration, not subtraction. And because it proceeds over many generations as each organism single-mindedly pursues its own life way, succession transcends the memory and awareness of each individual. It may be thought of, therefore, as an unconscious process. Over time natural systems tend always to accumulate and embody history as they self-organize in response to disruption; the result is increased complexity, expressed on the species level as adaptation and on the landscape level as resilience and biodiversity. Natural systems always grow older, and as they age, they grow wilder, becoming more whole, more harmonious, and more radiant. This process always moves in the same direction, always toward old growth, never toward youth or abstraction.

Wilderness, therefore, appears not as a state but as a direction. Wildness is the arrow of biological time.

In mechanical, linear systems, time's arrow follows the second law of thermodynamics, according to which both energy and information dissipate toward homogeneity and inertia. Time runs out like sand in an hourglass, fuel in the tank, or money in the pocket: time is granular, Newtonian, and ahistorical, admirably suited to a capitalist system of exchange with all its seductive powers of transformation. But biological time is all history, all story, where there is no distinction between meaning and information.

Our urban forests, I realized, were affected by both kinds of time. The sense of degradation and damage resulted from the constant disruptions inflicted by changing ownership and a view of land as commodity, location, or raw material—"natural resource" or "real estate" in the local vernacular. But biological time was also constantly at work, introducing new species and sorting out relationships. Every patch of green shadow in Cincinnati was undergoing succession. Each disruption, whether it consisted of mowing, planting, clearing, demolition, or landscaping, simply reset the biological clock. And here, I realized with some excitement, were two good reasons for hope. In the first place, no matter what we do to the land, we can't change the arrow of biological time, and this means that wilderness is always growing back. And second, the key to reconciling the wild and the human lies in relationships of intimacy and interdependency. For, viewed from the perspective of old growth systems, wilderness manifests order, vitality, and wisdom and therefore corresponds not to the worst but to the best in human relationships.

The Wild Not Less Than the Good

In natural systems, old growth emerges unconsciously as organisms, each living single-mindedly, sort out their relationships over time. But human life works differently, because we are myriad-minded beings. At every moment, we can choose which way to go, and we often choose half-consciously, moved as much by mood, caprice, fear, lust, anxiety, or felt need as we are by wisdom, virtue, or consideration. No wonder life seems so busy and confused, especially in cities with their abundant distractions and demands. No wonder we grow dizzy and burned-out, caught between prosperity and pollution with therophilia repressed and the very idea of progress called into question.

The great religions have long recognized this self-stoking cycle of desire, suffering, and addiction. Their solution, like Thoreau's, was to live deliberately, to embark on a life of attentive practice. But what can that mean, especially in relation to the wild? Practice is action, but action willed, directed, and repeated to give life a direction rather than to achieve a particular end. One practices a musical instrument in order to gain facility, to learn the notes and fingerings so that eventually one can begin making music. We say that practice makes perfect, but actually it makes us more transparent, so that the music can begin to pass through us into the world. After composing *The Rite of Spring*, Stravinsky told his awed listeners that he was only the vessel through which the music had passed. Likewise Michelangelo, hauling away stones that the builders had rejected, told an incredulous foreman that each stone contained an angel it was his duty to set free. Michelangelo had devoted himself single-mindedly to his art—in charnel houses dissecting cadavers by candlelight, in freezing studios, or teetering on scaffolds high above altars—so that when handed stones he would no longer be tempted to think of them only as bread. Practice gave Stravinsky ears to hear the unheard-of and Michelangelo eyes to see the unseen.

Similarly religious practice is meant to strengthen the soul by combining right thinking with right action. The Benedictines believed that salvation could be won by aligning one's life to a rigorous pattern of devotions. The Zen masters teach that the simple act of sitting day after day will confer a wonderful power that is, paradoxically, "nothing special" because it is "just you yourself." The proof of Zen lies in its effects on one's life. The master archer, who through diligent practice has reached the point where "It" shoots and the target is struck without aiming, has become a vessel of grace. His art is artless. The arrow passes through him.

One practices, in this sense, not to score points or win contests but for the sake of grace. Practice becomes an end in itself, a way of life. The path of practice is an endless, goalless journey of faith whereby we live, as Thoreau said, "in infinite expectation of the dawn." Think of the trajectory of his own life, which, though it began with rambles in Massachusetts and mountaineering on the dark flanks of Katahdin, ended with a sedulous, almost prosaic devotion to natural history. The path of adventure and the path of practice as embodied in Thoreau's life resemble the two sides of an arch, each supporting the other. Early on he was a visionary moral philosopher, a reformer and social critic who sought out wilderness in order to expose the contradictions of the age while exploring his own "higher latitudes." Later he sought the depths of local nature where, perhaps, he might catch a fact at the moment when it flowered into a truth. Early on he wanted to change the world; later he was content to let the world change him. He matured from a teacher into a learner, and his practice of the wild was natural history.

In youth, with its restless hunger for affirmation, the path of adventure leads straight to the wilderness with its peaks and rapids and labyrinthine canyons drier than bone, to sunbaked rock and the vertiginous geometry of exposure, to hours of solitude engraved with the slow rotation of stars. There, suddenly, an animal or tree may stand forth in the radiance of its personhood, piercing the soul with the certainty of I-Thou encounter. That's when you understand the myths where animals speak, the sense of obligation felt by hunting peoples, the necessity of ritual. Youth craves such moments, when identity is certain. You are alone: life vibrates between the dream and the ascent. But in middle age, as a householder with spouse and children, you are not alone. Life no longer appears as a beckoning dream to be embraced and perfectly fulfilled, but as a story that has grown by odd yet expressive turns, like a twig with your soul at the growing tip. The difference between these two phases of life is history, the burden and the blessing of the stories we bear. And so the eye of middle age looks both forward and backward, outward toward adventure and inward toward memory and knowledge. It encompasses our manifold relationships and obligations to people as well as to other beings in nature. It takes account of such complexity.

That's why the path of practice appeals to the generative heart of middle age and why old growth forests inspire our therophilia. Wild things in their resilience, endurance, and vitality appear to be living with perfect grace. Their lives seem guileless and unaffected, not without struggle or danger yet still blessed with facility and integrity. To be who they are appears unproblematic. At every moment they seem to speak with their whole being. This is their practice, to enact at each moment exactly who they are. No wonder that we, the protean species, regard them with fascination, even a touch of envy.

At midlife, too, one appreciates the cleansing effects of ritual, the slow percolation of time through form as water is purified by trickling through fine sand. Practice cleanses the mind, centers and frees it from distraction, and thereby restores the soul. For the mind thus purified is freed, not to wander but to be empty and still, so that it can be filled with form and thereby achieve serenity.

City living has made me realize the importance of practice as an antidote to the corrosive effects of urban time. Thoreau chose to live deliberately, but here one must—that is, if one aspires to make peace with nature. For practice bends time into a circle and so brings one's life into accord with the cyclical rhythms of the living world. It leads to a fusion of human and biological time.

What would it be like if we practiced the wild under the sign of old growth, aligning our lives with the arrow of biological time? Wild practice is first and foremost a local practice. You always have to do it right here. Wild practice has an aspect of attentiveness: learning the other creatures and their ways, keeping watch, waiting for things to emerge, learning to see the unseen. There is also an aspect of mindfulness, of repeated acts deliberately composed, of discipline projected over the long term. There is an aspect of relation: dancing with the wildness of others, participating in local flows of energy, nourishment, and information, all of which comprise what I call husbandry. There is an aspect of homage to one's origins in landscapes of learning or transformation—call it pilgrimage—and an aspect of reflection and witness that preserves the land's gifts by sharing them through stories. Five disciplines, in sum, are necessary: attentiveness, mindfulness, husbandry, pilgrimage, and witness.

Now imagine what life would be like if such a wild practice infused our relationships across every scale from the individual to the community to the landscape.

When I think of wildness in personal relationships, what springs to mind are not images of glamour, wealth, or violence but the faces of radiant old people who have lived enduringly through marriage and parenthood. They have a way of creeping up on you, like an animal suddenly appearing at the wood's edge. Youth's eye is too inward looking, too stunned by glamour to appreciate the calligraphy of such faces, intricate as an illuminated gospel from the age of Aquinas. And yet how convincing a life they lead! One yearns in middle age for exactly that balance of humor and compassion, weighted with lived truth and edged with the ineluctable bitterness of life in a fallen world. One knows by now that, just as a mountain is climbed by taking one step after another, a marriage endures by succeeding one day at a time. There is no way to seize on a good marriage. It can't be purchased like a house or a car or a piece of land: you have to put in the time. The path of marriage is a long journey sustained by eros and therophilia, for love viewed under the sign of old growth is not a mood but an action, not an emotion but a form of perception that allows us to see and appreciate the unseen. How else could people ever stay together?

In the beginning body calls to body, craving completeness. We take the surface for the essence, seeking the one who will answer effortlessly to desire. Drawn by the spirit of romance, how sweet it is to believe that once we find, bond, and mate we will be *there* at last, secure, at rest, no longer suffering and incomplete. We can almost hear the click of the golden key opening heaven's gate, as if the outer circumstance could stanch the hidden wound. But love is a life's work.

Old-growth eros differs from romance the way the fruit differs from the blossom. It requires aging, like the bouquet of wine or the rich scent of vanilla. Feeling and touch gain ascendancy over looks as intimacy deepens. Desire may drive you together in the beginning, but therophilia holds you for the long term. For what could be wilder than another soul encountered up close and personal day after day? In this respect, husbandry appears as a conversation between souls who, growing together in a lifelong dance, weave a home for one another. Love is a matter of learning and a form of practice, answering to and calling forth our deepest, most beautiful resources. In romance the beloved answers effortlessly to desire; love takes no work, but it's always starting over, always seeking perfection. In old-growth marriage, where love consists with wildness, the beloved resists desire and so helps you to learn and grow. Eros is fueled by attentiveness, mindfulness, and deliberate imagination. It lights the hearth and heats the house; it throws your partner's face into relief. How much sweeter is this deep history— complex, ambiguous, and intimate—than some fantasy image as smooth and hard as a green apple. You can't gobble maturity. Old lovers have learned how to make the music that is the food and figure of true love. Through years of practice, they have become virtuosos of each other.

On the community level, wild practice and the struggle for intimacy play out in terms of war and peace. Like marriage peace has no end but its own continuance; it aspires to sustainability, whereas war seeks only its own end through victory. War ends with the suppression of the Other; it is what theologian James P. Carse would call a "finite game" like gambling, clear-cut logging, or seduction, in which the prize for the winner is the loser. But peace is an "infinite game" in which the prize is play itself: all players go on together in life, learning, and the pursuit of happiness. A region at peace is most like an old-growth forest with its diverse inhabitants, complex networks of energy, nutrient, and information exchange, and deep reservoirs of embodied history. Political leaders and desperate populations embrace war in hopes of a quick, decisive return, stumped by the Gordian knot of history or fearing a true encounter with wildness in the person of the Other. But peace requires listening and learning, both of which take work and may cause pain as they abrade and tear at the old self with its sleek, close-fitting epistemologies. How much easier, even nobler it seems to fight than to listen. But as Thoreau observed, it is a characteristic of wisdom not to do desperate things.

Surely making peace is harder than waging war, but it keeps paying dividends. By demanding attentiveness, respect, and adaptability, it builds the soil. This is culture in the truest, most humane sense. You don't "keep the peace" as if it were cheese; you grow it and tend it, because it's alive. It is not a commodity, but an ecosystem in which even mortal enemies have a niche, and conflict is subsumed into a greater good. Viewed under the sign of old growth, peace is not the absence of war but war's antithesis, as love is the antithesis of addiction. Peace is a deliberate practice and a life's work. If we practiced the wild in our communal relations, we would always be making peace, always learning from and therefore loving our enemies, always seeking transformation, always aspiring to become a truly generative culture by aligning our own political history with the arrow of biological time.

On the level of our ecological relations with other species, wild practice manifests in terms of husbandry. How can we dance with the wildness of other beings on whom we depend so that humanity and the earth become, as Thomas Berry imagines, a mutually enhancing presence to each other? Heretofore, our husbandry has focused on a narrow array of species that yield rich, immediate harvests of food, commodities, or beauty. Our common practice has been to arrogate vast tracts of land to monocultures, pruning the ecosystem to a single niche and seeking to control the flow of energy, nutrients, and information by mechanical means such as irrigation, poisons, or cultivation. Historically, such practices have produced dramatic results of the sort described by Jared Diamond: the expansion of cultures across and between continents, the diversification and stratification of society, priesthoods, bureaucracies, armies, technology—everything, in short, that we think of as advancements in civilization. But these have led to massive and sometimes fatal environmental problems: the deforestation of Greece, the salination of Mesopotamian soils, the desertification of the Sahel, the drying-up of the Aral Sea, the "dead zone" at the mouth of the Mississippi River, not to mention global warming, the shaving of Amazonia, and soaring extinction rates worldwide. Seen in this light, human history appears as a parasitic infection.

But the ultimate cause of all these problems may well be the shallowness of our husbandry. If one takes a limited view of the organism, focusing on some useful feature and ignoring the rest of its complex relationships and potentialities, one is bound to be shocked when imported species don't stick to their job descriptions. Their wildness, their creativity soon create problems for us. But it is our fault, because we have wistfully thought of them as little machines rather than as self-organizing learning systems. We have not invested the time and attention requisite to a capable understanding. We have shunned intimacy. And so, as in a troubled marriage or a state of war, the partners have become mutually destructive presences to each other.

But it has not always been thus. History reveals that numerous cultures have developed forms of husbandry that enhance the biological productivity and diversity of their home landscapes. The farmers of northern Europe discovered how to build the fertility of cold glacial soils by working in compost and manure. The Tohono O'odham of southern Arizona developed intensive, small-scale farms on Sonoran desert oases that supported vital and diverse populations of birds, insects, and plants. Gary Paul Nabhan reports that when Organ Pipe Cactus National Monument was created, its wilderness management plan called for the acquisition and closing down of these farms. Ecologists, expecting a return to "natural" conditions, were surprised to discover that bird populations declined after the people left. Numerous species of plants, insects, and reptiles eventually disappeared as well; the overall productivity of the oases was markedly reduced. Nabhan concludes that native husbandry was holding everything together. In classic ecological terms, humans were the keystone species.

Another inspiring example comes from Amazonia. According to anthropologist Darrell Addison Posey, the Mebêngôkre, who inhabit the ecotone between forest and savanna, practice an intensive horticulture that involves hundreds of food and medicinal species. Generations of observation and experiment have given these people an unparalleled knowledge of local flora, not just their useful properties but their interspecific relations. The Mebêngôkre know which plants repel insects or attract pollinators, which companion plantings provide the best synergy, which fertilizer recipes (combining compost with various kinds of ash) work best for which combinations of plants. Because their husbandry embraces such a diversity of species and extends to a horizon of many generations, they have been able to establish forest islands by building up the soil in low-lying parts of the unproductive savanna. So subtle and refined are these methods that the achievements of Mebêngôkre horticulture were not recognized as such until recently. They were thought to be the spontaneous productions of unassisted nature.

In North America the burgeoning practice of ecological restoration offers another hopeful glimpse of the path toward deep husbandry. The very idea of working to bring back the wild by assisting nature, as it were, requires one to think systemically, considering the needs, life ways, and productions of a whole community of organisms rather than just two or three. This means paying close attention even to those species that appear trivial, modest, or disgusting and to consider each in the complexity of its relations. It also means involving oneself intimately with a place and committing to work with it over a long term, perhaps even to the seventh generation. It means entering into the green world's dance of transformation.

In this respect, ecological restoration seems like a form of gardening, but its crop is wilderness on a small, local scale. The restorationist assumes responsibility for cultivation, maintaining diversity, balancing populations, and ensuring succession. What's different is the focus on a whole system as opposed to a few privileged species, and the value of wildness itself, rather than decoration or commodity, as the prime motivation. Surely the idea of gardening for wildness itself is a new thing under the sun, as radical as mourning for a vanished species. As with Aldo Leopold planting pines or Thoreau hoeing beans, it also yields a spiritual crop. Soil building becomes soul building as outer and inner landscape move into phase. The path of practice returns us to wilderness at last with its deep humus and ancient greens. Will and wild hardly differ, and each sustains the other. Perhaps one day we will be able to say with Thoreau that we too love the wild not less than the good.

I admit that it's hard, even painful, to entertain such hopes when one lives deep in the city surrounded by artificial deserts, alien species, and teeming predatory populations with no inkling of biological time. There are days when the snarl of a mower grates on my ear like fingernails on a chalkboard. A bulldozer snorting to life makes me jump. I start looking for books to throw at big, glassy buildings. But it's always already too late. On especially bad days, I just collapse back into fantasies of Yosemite.

Imagine, then, how exhilarating it was to hear that a tract of old-growth forest still existed right here, inside the city limits of Cincinnati.

Caldwell Preserve is located on the west side of the Mill Creek Valley, the city's industrial gullet. Two decades after the Revolutionary War, a certain Major James Caldwell purchased 348 acres from the land speculator John Cleves Symmes and opened a sawmill to cut timber for settlers' cabins. After more than a century of profit, the family donated 122 acres to the city, about 60 of which had never been logged. Here, then, was a specimen of ancient Ohio Valley hardwood forest mercifully spared, as if the loggers themselves had felt some visceral misgiving at the eleventh hour.

I had to go out there. But the drive up the Mill Creek Valley was hardly inspiring: first the rail yards, then the Kahn's meat processing plant, Ryerson Steel, the old Procter and Gamble works at Ivorydale, where floating soap was still produced, the Jim Beam distillery stinking of peach schnapps. Nine miles upstream from the Ohio, I turned toward wooded hills, passed a substation and transformer yard, and crossed Mill Creek itself. The road climbed steeply and passed a huge auto graveyard, across from which I saw the modest sign and parking lot for Caldwell Preserve.

The trail led through a screen of brambles and honeysuckle to a steep slope that fell off into a ravine full of beeches and oaks that must have been three or four feet in diameter and branchless for thirty feet up. The ground was strewn with a mixture of native and alien species: wild ginger and dicentra holding their own amid English ivy and garlic mustard. I knew that the preserve occupied three ridges between which seasonal tributaries drained into Mill Creek. By the second ridge, the invasives had disappeared, and the understory was dominated by ferns, wildflowers, and pawpaws, thin trees of human height with dark, broad leaves and edible fruits much esteemed by Indians and settlers alike. Here the trees were even larger, forming a closed canopy sixty or seventy feet high. Something had dampened the sounds of traffic and industry to a murmur. In the vast open spaces beneath the trees, the air felt cool and still, as if protected by thick stone walls.

I found myself taking slow steps, looking up and around as I walked. A great horned owl took off from a high branch, glided away, and disappeared without stirring so much as a leaf. Huge logs lay rotting here and there; one sported a bright yellow fungus crumpled like a bath towel. Nearby a pileated woodpecker was deconstructing a dead white maple; he worked methodically, knocking off chips as big as crackers. Everything seemed slow and unhurried. The sense of embodied time was very strong. I felt composed, relaxed, and alert, the way I had after many days on the trail.

Of course, this old forest was merely a remnant, beset on all sides by the city with its energy and pollution and the overwhelming pressure of its myriad disruptions. As I came to the end of the third ridge, I could see Mill Creek sparkling below where its elbow truncated the forest bluffs. The water looked cleaner here, above much of the industry, yet it was still tainted by sewage from combined sewer overflows. For a moment, I imagined stepping into a canoe and floating down the Ohio to Saint Louis, then ascending the Missouri through the Dakotas all the way to Montana and the Great Divide. I could imagine how one might connect the vast, untrammeled western wilds to the modest shrines and remnants of old growth where we live. For an urban practice of the wild pursued with deliberate imagination needs story and pilgrimage to sustain it, just as migration sustains the life of Canada geese, who mate for life and embrace the continent on their journeys.

As I drove home from Caldwell Preserve that day, passing the scraped ground of construction sites, the shorn lawns of suburbs, and the burgeoning wildness of park borders and vacant lots, I realized that greater Cincinnati manifests landscapes in every stage of succession from artificial desert to old growth. Let it stand, then, as a figure for the continent as a whole, betokening every crisis and every opportunity that we confront on the threshold of an ecological age. If deep husbandry can be imagined here after two centuries of human impact, it can be imagined anywhere. And the path of practice begins with imagination.

Farther and Wider

ESCALANTE

The Perfect Seminar

You know you are home when you begin dreaming of journeys. After five years in the dean's office, I had learned all I cared to know about administration. I missed teaching; I missed writing; I missed thinking about truth, beauty, and the universal questions instead of how to unscrew this nut or tighten that bolt. Deaning was too much like parenting, and I was tired of cleaning up other people's messes. The old urge to escape began to stir. After walking the neighborhood with my children and discovering the grass forest, after experiencing the circulation of wildness in space and time, I felt very much at home in Cincinnati, naturalized as it were. But this only made the dreams more vivid. Especially in summer, when the air sagged with humidity, I'd get visions of snow peaks, red monoliths, or sandstone arches framing blue shards of sky. I'd long for the skin-puckering dryness of desert air, the searing, ultraviolet clarity of noon in the high mountains. I'd think back to great trips of the past, all the places I had visited and all the places I had missed when I lived in New Hampshire, California, or Utah. And so I resigned my deanship and went back into the faculty and almost at once began dreaming of Escalante.

I know now that this sort of thing happens repeatedly as part of making a home. Settling in is only the first step. To know where you are, you have to leave and return. You have to travel the full trajectory of the arch, heading out farther and wider before bending back toward the place where you started. And when you get there, it is no longer the same place, because you are no longer you. You have new eyes. You have a new story. And so it feels that you now know the home place for the first time.

You can take such a journey at any age, but at midlife it acquires an aspect of pilgrimage. Exploration, once used to build identity, becomes a mixture of homage and aspiration. The eye of midlife gazes back toward one's origins and ahead to everything that one still yearns to achieve.

Youth craves power and affirmation; midlife aspires to honor and completion. Pilgrimage, like practice, appeals to midlife's taste for resonance, depth, and meaning. One seeks out companions who understand the pull of home and community that bends adventure into a long parabola.

But I knew little of this when I started to dream of Escalante. It was the last American river to be discovered, draining a part of the Colorado Plateau so remote that even John Wesley Powell had missed it. My Utah friends had spoken with awe of its mazes of sculpted, tributary canyons. Ed Abbey had written a book about it, carefully omitting directions for how to get there. The Sierra Club and *National Geographic* had published stunning pictures. But I had never been there during all my years of teaching. What better place to begin a new practice with adult learners? We could study wilderness from the twin perspectives of urban nature and middle age.

In those days, too, Gary Snyder had finally published *The Practice of the Wild*, his sinewy blend of literary criticism, Zen practice, deep ecology, and Native American myth. Snyder had hard words for the twentieth century and the crimes of industrial capitalism, but if you chewed on them long enough, you would crack into the soft marrow of compassion. Aspiration, attentiveness, and devotion to work and family, even while he yearned for remoteness, infused his text. His vision of "future primitivism" spoke to the deep ambivalence that I, too, felt toward urban life.

Yet, rather than promoting an action plan, Snyder's inquiry led to mystical claims that practicing the wild meant stepping off the trail, any trail, and onto the path, which was nothing more that the wild itself, that is, the world. To me that sounded too much like getting lost. Where was the discipline? As a teacher and thinker, I felt it was my job to break trail for others, to act as a path maker. What was a "course" after all but a path or track through intellectual terrain that one had learned by traveling oneself? Pilgrimage was the same sort of thing, a known route aligned with a pattern of spiritual growth along vectors of homage and aspiration. I thought that both could be realized in a seminar held in the Escalante, which was not the whole world but a specific region. I could follow Snyder that far, but not off the trail, not yet. However, I did know what it felt like to step out of a car and onto the wilderness path. I could relate to that, even at age fifty. So I put Snyder back on the shelf and took down my backpack and topo maps.

As for the course, it began to design itself: an interdisciplinary exploration of the desert as landscape and idea, human and natural history woven together with bodily experience of the place. I worked with Ed Grumbine, an activist and conservation biologist who had done his doctorate at Union and had been taking students into the Escalante for years. He led our first group to a lush side canyon seven hours by car from Salt Lake City. We slept in sandstone alcoves, admired Anasazi ruins, and hiked all the way to the river itself for a cleansing mud bath in the heart of the labyrinth. Three years later we did it again, and each time I was thrilled to get out of the city and back out West. I remember a pleasure as gritty and hard as the red sand that, two weeks later, was still falling out of my shoes. I began to think it just might be possible to recuperate the old life of periodic migration to wilderness.

But the third time pays for all. Even out in the larger world, events seemed to be converging on Escalante. An old friend of Ed's, Tom Fleischner, had entered Union and written his dissertation on Escalante. He stepped in as guide when Ed moved on. Meanwhile, a long-running conservation battle over the coal-rich Kaiparowits Plateau had ended in victory when President Clinton had established the Grand Staircase– Escalante National Monument. Activists all over America rejoiced, and none more so than the Wilderness Society's T. H. Watkins. Burly, articulate, and indefatigable, Watkins had spent much of his career defending the canyon lands. Tom and I had often turned to his work for facts and inspiration, but cancer had claimed him just as we began planning our seminar. It seemed only fitting to hold a memorial for him at the point farthest in, on the banks of the great river itself. We wanted to lift him up to the class as a model of ecological identity. His practice of the wild deserved honor and emulation.

And so, sitting at my desk surrounded by maps and notes as a gray March rain pelted the windows, I felt a rising excitement at the thought of a third trip into Escalante. To return on the cusp of the millennium with the scent of victory still in the air, to work with the man who had written the book, to celebrate the ideas of Snyder and the life of Watkins in a great, good place accompanied by grown-up learners—all this seemed wonderfully auspicious. Tom and I fine-tuned the agenda to match academic topics with places in the canyon. We sent out route descriptions, equipment lists, meal suggestions, hiking tips, and study guides. On the day of departure, I hefted my new pack, savoring the feel of a snug, tight load of books and gear. I had never felt more confident or relaxed at the start of a journey.

Pam dropped me at the airport curb, and an hour later we took off, climbing toward thirty thousand feet as Cincinnati shrank into a map-like grid of buildings, streets, and parks. Banking against the roar and thrust of its engines, the whole plane seemed to shudder with the ecstasy of escape. The land unfurled like a gigantic scroll. Beside me two women heading for Las Vegas wanted to know, "Where *is* Utah anyway?" But I just pointed west, out the window, as green woods and cornfields gave way to the khaki of wheat and open range, and then to the tarnished silver of mountains, and finally to the baked-clay red of rimrock. In no time, it seemed, we were landing in Salt Lake City with the castellated spires of the Wasatch shimmering in the heat beyond Temple Square. It was just like my first trip twenty years before, at the start of my teaching career. The past clicked into phase: I could feel it turn and settle, secure as a key in a lock.

Tom and I met our sixteen learners at an airport hotel, standing around a pile of packs and books. We reviewed the schedule and the route, checked everyone's gear, then sent them off for a last civilized meal and a good night's sleep while we stayed up trading desert stories. Next morning we piled into rented vans and headed south on I-15, that open road that starts with every American Dream and leads only one way, into the wild.

On Coyote's Road

There's no direct route to the Escalante region, even today, though the going is easier than it was in 1872, when the first Mormon settlers arrived from Panguitch. They had heard of a place at the foot of the Aquarius Plateau where edible tubers grew, and before long "Potato Valley" was planted with ranches and stout town homes, all watered by the river itself. A few years later, the town of Boulder was established twenty miles to the east, across a dizzying maze of slickrock and tributary canyons. Today you can drive the old Mormon wagon roads or take the new state highway over Boulder Mountain, stopping, as we did, for panoramic views of the Colorado Plateau. From high above, the land looks austere but inviting, its rugged canyons softened and blued by distance, while the vast geometry of its bedrock lies fully exposed. Tom lectured on the geography and history of the plateau, pointing out the main Escalante canyon and its wriggling tributaries that had cut into cream white Navajo sandstone. Twenty miles west of Boulder, we left blacktop and turned south on the dusty washboard of the Hole-in-the-Rock Road, which Mormon pioneers had blazed a century before on their way to colonize the San Juan River country. It had taken them two months to cross the Colorado; they had had to blast a path through the thousand-foot walls of Glen Canyon and lower their wagons in pieces. Today their road, still unpaved, offers the best access to Escalante country. We took it for ten miles along the base of the Kaiparowits Plateau, then turned onto a jeep track that wound nine miles through overgrazed, tomato red hills before it ended in a salt-cedar thicket strewn with cow pies. This was the end of the road, the beginning of the trail.

The class piled out, stiff from the seven-hour drive. Packs were hoisted, water stowed, belts cinched. A few people were already heading down the path. "Wait up!" Tom called. Then, "You think we should let them go?"

"Why not?" I said. "We went over the route. They can't get lost."

Tom gathered the class. "Remember, the trail follows the wash. Up here it's just a dry streambed, but the walls soon rise up. In about two miles, you'll come to a barbed-wire fence. We'll meet there. If you want to save some distance, you can follow the jeep track that cuts across some of the bends." A few moments later, we were alone.

We closed up the vehicle and signed the trail register, then headed down the path. It felt good to be together. I liked coming last, not only to sweep the trail but also to enjoy the land for a few minutes by myself. Solitude is hard to come by when you are leading a class. Tom and I smiled this shared thought as we broke out of the thicket and entered the wash. There was no water here, though we could see its traces: wide, sweeping gravel bars cobbled with black lava pebbles from the Aquarius Plateau, each one fringed with a white crust of alkali. Across the wash, the road climbed into open desert, rutted and brushed-in. We turned downstream, following the muddle of boot prints and cattle tracks.

It was a beautiful day, sunny and cool. At 5:00 p.m. the light lay long and mellow on the land, softening its abrasive hardness. Even the dust seemed to glow. After a long, indoor winter, the feel of sunshine on my skin was blissful, rejuvenating. My body limbered to each long stride, the pack riding high and easy despite its weight. All backpackers know this buoyancy, this rush of freedom that comes as you head into the wild under your own power, carrying everything you need. Even my left leg, which I had pulled while jogging, felt pretty good.

The canyon walls began to rise up, bluffs of red sandstone rounded like loaves by rain and wind. The wash swung back and forth in long meanders, overgrown with cottonwood and rabbitbrush. A crude jeep track dipped in and out of the streambed, cutting across the meanders just as Tom had said. We followed it, often losing sight of the streambed altogether. It was hard to know which way the class had gone, since there were plenty of tracks in all directions. After twenty minutes, Tom said, "I'm getting a bad feeling. We should have caught up with them."

"Do you think we could have passed them on one of the bends?"

"Maybe. You think they're ahead of us?"

"Could be. They did go charging off. But they can't get out of the canyon. We're sure to meet them at the fence."

"Unless they took that BLM road across the wash."

"Come on. We told them to follow the canyon. Even if they went that way, they'll figure it out and turn back."

"Let's hope so," Tom said, quickening the pace.

A half hour later, we reached the fence. There was no one there. We threw down our packs, pulled out water and gorp, then propped our gear against the fence for a sign. We charged back up the trail. It was 6:00 p.m., and we had only three hours of daylight. Almost at once, we ran into two learners, Paul and Martha, looking flushed and excited. "Thank goodness!" exclaimed Martha. "We thought we'd taken the wrong trail."

"Are the others close behind you?" I asked.

"I don't know," Paul said. "They got off before we did and took the road across the wash. We were last and were worried about keeping up because, you know, we're the oldest—we're both sixty, and this is Martha's first backpack trip. They got ahead of us and were out of sight by the time we turned around. You had explained that the trail followed the bed of the canyon, but the road seemed to be heading into the open desert. I knew it couldn't be right."

"Let's hope they figure it out," I said. "Why don't you make camp while we go look for them. There's an alcove hidden in the cottonwoods just past the fence."

Without packs we made better time. It would be dark by nine, but we'd be fine if the group had turned back. It had taken us an hour to hike in, which meant we were already two hours behind them. We hurried along, our feet sliding in the loose sand.

"Tom," I panted, "have you ever lost a class?"

"Never," he said. "I did get lost *with* a class once, sort of. We were in a canyon system I knew, and it was only for about an hour."

"They'll kill us."

"We have to find them first."

Even with the jeep track cutting bends, it took forty-five minutes to reach the trailhead. Two haggard learners, Fran and Jerry, were sitting under a cottonwood. We ran up to them. "Are you OK?" Tom asked. "Where are the others?"

Fran almost shouted, "How should we know? They were way ahead. Jerry here collapsed about half a mile in. I had to help him back! Of all the stupid, irresponsible . . . ! How could you let us go off like that? Who knows what might have happened!"

Tom stared at her. "It's my fault," he said. "I forgot about the other road. I'm sorry."

"We're just glad you're safe," I put in. "We've got to find the others and bring them back. Do you want to camp here, or do you think you can make it down to camp? Paul and Martha are there, and they have water."

Fran slumped and sighed. "I think we can make it now," she said. "What a way to start! I'm sorry I yelled at you." And she gave Tom a hug.

We watched them load up and set off down the wash. Tom shook himself. "Ever been on a fire line?"

The jeep road climbed out of the wash and into red, denuded hills. It was full of boot prints. We tracked the class for more than an hour, watching for any sign that they might have cut back across country, but the prints just stuck to the road. There was no indication that they had ever stopped. The road pitched and curved through tumbled, open country that rose in the north to low, cream-colored cliffs and rolled off southeast toward the main canyon of the Escalante. It was, in truth, a beautiful landscape, but we were in no mood to enjoy it.

"Tom, how many years of outdoor experience do you have?" I asked.

"Oh, about two or three decades."

"Same. Has anything like this ever happened to you?"

"Never."

"Why haven't they stopped?"

"I don't get it."

Meanwhile, the sun had dropped to the edge of Kaiparowits. The air was cooling fast. My left hamstring began to ache. The class was nowhere in sight. Another half mile, and I started to limp.

"Tom," I said, "I can't keep up. My leg is going."

"I'll jog ahead," he offered. "Maybe I can catch them." He looked off down the road and shook his head. "Coyote is messing with us." He loped off and disappeared over a rise.

I looked around, awed by the sudden silence, the immense, pastel serenity of the landscape. What was I doing out here all by myself, five miles from water with only a pint left, a few handfuls of gorp, and no sweater? At least the learners had full packs. We had expected to hike a mere two miles today but were now hiking eight at least. So much for advance planning.

I trudged on. Sooner or later we'd meet the class. At least, with food and gear, we could make a dry camp or else cook a meal and walk out at night. In my dazed state of mind, all choices seemed equally attractive. I had no idea how to salvage the seminar, apart from admitting our mistakes and offering alternatives to the group. Academically, experientially, it was a disaster. Some people might just want to go home.

Cresting a low rise, I noticed a strange, dark object in the road. I bent down for a closer look. It was a coyote scat, still warm and full of rodent teeth. I looked for tracks, but with the welter of boot prints, it was hard to tell.

I stood up. The sun had set, leaving a tangerine glow above Kaiparowits. The land began filling with shadow. Cool air flowed downhill from the bluffs. Shivering, I munched on gorp, hoping my body heat would last. There was nothing to do but keep going, trudging from one low rise to the next. Finally, just as it was getting dark, I spotted a couple of lumps by the side of the road that resolved into learners with packs. It was Barb and Jim, two novice hikers. We embraced. I felt tears start.

"We stopped about an hour ago," Jim said. "Tom said to wait for you. He ran ahead."

"I am so sorry!"

"It's ok," Barb said. "We began to have second thoughts a while back, but everyone was really into hiking. It was hard to stop."

We debated what to do. Six learners were now accounted for; eleven were somewhere up ahead. Perhaps Tom had already reached them. It seemed important for one of us to be with each group. I figured it would take about two and a half hours to get back to camp, where, presumably, Fran and Jerry had arrived. We decided to leave a note for Tom in the middle of the trail. I took Barb's pack, which she had carried for three miles. It felt like a dead body.

In the fading twilight, we picked our way down the trail. With no moon, it was hard to judge depth, and we kept stumbling into rocks and holes. The black sky had filled with stars that sparkled like diamond dust. The road glowed faintly in their light, but it was barely distinguishable from the shadowy desert on either side. We had to feel our way along; a turned ankle would have been disastrous. And yet, despite the anxiety and fatigue, we became aware of wonder. I had never been out in the open desert on a clear, moonless night miles from camp. It was exhilarating to look up into the vast, archaic depths of the universe, to stop for a sip of depthless silence and feel the prickle of ancient starlight on your skin. These were not things you could do in the city nor, for that matter, on the trip we had planned. Down in the canyon with each hour closely scheduled, we'd all have been fast asleep, safe and sound instead of lost and wide-eyed in the dark.

Three hours later, near midnight, we staggered into camp. I nearly tripped over Jerry, who was sleeping curled up in my sleeping bag right in the middle of the trail. A groggy Fran explained that he had collapsed again and abandoned his pack a mile up the trail. Paul and Martha had made tea and fed them dinner. After settling the others, I took Tom's sleeping bag, figuring he would make camp with the other group. I lay out on the dry sand and tried to rest, but my mind was still churning anxiously. Hopefully, no one had been hurt. Once we were all back together, we would have to deal with the seminar. But how? As a learning community, we had been torn apart, dismembered and scattered across the desert in pitch darkness. How could we ever complete our journey? Tom and I were finished as leaders.

By 2:00 a.m. I was sliding toward sleep when I heard someone bellowing up the wash, shouting my name. As I scrambled into clothes, five learners came stumbling into camp. Tom had finally caught up with them about four miles in. The rest were camping at the cars, and Tom had gone back to take them water. By 2:30 a.m. he finally arrived, collapsing onto the sand without a word. I hugged him and handed over the sleeping bag. I had hiked ten miles that day; he had hiked sixteen. We decided that next morning the first thing to do was to get everyone into camp; then we could hold a council, encouraging people to air their feelings. We would have to take it, all of it, without saying anything. The group would have to reconstitute itself. If they decided to go on with the seminar, we would suggest spending the day here, to rest up before heading further into the canyon.

After Tom fell asleep, I lay awake watching stars drift over the canyon rim. Paul and Martha had loaned me one of their sleeping bags, but I still shivered in the chill that flowed downstream from the slickrock plateaus above. It was good to know that everyone was safe, but I had no idea where we would go from here. As a teacher and guide, I still felt hopelessly lost.

Regrouping

A Russian proverb says, "The morning is wiser than the evening." Perhaps so, but as dawn's early light seeped into the canyon, all I could think of was coffee and oatmeal. Tom was already up; he had let everyone know about the council. Bleary eyes, grunts, and sullen looks did not bode well. We drowned our misgivings in coffee, then started back up the wash. The walls glowed in the morning light; the sand rustled underfoot like silk. Even the cobbles, so treacherous the night before, seemed to shine like the beads of a necklace.

"This trail is getting familiar," I muttered.

"Five times for you, seven for me."

"What a fiasco."

Halfway to the road, we spied a green lump on the bank—Jerry's pack. Directly above, high in the sandstone cliff, was a round hole with a bundle of sticks poking out. White streaks of guano ran down from the hole. It was a raven's nest. As we passed, a raucous croak sounded. To me it felt like a laugh.

Three bends later, we met the first learners coming down. Everyone was on the move, they said. A coyote had come into their camp just before dawn. We pointed out the raven's nest and helped ferry packs. Before long we were all back together, sitting in a circle in the big sandstone alcove where some had spent the night. It was a cool, private place, screened from the trail by cottonwoods. Tom began by apologizing once more for suggesting the jeep trail. I acknowledged that we had failed as their guides and leaders; we were ready to listen. Someone produced a "talking stick" that passed from hand to hand as people spoke their minds. I felt as if that stick were twisting my guts. We were castigated, cursed, understood, sometimes forgiven. One learner, who supervised dozens of school principals, spoke of the seriousness of leadership, how unconscionable it was to put students at risk. Another wondered why she had gone so far along with the group despite her misgivings. Jerry spoke of his work in organizational development and a concept called "group think" that describes how people who are excited about working together can arrive at bad decisions because no one wants to break the mood. The Bay of Pigs invasion was a classic example. Several learners had experienced fear and exhaustion combined with a "runner's high" and a breathless awe at the beauty of the landscape. Others shared leadership crises of their own. Paul told of taking a high school class on a bike trip where he made every turn correctly, except for the first one.

As the talking stick moved around the circle, the stories and statements became more probing and heartfelt. By the time it was halfway around, I was staring into the sand, fighting tears. People had begun to speak from a very deep place, drawing up midlife wisdom as cold and clear as artesian water. I could hardly bear such candor, such love. The mood was shifting from anger and blame to reconciliation and resolve. People wanted the seminar to go on.

The talking stick appeared before me, but I had no words. Tom picked it up. "Thank you," he said. Then, after a moment, "Perhaps we should stay here today." Heads nodded. "This is a good place for natural history," he went on. "Let's meet for a walk after lunch."

We ate, we rested, some people slept in the shade of cool, overarching stone. An hour later, Tom gathered us by the stream, which had emerged from its subterranean bed just before the fence and now ran half an inch deep over red pea gravel. I felt as drained and empty as a bowl. Tom said, "The first step in knowing a place is to pay attention. So, let's walk downstream a ways. Just notice what you notice."

We began moving down canyon, alternately wading in the stream and clambering onto terraces. Here, close to the water, grew a forest of horse-tails, living fossils from the Coal Age with delicate green fronds that tickled my knees. A bit higher up grew the brown wands of tamarisk, filigreed with dusty green and topped with pink tassels, along with the head-high whips of ubiquitous coyote willow. Still higher grew cottonwoods, their kale green foliage rustling in the breeze, and Russian olives, whose sweet, creamy blossoms were full of bees. These were the same European honeybees that had been decimated by tracheal mites all over the rest of the country. For them this canyon's wildness was a refuge, though they were alien species just like us. I noticed vermilion dragonflies cruising low over the water and cliff swallows high above, darting from wall to wall. At times I was hardly aware of walking. The canyon felt vivid, exotic, even though I had been here twice before. It was as if I were seeing through my skin, as if my whole body had been scraped with a sharp flint blade.

Back at our starting point, Tom took up a pinch of sand. Seen though his hand lens, its pink uniformity broke into a many-hued mosaic: reds, blacks, grays, whites, each grain as angular and distinctive as a boulder. There are many stories in simple things, Tom said. If we could read one of these grains, we could read the whole history of North America. He looked up at the walls where the grains had come from, pointing out the oblique striations of cross-bedding that showed how the sand had been laid down in dunes by desert winds. This Navajo sandstone was the largest system of sand dunes in the history of the world; it covered a vast area of the West, from Las Vegas east to the Four Corners and north all the way to Yellowstone. At Zion National Park, the formation was three thousand feet thick. Yet no one had been able to figure out where all this sand came from.

Show me what you found, Tom said, and he elaborated each discovery. Those dark crusts on the sand were "cryptogamic soil," a complex of lichen, algae, fungi, and bacteria that's the main locus of nitrogen fixation in the desert. It's the first stage in soil formation; be careful not to step on it. Tamarisk, or salt cedar, produces abundant seeds that can sprout within days; mature plants have deep roots that suck up a lot of water; you could say that's greedy, but as a species, we are the real water hogs. Coyote willow is one of the West's most abundant and widespread native shrubs. Notice how flexible it is, always pointing downstream. That's due to floods; there's adaptive value in being graceful.

As the afternoon went on, I felt myself turning outward from shame and depression toward the beauty of the canyon. Perhaps it was Tom's love of the place, shared with such generous imagination, or perhaps, as the sages say, attention is really a form of prayer. In any case, I could feel the class drawing together, held in by the canyon's walls that began to feel like cupped hands or cradling arms. Each bend was an arch that could hold me up or, lying on its side, contain me like a bowl. Tom's expertise, concrete and gentle, connected us to the land like probing roots. We could feel its order and harmony seeping into us like water.

Later that evening, Tom and I met to consider the next day's work. My leg still felt very sore; there was no way I'd be hiking to the river. Tom offered a fistful of ibuprofen but confessed that his own feet were badly blistered; he probably wouldn't make it either. As for the rest, they liked the idea of a short day. So we agreed to stop for lunch a few miles in and take stock. As darkness fell, we gathered in the alcove and lit a cluster of votive candles in lieu of a campfire. Tom and I lectured on wilderness and the idea of nature from biblical times to modern environmental writing. This was still a graduate seminar, after all; people had done the reading. As we talked, I imagined each text as a sand grain, uniquely chipped and colored by the flow of human time. Nature, too, was an open book that we were just learning to read, not only here, but back home as well. It was strangely comforting, as I lay down for the night, to feel the firm sand shifting to the contours of my body, as if the continent's history were bearing me off to sleep.

The Great Alcove

Tom said, "In the canyon there are only two directions, upstream and down. Today we walk with water and in it." He laid out the map. "Notice how the contour lines bunch together here. Those are cliffs where the stream flows through a narrow slot: the walls are almost close enough to touch. That big bend to the left, like an open *C*, is where the stream used to flow; it's called an oxbow. We'll stop there for lunch. It's about two miles."

"Including shortcuts?" someone cracked.

Tom grimaced. "Not today. I will go first and meet you at the narrows."

It was a bright, cool morning. Swifts darted among the trees as we hoisted packs. My leg still ached, and Tom limped slightly as he started off. There was no telling how far we'd get beyond the oxbow, whether we'd make it to the base camp that Ed and I had used, a good five miles in. Beyond that it was five more miles to the river. I had been so looking forward to a memorial moment for Tom Watkins, followed by a cleansing swim. But now all bets were off.

The class set off at a meditative pace and was soon strung out in groups of two or three. There was no maintained trail, just a footpath worn by other hikers that often forked or wandered confusingly. We picked our own course but had to keep weaving in and out of the stream, for the vegetation was often too thick or prickly to bash through, especially the Russian olives with their two-inch thorns. I came last in order to sweep the trail, even though there was even less chance of getting lost, now that we were down inside the canyon. Several learners were still suffering from blisters, fatigue, or stress. At breakfast everyone had wanted to try for the river, but we knew that some had misjudged their own strength. Tom and I had agreed to take no more chances.

Coming last had other attractions, of course. I remembered the thrill of entering the green, lush world downstream from the fence, which had closed the canyon to grazing. Upstream, the red, denuded hills and washes choked with tamarisk showed how much ecological damage cattle could inflict on this dry environment. Such areas would take many years to recover. This was poor beef country, despite the cowboy myths so dear to ranchers, county commissioners, and other "Sagebrush Rebels." I gave thanks for whoever had built that fence. It demarcated two kinds of husbandry, and you could tell at a glance which kind was deeper. On one side, they were raising beef and weeds; on the other, wildness.

The fence made clear that here in the Escalante, wilderness was not only growing back but also growing on. Downstream the plant community was a lush mix of native and alien species. The aliens were doing fine, but the natives seemed to be holding their own. Instead of dense stands, I found tamarisk mixed in with willows, and Russian olive growing alongside cottonwoods. I found alfalfa with its spruce green foliage and deep blue flowers sprawling like lupine, but also scarlet pentstemon and the sweet, minty purple sage. The plant community here seemed as international and diverse as the one in Cincinnati. I even noticed some common species, such as the native box elder and alien yellow sweet clover. The Escalante flora, though free, wild, and lovely, was hardly pristine. It was a mix, a hybrid community like the one in my backyard.

As I walked, I began to feel a strange double consciousness. There was the wholeness, harmony, and radiance of old growth, yet also a teasing familiarity. I was about as remote from Cincinnati as you could get in the lower forty-eight states, yet here were plants that also grew in Ohio. I had been here before, yet today everything looked fresh and strange. As I moved downstream, the sense of paradox only deepened. In desert country, you are aware of rock, of hard, corrosive light and baking heat. You can feel the air sucking moisture through your skin. Sweat dries instantly, leaving a salty crust. Water is something that disappears; it carves the landscape, then vanishes like a ghost. Its curved, graceful movements haunt the traveler. But here in this canyon, water stayed with us at every step. In less than half an hour, our boots were soaked, our socks caked with red sand even though the stream was seldom more than an inch deep. Glancing from the high, rounded walls to a sandbar underfoot, where the stream purled over pebbles, I could see the grand contours of the canyon reproduced in miniature. The stream, I realized, was older than its bed, yet it seemed as fresh and innocent as a newborn spring. There was something perennially youthful in its flow, with which we and all other features of the landscape were now aligned. It was easy hiking downstream through willow thickets, for they all bent our way. The cottonwoods all tilted with the flow, pointing toward the river miles away. Dried leaves and stalks lodged high in their branches by floods seemed like notes left by passing pilgrims to encourage us. The canyon had gathered us and was now giving us direction. We were becoming coherent, moving into phase with the landscape and with each other. "Water's my will and my way," said Roethke. Yes, but here it was water shaped and contained by rock—by rock that the water was also shaping as it moved. That was the way of this landscape, hard and soft, still and moving, red and green, the obdurate fixity of stone and the lush complexity of life.

By noon we had reached the narrows. Coming out of a thicket, the stream flowed directly toward a huge red wall, but instead of turning and running along the base, it cut right through, clean as a knife through butter. We walked into the slot, wondering at the cool, vertical walls that were close enough to touch. It felt like walking through cathedral doors. On the far side, Tom led us up through dense brush into the oxbow, a great bend that had been left high and dry when the stream broke through the wall and began cutting the slot.

Imagine a pro football stadium two hundred yards across with a roof arching over the topmost row of seats. That will give you an idea of the alcove we now entered. It swept up-canyon in a great arc, the inside wall curving back so that a forty-foot swath of ground was protected from sun and rain. There was room for dozens of people to camp out of sight or earshot of the trail. Scattered charcoal marked the fires of former users, backpackers for sure, but also cowboys, and perhaps even Anasazis. Near the drip line grew clumps of coarse, wooly plants with pointed leaves and white, trumpet-shaped blossoms, the sacred datura used by southwestern tribes to induce visions. It seemed fitting that they should grow here, for the alcove seemed to gather and focus the entire landscape like a huge parabolic mirror. Sitting at the center of the arc, I realized that its two ends reached just to the limit of peripheral vision.

Meanwhile Tom had gathered the group for lunch and was asking how the morning's hike had gone. Several reported foot problems—bad blisters, a turned ankle—while others were having pack trouble. Two had needed a friend's arm. But everyone else seemed fit and exhilarated, apparently fully recovered. They still wanted to try for the river. But Tom said, "It's too far to go today. There's a bunch of neat stuff we can do around here. The Anasazis farmed this canyon. It's rich with the human past."

We sat down in the shade, spread peanut butter on bagels, guzzled iced tea, and discussed what to do. Ed's old base camp was another two miles in, and the river four or five miles beyond that. We knew some could never make it. Someone asked if we could split the group; those who wanted to could try for the river, the rest could stay here. But Tom and I were too gun-shy for that, and besides, there was the learning agenda to consider. So we decided to play it by ear. If we kept checking in with the group, we could not go too far wrong. Everyone started to relax. It was good to sit cross-legged on clean sand, eating our fill and watching swifts dart past the red cliffs singing in the sun. It was wonderful to be doing without clocks or calendars, to simply sit and eat and feel your body rejoice. I thought of saying grace; it was something you could do anywhere, even in the city.

Afterward Tom led us downstream to a wide terrace where a tributary came in out of a big amphitheater. Dry waterfalls stepped back and up, all the way to the rim. "Coyote's anthro," Tom began, sweeping his arm across the view. "Anasazis lived here a thousand years ago, farming terraces like these all through the Escalante. Then they disappeared; no one knows why. Some say they were the ancestors of the Hopis." He began pointing out their traces: a row of handholds chipped into sloping rock, patches of Indian rice grass marking a garden site, an intact stone granary tucked up on a shelf under an overhang. No larger than a keg of beer, it might have held a bushel; the closely chinked sandstone slabs, mortared with mud, would have kept out mice and rats. "Imagine," Tom said, "relying on this country for all your needs, making sandals from yucca fiber, weaving robes from turkey feathers, raising corn, beans, and squash as well as native plants like wolfberry, making pots from river clay, chipping knives and arrowheads from chert nodules washed out of the cliffs. Wild and beautiful as it is, this land is full of human history. Go up into some of these alcoves, and you'll see the black stains of cooking fires. Next to them are tiny hand prints in red ocher, left by children. You can pick up corncobs no bigger than your forefinger, ancestral varieties only recently domesticated, much closer to wild grass than today's corn. None of my Indian friends will sleep in these alcoves; they say they can feel the presence of the ancient ones, who are not friendly. My students report having weird dreams; some have even felt hands pushing them away."

Tom asked, how do we compare ecologically to the Anasazis and the Mormons who followed them? Escalante was uninhabited for hundreds of years. Then came the Mormons with European agriculture. Cattle allowed them to exploit grass, which the Anasazis could not (their only domesticated animal was the turkey). But the Mormons had only small, widely scattered settlements, and none in places like this. No doubt the Anasazis were more numerous. As for us, we have to bring in everything we need, except for water. We're tourists, the ultimate alien species. We take a lot away: fun, beauty, knowledge, maybe wisdom. What do we give back?

No one had thought of that. We were too busy worrying about dry socks or where to sleep or what to write in our journals. We were busy adjusting to a place that was rich and strange. Tom let the question hang as we wandered back to camp.

Later we cooked dinner in the alcove, then gathered around our votive candles. It was amazing how much light and psychic warmth a few small flames could provide. They threw our shadows high against the walls, looming and flickering. But this was not Plato's cave: it opened generously to the desert sky. Someone asked, what is the significance of this place to the biosphere? Does it make any difference in the global ecology? It does not regenerate the atmosphere like oceanic phytoplankton nor harbor myriad species like the Great Smoky Mountains or the rain forests of Costa Rica. So, what difference does it make? Not much, Paul said, if you look at it that way, but think of what it's doing to us. Think of the stories we'll bring back. There's a ripple effect. Nature writers like Snyder and Muir had experiences that they put into stories and poems that mattered, that changed how we treat the land. Barry Lopez says that the stories people tell have a way of taking care of them, that sometimes we need a story more than food to stay alive. Maybe the land does too.

We talked far into the night, sharing accounts of adventures in the wild and especially of meeting birds and animals: a bear or coyote coming into camp, a loon popping up next to you as you swam across a northern lake, a cougar glimpsed across rocks, a white-faced ibis appearing suddenly at a bend down-canyon, a raven flying overhead and dropping a feather at your feet. It was a Paleolithic scene, human beings hunched together in a small circle of light, creating culture out of animal dreams. That night the warm sand felt as soft as fur. The moon rose, washing the alcove in pale blue light. A storm cloud rumbled past, flashing briefly, but left no rain.

Walking Meditation

Next morning, as the sky turned silver, I watched swifts soaring across the alcove. A raven flew in and perched on the rim. In the center of my view, a great rounded tower caught the hot gold of sunrise. I remembered one Easter morning back in New Jersey, when I watched dawn break over Manhattan: the skyline glowed pink and gold as if it had just been made. For a moment, the whole world had seemed fresh and full of grace.

No one was up. I slid out of my bag and walked barefoot across the cool, Zen sand, skirting the Gambel oaks, whose dry leaves crackled like cornflakes underfoot. Down at the narrows, it was very cool. A slow breeze carried the perfume of Russian olives, musky and sweet with a salt edge, faintly pungent. The water chuckled and whispered in its bed. Wading in, I felt embraced by tenderness. No wonder Ed Abbey had found the desert feminine and mysterious. Yet Tom had once been stranded here for two days by a flash flood. Imagine red water surging ten feet deep through this cut, carrying all manner of debris, even a dead cow! It was important to note the signs, to pay attention to the unseen as well as the seen. In the Boundary Waters, the invisible hand was fire; here it was water.

Back at camp, people were already sitting in council. Some still wanted to try for the river; others had fallen in love with the alcove and its environs. With sore muscles and broken blisters, many could not hike far. Several wanted more time to discuss the readings. Finally we agreed to spend the morning here and split up in the afternoon, with Tom leading one party downstream while I stayed put with the other. We asked everyone to consider what this arrangement would mean. It was not the pattern of experience we had envisioned, an excursion in which the group would always be moving through the landscape in the fashion of explorers. That had been the classic pattern in American nature

writing, and it had shaped our environmental thought. What consequences would such a pattern have for our experience of this canyon?

Well, Barb said, if you are always moving, you form quick impressions
at a distance, and you have to rely on preconceived ideas to fill in the
blanks. You bring a lot in with you, just as we do with our food and gear.
You tend to think in terms of scenery. But when you stop, as we did the
other night, the place really begins to sink in. It's beautiful. It reminds
me of architecture, Paul said, all these massive, geometric forms—just
think of the names: Music Temple, Castle Valley. Maybe the sense of
beauty comes from the fusion of human and natural form.

There was no doubt that Escalante, and the canyon country in general,
would be high on anyone's list of beautiful places. It had been featured
in numberless coffee-table books and creamy magazine spreads. Envi-
ronmentalists had turned it into an icon. But history shows that beauty
is something learned. We all agree that the Tetons are beautiful, but it
was not always so. Until the seventeenth century, mountains were
considered ugly, deformations of once-perfect nature brought about by
the Fall. Only when the microscope and the telescope began to reveal
unseen dimensions of order and magnitude did nature begin to take on
aspects of sublimity that had hitherto been reserved for God. By the end
of the eighteenth century, Romantic poets and philosophers were
celebrating alpine landscapes as sources of inspiration and virtue.
American writers like Emerson, Thoreau, and Muir adapted such ideas
to promote a vision of American culture founded on intimate contact
with nature. In a similar vein, artists and photographers like Albert
Bierstadt and Ansel Adams had projected an indelible concept of
sublimity onto the landscapes of the West. Through such a lens, nature
was always a New World that beckoned warriors and explorers, even at
midlife.

But another aesthetic was also at work in America, informed by
naturalists and ecologists. The close observation required for botanizing
or taxonomy led to an interest in small things and relationships. Writers
like Aldo Leopold and E. O. Wilson had taught us to appreciate the
significance of minute organisms, the music of migrating geese and
cranes, the dancelike change of floods, winter storms, or ecological

succession. Photographers like Eliot Porter had discovered how to express the variety and intricacy of ecosystems by using texture and color. But as recent nature writers had realized, only narrative could convey the relationships that, like harmony in music, formed the true beauty of any landscape. Only stories could teach us to see the unseen.

In the canyons, we all agreed, it was easy to experience the great rocks photographically, especially when they were set off against the sky or juxtaposed against one another to stunning effect, like skyscrapers, monuments, or statues. Surely we had all grown accustomed to that sort of view through years of living in cities and reading magazines. That being the case, how much of our trip was really new experience? Weren't we just finding what we came to see? I don't think so, Barb said. It's the greenery; I never expected so much greenery in the desert. It's the water, Martha said, and the sounds. Running water, all those birds. But there's not too much of any one thing. I get it about the architecture, Jim said, but the rocks aren't set up on the land; they're part of it, and we're down inside it, inside the land, and yet we're outdoors all the time.

Tom said, "Each of these metaphors is a lens that offers a certain kind of insight. What sort of world do you want to see? There is always more here than meets the eye, always more to the scene than scenery. Suppose we did a walking meditation, paying special attention to our nonvisual senses? We could go in two groups, circling in opposite directions through the narrows. No talking, especially when we meet! When you're done, go off and write down everything. Take a break from ideas. We can compare notes over lunch."

So we got up, creaking a bit, and began to move, placing each foot firmly before taking the next step, as Zen directs. I became aware, first, of how the sand felt underfoot, firm yet shifting in its support, so that you had to take on a sailor's rolling gait. Emerging from shadow into sun felt like opening an oven door; the heat was hard, almost solid, with a cutting edge. Dry, straw odors filled the air. Cheat grass crackled underfoot. Bird calls caromed off the high stone walls. I felt the swish of rabbit-brush, prickly as spruce, against my legs. Down by the stream, head-high willows forced me to use both hands and arms; they parted easily but snapped right back. I could not walk straight through but had to weave in and out. It felt as if I were wrestling with the land. The willow leaves yielded to an upward stroke, like cat's fur, but the wands were stiff and resilient; they could lash.

Along the water's edge, soft filigree of horsetails tickled my shins; tiny dark cones at the tip released a pale, purple puff of spores when flicked with a finger. The rustle of cottonwood leaves and the hiss of running water softened the crunch of boots on pebbles. As I entered the narrows, a sudden breeze cooled my forehead; I realized that the walls funneled and focused the canyon's many air currents to a steady downstream flow. I ran my hand over the wall, feeling its fluid curvature and hard, abrasive texture. It resisted my touch, even as surface particles came loose and fell away. This was erosion; I was doing water work. What was my body anyhow but a tissue of moist salt cells, a form of walking water? Everything felt so cool and close after the fierce, ceramic heat up in the alcove. Down here things were damp, hairy, complex, trembling with life, and fragrant with many odors. It all reminded me, somehow, of childbirth and that first week spent at home with my wife and daughter. I realized that travel here meant more than just watching scenery; it was a dance in and out of intimacy carried on with every sense. Even the change in temperature as you moved into and out of shadows played a role. Beauty was a weaving of sound, light, shape, touch, and movement across many scales. It was not something seen but absorbed. To appreciate it, you had to remain in one place, as we had been forced to do.

Back in the alcove, there seemed to be much less enthusiasm for going to the river. We ate a slow lunch, then separated into small groups, agreeing to meet for dinner and share what we had found. Tom took one group downstream toward the beaver dams and bends with hundred-meter walls, while I stayed closer to camp with another group to talk about the writers and practice in our journals. We wandered downstream, slow as philosophers, and stopped in a shady alcove for snacks and talk, but a wind sprang up and blew sand in our faces. A gray cloud boiled up over the rim, spitting rain. So I gave up class as a bad job. That day we were destined to learn mainly through our skin.

Back at camp, Tom asked how it had gone. Everyone agreed that this canyon was beginning to feel like home. We had experienced many kinds of beauty, but how should we respond? What was the link between aesthetics and politics, between experience and action? Tom said, "The larger your sense of self, the greater the scope of your self-interest." Could a wilderness such as this be "managed"? That would be our question for tomorrow.

Later, as darkness fell, Tom read his own description of the oxbow, explaining how, right here, he had realized that love was a form of perception. As he spoke, a kestrel soared from its nest high on the rim. I thought of my own daughters and how much they had taught me, especially that day we discovered the grass forest. How they would have loved it here! The same stars were shining on the roof beneath which they slept as on my sleeping bag stretched on this desert sand. I could almost feel a slim, electric current humming through the earth between us, all the way back to Cincinnati.

Emergence

When dawn came with the first bird calls, I had no desire to move. I felt cemented to the ground. My eyes traveled up and outward along the great, curving walls of the alcove, but my mind was completely still. It was as if the whole landscape had come to rest on a point of precise, delicate balance located somewhere behind my eyes. Tom was right about one thing: staying put had allowed us to sink in. I had never felt more connected to the earth.

I became aware of the double curvature of the walls, which bent horizontally to the stream's ancient meander while arcing vertically inward as the current had worn away the outer edge of each bend. No doubt these curves, so unlike the geometry of monuments or buildings, accounted for some of the strangeness I had been feeling on this trip. Hiking past such formations would give only a glancing view sufficient for a quick and easy comparison to stadiums or capitol domes. But staying in one place made us all aware of water and its process, the curve of flow that inscribed both rock and memory. Here I had to take issue with Tom: there were not two but three directions in the canyon—

upstream and downstream, yes, but also a third direction, inward. You could move that way only by staying put.

After coffee we gathered for one last session. Tom wanted to know what we thought about his question. Now that the time had come to go home, what were we going to do? What did it mean to manage a wilderness like this? Recall, he said, that humans managed this land a thousand years ago, and that "manage" derives from the Spanish word for hands. We manage anything we set our hands to. We cannot avoid the challenges and obligations of husbandry. We can't just leave things alone. Nonaction does not equal nonmanagement when it comes to the more-than-human world. The drift fence up-canyon is a slow, deliberate, and recent action. After the Anasazis, no one lived here or cared about it except for a few Mormon ranchers. It took years of conspicuous degradation before people started thinking about grazing policy. And it was only in the last thirty years that backpackers had come to the Escalante seeking adventure, purity, or visions. Now you and I are the cutting edge of human time. Our hands are laid on this place like moving water. What sort of traces will we leave? What do we want our chapter in the story to be?

But, Ben said, we're going back. We can't live here like the Anasazis. We had to carry in everything we needed. Three days ago, these were heavy packs! None of us could begin to live off the land. Ecologically, we're tourists, not inhabitants. We only taste the wilderness; we don't *live* with it. We might as well be visiting the moon. It's curious to think, said Jim, how much we still depend on our city life, even so far away. Back home everything we use is brought in too. Not to mention, added Barb, the planes that brought us here, using imported oil. And while we're at it, Ben put in, let's not forget the famous drift fence that keeps this place so wild. It's a result of the Glen Canyon National Recreation Area, which results from Lake Powell, which was created to supply electricity for Las Vegas and L.A.! You could say this wilderness depends, finally, on those awful cities.

Tom laughed. "One thing's for sure: we all have to go back. Our relation to this place must be enacted elsewhere. Think about what you are taking home. Remember that taking confers responsibility. The circle of the gift is a sacred circle. As we walk back, think about giving back."

We hoisted packs and filed out of the great alcove. Tom and I came last. We no longer had any fear of people getting lost. It felt good to linger as voices faded up the trail, until we stood alone in that great parabolic space. What was it about this stone that so tugged memory? Neither sculpture nor architecture fit. The walls wore the face of water yet stood as hard and stiff as bone. Up ahead Tom gave a dove call. I bowed once to the soaring walls and once to the open landscape they embraced, the distant rim, the hot, blue sky, the creek's green, tangled banks. My pack was lighter now. My leg felt fine.

We walked slowly back to our first night's camp, pausing by ancient cottonwoods or expressive boulders. Although the canyon sloped imperceptibly, we felt a real effort hiking upstream. The willows all bent against us; the thickets seemed dense and prickly; even the terraces seemed higher, their banks crumbling and treacherous underfoot. Perhaps there was an emotional tug as well. We had been scattered and gathered, broken and then healed by the land's coherence and wild beauty. The group had survived in spite of getting lost. We had reconsti-tuted the seminar and accomplished our learning goals. The one thing we had failed to achieve was a deeper entry to the river, where we had hoped to celebrate Tom Watkins. That was a sorrow. What would he have thought of our getting lost? No doubt he would have loved the night hike across open desert, miles from nowhere under the ancient stars.

Approaching camp, I met Paul and Martha filtering water. They jumped up and offered me a cupful. "I can't believe we made it!" Martha exclaimed. "You know, we're the oldest, and this was my first time backpacking." I laughed. Paul suddenly asked, "Do you regret losing the class, now that we're done?" I stared at him. "As a teacher, I mean," he smiled. "I'm asking you as a teacher."

I thought of our eagerness, the joy of fellowship with Tom, alarm, anxiety, breathless effort, the hurting leg, the coyote sign, the starlit beauty of the land, the talking stick, the agony of council followed by healing immersion in the canyon. It all flashed by in a moment, leaving a raw tenderness, like a burn. I stared at Paul, then stammered, "I don't know."

When we got to camp, people were already cooking dinner. A communal feast had been organized, and leftovers were being turned into delights. I threw down my sleeping bag in its old spot beside the fence, then returned to eat with my companions. After hauling in all that food, why carry it out? Besides, you always feel reluctant to break the fellowship. So instead you break bread together. That's what "companion" means, after all, someone with whom you share a piece of bread.

The talk fizzed and swirled around our various expectations of the desert and how the reality had cleansed our imagination. This was not a place for arid fanaticism or ascetic rites. It had nurtured us with living water, embracing stone, deep human history, and rich communities of life. Several people had already resolved to come back with friends or families. Next time they would go all the way to the river, or at least find a way to get up to the rim.

Tom jumped up. "We can get up to the rim from here!" he said. "It's tricky, but there's still enough light. I'll show you." And he led us across the stream to a slickrock spur. It was steep, with gut-wrenching exposure, but we all managed to pick our way up. As we reached the top, the landscape suddenly flew open. Acres of smooth, bare rock pitched eastward like frozen waves, all the way to the horizon. I felt momentarily dizzy, as if I had stepped onto the deck of a storm-tossed ship, but the only thing moving was a soft evening breeze. Imagine what a real storm would feel like up here! Wind had scoured this country clean. It was now eroding these fossilized dunes it had once laid down. Above the rim, there was no protection. We could see where the canyon was by the green tops of cottonwoods, and it looked like a slender thread indeed. Shade, water, everything life needed was there. The canyon had sheltered us, but it had also kept us in. It had restrained our vision. Perhaps that was part of the cost of healing.

Up ahead people were scattering like deer, running and leaping across the slickrock. Such breathtaking expanses of space had seemed inconceivable during our five days of hiking inside the earth. Climbing out felt like being born. And at that moment, I realized why the famous landforms of alcove and arch had seemed so different this time. Encountered up close as part of a healing journey and animated by a sense of biological time, they no longer felt like works of sculpture or architecture, but living bone. These arches and alcoves and openings resembled the first landscape we had ever known, that of our mother's body. They had cradled us like the pelvic bones of a woman. No wonder hiking back had felt so hard. Downstream the canyon was a funnel; upstream it was a birth canal. Without immersion there could be no emergence. And emergence was effortful, even painful. It was labor. Yet that was the price of all new life, whether of the body or of the mind. That was the price of freedom. No wonder the native people of the Colorado Plateau had imagined themselves emerging from lower worlds into this present one with all its challenge and opportunity. Perhaps they had chosen the canyon for a home, in part, because they wanted to honor their origins.

Up ahead the learners had gathered at a high point where a ring of rocks made a sort of natural lookout. By the time I got there, they had already traced Coyote's Road running along a line of bluffs to the north. To the west, Kaiparowits formed a dark wall against the sunset; to the south and east, the horizon lay fifty miles off, beyond the Escalante and the Colorado. That's what emergence did, I thought; it changed the horizon. Now we could see our path, and it all made sense, even the traumatic events of day one. We had to be broken before we could really come together. We had to go down and in before we could rise up and come out. Indeed, there was a fourth direction to canyon travel, the one that led up to and beyond the rim. I felt like bowing to them all.

Someone asked about Tom Watkins. Had he ever come to this place? It was possible, I said. He had traveled all over the canyon country. It was his spiritual home, even though he spent most of his life in Washington, DC, as a writer and activist. He was a pilgrim to the wild, just like us. This country had nurtured him, and in return he had fought for its protection, which meant, actually, that he was fighting for us. Tom was a warrior. His love was as abrasive and rugged as the rock we were sitting on. His politics were as clear and refreshing as water; they inspired and sustained so many of us who had to live far from places like this. In my mind's eye, I imagine him hiking along with people like Ed Abbey and

Wallace Stegner, in a place where boots never wear out, and the slickrock goes on forever.

We sat in silence as the sun dipped below Kaiparowits. Wherever Tom Watkins was, I hoped he was carrying his stories. He had left the earth to us. What would our story be? The air turned purple as the last sunlit hilltops winked out one by one. Shadows pooled in the slickrock hollows. Camp was close by, but some people decided to sleep up on the rim. Tom and I helped the others work their way down. Nothing had gone as planned, but somehow everything had turned out all right. We had even celebrated Tom Watkins in a place that was much more fitting than the river. I felt the group's forgiveness flowing around us like cool night air.

Perhaps compassion comes more easily to those who have experienced brokenness. By the age of forty, everyone is a survivor. At midlife you get the sense that brokenness and healing are not isolated events. You become aware of emergence as part of the life process; you learn to embrace its pain as a sign of transformation. Gary Snyder had said that to find the path, you had to step off the trail; then you would discover that the path was everywhere, everything, the wild itself, and at that moment practice would begin. I could see the wild now as an ongoing process of emergence. To practice the wild meant to live with that process, and to live for it as well, even in cities where we work and raise our children and struggle with politics or art. To practice the wild meant to step off the trail of received ideas about people and nature, to embrace learning and metamorphosis. The wilderness journey was no longer an act of rebellion but a pilgrimage. You could bow with a whole heart to the four sacred directions. It would no longer be an ordeal to return home.

Next morning we joined hands in a circle to give thanks, then hiked out in silence past the drift fence, the raven's nest, and Coyote's Road to our waiting vehicles. In no time, it seemed, we were back in Salt Lake, and next morning I was airborne again, watching the vast West curve away from six miles up. Yet when I closed my eyes, I saw only a thin green oasis full of willows and secret shoals enlivened by bird song and the perfume of Russian olives. I could feel the sand grains lodged in my hair and fingernails, the long scabs of willow cuts on my legs and arms.

Back in Cincinnati, Pam and the girls met me at the airport. That night I ate at my own table and slept in my own bed, which felt disturbingly soft after six nights on firm desert sand. The next day, running errands, I noticed a hedge of Russian olives that someone had planted along the road; they were festooned with blossoms as white and creamy as those in the Escalante. I noticed pink tassels of tamarisk nodding over the wall of Spring Grove Cemetery. Tufts of cottonwood down had caught in our screen door. And in the stack of accumulated mail, I found a note from Tom with an interview that Gary Snyder had given during a trip down the Ohio Valley two decades before. Asked what advice he would give to someone local, Snyder had replied, "Learn about Cincinnati. It could be beautiful!"

A SMALL PIECE OF LAND

A Family Resource

Emergence myths speak to the mystery of human origins, which must be as old as consciousness. They tell of human beings climbing up from the underworld, issuing from a spring, slipping out through the bole of a great tree, or being formed by God from the dust of the ground. They connect people with their home landscapes and express a sense of belonging at the root of the group's identity.

But emergence myths also speak on a more intimate, personal level. Psychologists say that the years between nine and twelve are crucial to forming one's ecological identity. During this period, children turn outward from the family toward the surrounding world, wandering farther from the house toward the woods and fields, where a stream, a thicket, a mossy boulder, or a rotting log may suddenly captivate their attention. All it takes is a few such encounters for the mind to begin putting down roots. And when the kids run home, excited to tell their stories, parents often respond with stories of their own. That's how one's experience of nature becomes interwoven with family tradition and the myths of the culture at large.

When we speak of having roots, we are really talking about this tissue of story and landscape. A move may tear us away, but the stories always come with us. This accounts, in part, for the nostalgia we feel when the novelty of a move wears off. The new country may dazzle and exhilarate—it may even become home eventually—but it can never replace the landscape that formed us, the native ground to which we will always belong.

For me that native ground is New England. Despite lengthy sojourns in Utah, Minnesota, and Ohio, I've always felt like a Yankee. I cherish cold winters, glaciated hills, clear lakes, and mixed forests of pine, birch, and maple. Summering in Connecticut exposed me to these things during the crucial years, even though we lived and worked in New Jersey. My father and grandmother, too, were always talking about the old homestead up in New Hampshire, where they had spent summers when Dad was a boy. We still had some farm tools from the old place: huge scythes, a posthole digger, sickles, crowbars, a two-man timber saw, peaveys for rolling logs, hay rakes with wooden tines, a block and tackle, plus various hoes and shovels with wooden handles shiny from use. These pioneer implements evoked for me a life of hard work in the open air and a yeoman ancestry more virtuous in its connection to the land than the urban, industrial culture in which I was growing up. I could hear the nostalgia in my father's voice as he spoke of those childhood summers when he learned to fish in the Contoocook River and, later, canoed through Canada with Indian guides or cast for salmon in the rivers of Nova Scotia. I could see why it had been so important for him to buy a small piece of the old homestead when it was broken up and sold off at the end of World War II.

As a returning GI, my father had few assets apart from a pregnant wife and three months of paid leave. He could not afford to buy the house or the main lot by the river. But his Uncle Ed, who was managing the estate, offered him the old maple-sugar orchard on the mountain above town, a forty-acre interior lot with no road access or surface water. There were lots of rocks but no mature maples; it was covered by spindly second growth. The tax collector had assessed it at fifty dollars, his uncle said, and he'd be happy to take that much for it. They shook hands, and Dad forked over two weeks' pay. He was now a landowner and taxpayer in the sovereign state of New Hampshire.

For the next fifty years, the land sat idle while my father worked in a factory and raised a family. His wilderness days were behind him. We visited the property once when I was about four years old, but all I re-member is camping out in a sandpit and riding through the woods on my father's shoulders. He was a big man, with shoulders to match, and I felt very secure up there, pushing branches away with my little hands and looking all over the place. I felt as if I were sitting on top of a moun-tain.

Even though we never went there again, the New Hampshire property often crept into family conversations. My grandmother reminisced about her Yankee relatives and their wonderful old house. I could tell that my father was proud to have kept a bit of the old place in the family. He had logged a few acres back in the 1950s to help pay some medical bills, but otherwise he had left it alone. The town classified it as undeveloped land, which saved a good deal on taxes. It remained a memory and a vision to us, a strange, remote place to which we were linked by law and family tradition but did not really know. As my own path in wilderness teaching began to unfold, I often looked back toward New England from the western mountains or the northern lakes, glad to think that our family still kept its ancestral link to a piece of land that was growing ever more wild. I imagined the property as our own private national park, rich with native species, an island of ecological sanity amid the sprawl, pollution, and wreckage that had marred so much of North America. At times I thought of building a cabin there. But the path I was on never seemed to lead back to New England.

Meanwhile we were all growing older. My father turned eighty and began to think about settling his estate. One day he called and asked what I thought about selling the property. "I don't suppose you kids would be able to do much with it," he said. "You're all scattered hither and yon."

I was surprised at my own reaction, a sudden tightening in the throat. "We can't sell it!" I blurted; then, recovering, "We don't even know what's up there. We should at least take a look."

"I've been thinking about that," he said. "Last year a guy called and wanted to log it for me. He had been working on an adjacent lot and noticed some good, merchantable timber, said we could net around fifteen thousand. That sounded pretty good to me, but I didn't know this guy, so I had a local forester mark the property line."

"I'll be in New Hampshire this fall at a meeting," I said. "I could go over and check it out. I have a learner who specializes in land inventories."

"Fine," Dad said. He paused. "I'm glad someone's taking an interest. You know, we've never done anything with the property in all these years."

"We didn't have to," I said. "It's been growing wilder. That's something in itself."

"Perhaps," he said, "you'd like to take it on?"

"Let's find out what's up there first," I said. "We don't need to decide right away." But I felt a tingle as I put down the phone. I had never owned land apart from our city lot, never been responsible for any wilderness except in the abstract, as a citizen of a democracy with millions of acres of public lands. Ownership in that sense meant something remote, impersonal, and governed by lofty ideals. It was much easier to fathom than legal title to and responsibility for a particular forty acres in a specific New England town. Somehow fighting for big, public wilderness felt more virtuous than actually owning land. Perhaps I was just shying away from responsibility, the effort it would take to learn enough about the land to manage it with care. On the other hand, I was thrilled at the thought of walking ancestral ground. Finally I would get to see the famous property where my father had gained his spirit of adventure and my Yankee ancestors had drawn their sustenance straight from the land. Returning as a pilgrim would prepare me for ownership in more ways than one.

But what, in fact, did it really mean to "own land"? The question nagged me for weeks, right up to the day I took off for Boston. As the plane climbed over Ohio's glacial plain and crossed the Appalachian escarpment, I watched the land spread out like a rumpled quilt, its corrugations of ridge, valley, and watershed clearly visible. I had enjoyed such views every time I took off for the wilderness, but now I was aware of something else: innumerable, invisible property lines stitched along roads, fences, or the edges of woods and fields. The vast landscape resolved into an intricate mosaic of individual properties, thousands upon thousands of them all patched together like one of those posters where a face emerges from a collage of tiny snapshots. Every one of those parcels had been surveyed, mapped, deeded, and filed in the tax books of a town or county. Each one belonged to somebody who had ideas about what to do with it. Even from thirty thousand feet, you could tell a lot about those ideas just from observing the varied colors and textures. America as a whole was largely made up of small pieces of private land, and ownership meant many things to many people. But what did it mean to my family or to me?

Ever Since Genesis

There's a big difference between enjoying, learning from, or managing land and actually owning it. We all grow up interacting with land—indeed, we can hardly escape it—but when we become landowners, these varied forms of relation draw into vivid focus on one particular place. In Dickens's novel *Great Expectations*, the young hero, Pip, gets a lecture on "portable property" from a law clerk who likes to wheel and deal. This gentleman has garnered enough liquifiable assets to finance a cozy suburban home, where he cares for his aged father and leads a private life of virtue and generosity. Such "portable" property contrasts with the "real" property of landed gentry, who, in the novel, have been corrupted by obsessions and old money. Dickens's point is not that owning land corrupts but that identity and integrity must be earned. One grows a life story out of the interaction between character and experience. Environment—in this case, wealth and class—is no predictor of virtue.

Nevertheless, land and identity are closely linked in our culture, no less so now than in Dickens's time. Owning "real property" gives one a real estate, that is, a real social position. Thomas Jefferson believed that owning land was essential for democratic citizenship. In the early days of New England, only landholders could vote at town meetings. For centuries whole classes of American people, including women and African American slaves, were barred from owning land, even though it had long been part of the American dream. No matter how poor you were, you were always somebody if you had a small piece of land. After the Revolutionary War, Congress rewarded veterans with grants of frontier land. George Washington himself received over a thousand acres near Cincinnati, which remained part of his estate even though he never saw it. The Homestead Act lured thousands of immigrants from Europe, where every square inch of ground had been spoken for. America became the "land of opportunity" because of the deep link between geographic and cultural space. To own land meant not only to be real, to have a social identity, but also to enjoy exhilarating freedom.

This aura clings even to my modest suburban homestead in Cincinnati, which amounts to about four-tenths of an acre, or 1 percent of the New Hampshire property. Nevertheless, ownership means pretty much that same thing in both cases. Being "private" property, my Cincinnati lot is off-limits to public use. I can fence it off or post the bounds and prosecute you for trespassing. I can cut down or plant trees. I can grow any shrubs, flowers, grasses, or vegetables that I choose. I can erect or tear down buildings as long as I follow the zoning and building codes. I can come and go as I please. I can study the weeds, feed the birds, raise my children, reside, work, eat, sleep, or party there to my heart's content.

As long as I follow the law. If one of my trees falls on the house next door, I'm liable for the damage. If I don't pay my taxes, the sheriff can seize the whole place and auction it off. My tax bill is a crude reflection of public desire, arrived at by polling the local real-estate agents. This may sound like divination, but it comes down to hard cash for me. Thank goodness Cincinnati is not San Francisco, where my little homestead would cost a cool half million in millennial dollars. Cash may be portable property, but it's worth a good deal less on the West Coast. Today you can move (or launder) money with the click of a mouse, but land stays put. Perhaps that's why we still call it real property. It's worth noting that only one letter separates "realty" from "reality," and that letter is *I*.

Meanwhile, as far as the law is concerned, my chief right as a landowner, apart from living there, is the right to sell it off. With 0.4 acres and a house, I am not homeless in Cincinnati, but I could pack up and move out tomorrow. Real-estate agents agree that the average home changes hands every five years, suggesting that there are strong nomadic currents in our culture. Americans are a restless people, always searching for the next best thing. We like to pull up stakes and exercise our options. Therefore, ownership for us has a fluid, ephemeral quality, like money itself. But this makes a shifting, sandy ground on which to build an identity.

However, there is another sense of ownership beside legal title that also lies deep in the American grain. To own means not only to possess but also to confess, acknowledge, or embrace. I can own up to an act, own an emotion or an idea, or celebrate a loved one as "my own." In this sense, ownership suggests intimacy, honesty, or commitment, things that cannot be bought but must be earned. They are matters of relation, governed by reciprocity rather than possession. Thoreau built his cabin on land that belonged to his mentor, Emerson. He never owned so much as a square inch of Walden or its woods, yet who is more closely linked to it than he? Thoreau made Walden his own through attentive devotion and diligent practice. Yet it never belonged to him; rather, he belonged to it.

I have always found it amusing that Thoreau, who gained so much value from land he did not own, should have made his living as a surveyor. He had long since concluded that the best products of any landscape were insights and epiphanies rather than timber, hay, or crops. That's why he never bought a farm. Moreover, he was deeply suspicious of money and the mercantile economy. "I have learned," he declared, "that trade curses everything it handles; and though you trade in messages from heaven, the whole curse of trade attaches to the business." Hence his contempt for the "model" farmers who had cut down the woods and polluted the ponds. He wanted a different relationship to land, one based on wisdom rather than money, where story played an essential role. To him real ownership was a matter of paying attention and bearing witness. It meant weaving the thread of his own life together with that of the land.

In adopting this curmudgeonly attitude, Thoreau seems to have been aware of the two great moral paradigms of land ownership that, as with husbandry, were set forth in the two versions of creation presented in the book of Genesis. Recall that in the first version, God creates the heavens, the earth, and all the other creatures before he makes humans in his own image and gives them dominion. In the second version, God first creates a barren, lifeless earth and then, for obscure reasons, fashions a man from the dust of the ground. Next he creates the Garden of Eden and puts the man in it to tend it, but somehow this arrangement does not work out. God decides that the man needs a helper, so he creates all the other birds and animals, but they don't work out either. Finally God creates a woman to help the man. And help him she does, after first helping herself.

These stories have exerted a tremendous influence on Western history, yet they project very different conceptions of how people ought to relate to the land. The first story offers the hierarchical model of dominion, which construes other creatures as resources. Humans are instructed to subdue the earth; they do not have to treat other creatures as equals, nor do they have to answer for their environmental behavior. Needless to say, this model favors private ownership, commodification, and the free commercial exchange of land. It speaks directly to the optimism of a pioneer or entrepreneurial mentality. It invests speculation with an aura of sanctity. It encourages short-term, extractive relationships and promotes "use," by which is meant the conversion of organisms and minerals into cash. Best of all, it absolves the owner of moral responsibility for long-term degradation, pollution, extinctions, or other delayed effects. James Watt, Ronald Reagan's notorious secretary of the interior, once declared that God wanted us to use up all the timber and oil today because the world was due to end in a couple of generations.

In contrast, the second creation story projects a model of stewardship rather than dominion. God creates nature as a walled garden in which he can take relaxing walks, and humans are put there to till it and keep it. The garden belongs to God, not to Adam and Eve. Their role is one of husbandry: to manage, nurture, and preserve the land for God, to whom, like any stewards, they must report. Their duties and ecological relations are prescribed. When they eat the forbidden fruit, they violate both and cease to be responsible stewards. At that moment, wildness erupts in paradise, and history begins.

It is significant, I think, that the authors of Genesis lifted up both paradigms without forcing a choice between them. Dominion and stewardship pull in opposite directions, yet both are sanctioned by God. Perhaps the authors recognized how complex and difficult it is in real life to manage one's relation to a landscape that, while sacred, must also provide a livelihood. The same tension runs through American environmental history, where preservationists inspired by John Muir's vision of

Edenic wilderness battle the forces of commodity personified by big mining, timber, or real-estate companies. Each side claims the moral high ground of stewardship and service to the public good. But the dilemma remains. For, as Aldo Leopold realized, to own land means to write your signature on it, even if you merely let it alone. Leopold knew that every tree he cut or planted made a mark and that the marks added up to a story. Everything he did to the land expressed his character and his values. Ownership, therefore, became a sort of dialogue.

As I flew over eastern Pennsylvania, I realized that the same tension was playing out in our family's relationship to that small piece of New Hampshire forest. Our ownership had been a mixed, ambiguous tale. We enjoyed the sense of privilege and entitlement, the feeling of being landed citizens of the town, of having a tangible link to the ancestral landscape. We liked the idea of being able to do more or less what we wanted there—of camping out, building a cabin, or even cutting some timber. We enjoyed having options: it was a kind of wealth. And the best part was we could enjoy this feeling without actually having to do anything to the land. We could leave it alone, letting biological time run on as the trees matured and the forest grew wilder and wilder. We could enjoy the feeling of dominion without doing any damage and the satisfaction of stewardship without doing any work.

But my father's age had upset this tidy equation. He wanted to settle the estate. Change was upon us. As the plane touched down in Boston, I realized that whatever we did, even if we sold the land, logged it, or let it alone, would still express our values and reveal the kind of people we were. We could not go on like this, having it both ways. What we did would always matter. Our life and the land's would always be woven into a story. The only question was what kind?

A Walk in the Woods

Rick Van De Poll met me outside the town hall in Bennington, New Hampshire. He was a lean, energetic man dressed in green wool pants and a red plaid shirt, every inch the professional Yankee forester. He was also an accomplished naturalist, as I had discovered during one seminar in the Boundary Waters when he had identified over a hundred lichens during a three-hour walk. He had written a seven-hundred-page dissertation on New England land inventories for his Union degree in natural resource management. I figured that if there was anything noteworthy on our land, Rick would find it.

We spread out our maps on the hood of Rick's pickup. The USGS topo for Bennington showed the western slope of Crotched Mountain with the town road running up and across it before petering out into a dirt track. Our land was somewhere up there, inaccessible by road. The old tax map showed it as the "Steele Pasture," a lopsided square. Dad had sketched in some barbed-wire fencing, a stream, and rock ledges along with several stone walls. The surveyor had told him that we would have to cross the neighbor's land, using a drive that came in just where the town road ended. The bounds had been marked with blazes and orange spray paint. It should be simple enough to find.

We drove out of town along the Contoocook River, where prosperous mills once churned out paper and textiles while my father fished for pickerel upstream. The road turned east toward the mountain, plunging into thick yellow woods that glowed with October light. "All second growth," Rick said as we bounced onto gravel. "Mostly young sugar maples. Probably logged about thirty years ago." We passed a few modest houses on small, cleared lots. The road started climbing, then bent sharply left a mile up the hillside. The forest opened as the maples gave way to older beech with some dark hemlocks mixed in. Above the road, to the right, the slope rose steeply with boulders strewn among the trees. The soil was thinner and drier up here; the trees looked older. The road appeared to have sunk into the ground; portions of old stone walls ran alongside. You could tell, Rick said, that this was a very old road. The land was too steep and rocky for crops; the stone fences showed that it had once been cleared for pasture. That would have been about two hundred years ago, several economies back.

We turned off just before the road ended in a blade berm, beyond which the track faded into the woods. A hundred yards brought us to a small hunter's cabin. "End of the line," Rick said, jumping out. "We ought to head northwest across this bog. Check those hemlocks for a blaze." I could see a stone wall abutting a dark row of evergreens. Down-hill and to the left was a logged area strewn with tree tops and slash; it looked naked, sunburnt, but on the other side of the wall was our land, cool and dark. Rick found an orange paint mark and sighted along it. "This is the east boundary," he said. "There's a blaze every thirty feet."

Once inside the tree line, it felt as if we had entered a dark, high-ceilinged room. Even with leaf fall in progress, the high canopy filtered out a good deal of daylight. We walked among trees of every age, from inch-thick maple saplings to giant red oaks a yard in diameter with no branches for thirty feet up. Sometimes three or four of these would be growing out of the same base, like points of a crown. Rick said they were sprouts from a stump left by the last round of logging, perhaps fifty or sixty years back. Now they were prime timber for furniture or veneer.

We moved deeper into the plot, looking for evidence of the sugaring operation that Dad had described, but all we found were some rusted buckets. The sugarhouse had fallen and rotted away. There were no mature maples to be seen; all we found were some huge, decomposing trunks. Rick said that a blight had devastated the sugar maples right after World War I, around the time my father had been born. Any left stand-ing would have been blown down in the hurricane of 1938, which cut through New Hampshire forests like a scythe. Some of this wind throw was still visible sixty years later: nurse logs bearing tiny forests of moss, ferns, and wild flowers and ending in shallow pits where the roots had been, or trees with thick trunks branching at breast height, where the wind had snapped off the top of a sapling. I was impressed by Rick's skill at reading the landscape. To me it was just a wild woods, lovely, dark, and deep, but to him it was living history. I hoped that our walk might also uncover secrets: rare plants, maybe a hidden spring. What animals lived here? I knew that bears, cougars, and fishers had returned to other parts of New England. Perhaps some had made it here.

As we tramped around, it became clear that the mountainside did not drop at a steady grade but rather in giant steps twenty or thirty feet high. Rock ledges alternated with shallow troughs full of rich, black soil. Flat places in the troughs marked the sites of vernal pools, where snowmelt would provide breeding grounds for salamanders and tree frogs. There might also be orchids, though at this time of year it was hard to tell. On the tops of the ledges, we found young hemlocks rooted in cracks along with thick beds of star moss. Rick found signs of porcupine, raccoon, and other small mammals. There were some caves that appeared to have been used for dens.

On the north side, light was pouring in from the adjacent lot, which had recently been logged. Many trees had been left standing, evenly spaced to ensure reseeding. Stumps had been cut to the ground, and most of the slash had been removed. "That's a clean job," Rick said, "minimal damage to the soil, not much erosion, though you can see from those tracks that they didn't use horses. Quite a few seedlings coming up along with berries. Lots of food for the wildlife." It was a different story on the south edge of our land, where the next lot looked like a war zone. Slash, brush, and even sizable limbs had been strewn helter-skelter among knee-high stumps. The loggers had cut everything but carted off only the prime saw logs. Rick shook his head. "There's a lot of firewood going to waste. It'll take that property half a century to recover."

We sat on a stone wall at the southwest corner, where a cluster of huge white pines had grown up. Three feet or more in diameter at breast height, they towered over the nearest ledge. I had never seen such great pines in the East; they reminded me of old growth in the Boundary Waters or the Sierra Nevada. We sat for a while enjoying the silence and the feeling of clean, wholesome wildness. Finally I asked Rick what he thought.

"Well," he said, "this is a mature second-growth forest. I didn't see any rare or endangered species, though it's hard to tell at this time of year. Those vernal pools would be a nice resource for amphibians. As for human use, you could build here, but water would be a problem along with access. Plus you'd have to cut down a lot of trees for any kind of view. Basically this is just a well-stocked lot."

"Meaning what?"

"Meaning you have a lot of merchantable timber. Prime red oak, white pine, and hemlock. In today's market, I'd guess you could get about a hundred and fifty thousand, in round numbers."

My skin prickled. Suddenly the forest disappeared, and I saw my father with dollar signs in his eyes. *Ka-ching!* I thought, "I can't tell him!" Then, "I've got to tell him!" It was his land, his investment, after all. His original fifty dollars had grown three thousand times over the past fifty years. That was a total return of 300,000 percent, or 6,000 percent per year at simple interest! Even subtracting production costs and inflation, that was an astronomical return. How could you argue against such numbers? Who would want to?

I realized that Rick was still talking. ". . . a good market for red oak that will probably last for a while. The trees are prime, but you would not have to cut all at once. You could use low-impact methods, horses for instance, but of course that would lower your profit. It's really a question of your own goals and values." He paused. "Of course, you could also just leave it alone."

"But what's the good of that?" I asked, recovering my breath. "We'd keep paying taxes; the timber would deteriorate. Plus, we'd never use it; the family's scattered all over the country. Couldn't we donate it for a nature center or something?"

"Not likely," Rick said. "It's really quite an ordinary parcel and not very big. No rare species, no unusual formations or scenery, hard to get to. Plus, as you see, most of your neighbors manage for timber. The town probably thinks of this as a working forest."

"But I hate logging!" I pleaded. "I like this old growth. I like the very idea of it!"

Rick smiled indulgently. "Hey, you don't have to do anything right now. These trees could grow for another decade before they start to lose timber value." He got up, brushing twigs from his pants. "Of course," he grinned, "in the meantime, the market could drop."

We walked back along the stone wall separating our land from the raped lot to the south. I wanted to fix in my mind the memory of cool, hemlock-shadowed depths where yellow sunlight played on the dry leaf litter. Neglected for half a century, our small piece of land had grown whole, harmonious, and radiant even while gathering value for distant markets. Thoreau had written, "Every tree sends its fibers forth in search of the wild. The cities import it at any price." I had always admired this insight but never expected that it would hit me in the face. My father would surely be tempted to log, and I doubted that the family would object. I was tempted myself. The profit from liquidating this timber would pay for a decent house in Cincinnati, finance an Ivy League education, or feed the family for twenty-five years. Yet even if done with care, logging felt too much like selling out. It stuck in my craw. As we drove away, I resolved to do what the government does when faced with a Hobson's choice: more research.

Stories in the Land

Back home in Cincinnati, I began reading up on the ecological history of New England. There were sound business reasons to manage our lot for timber. Logging had always been a key Yankee industry, especially in northern New Hampshire and Maine, where the ground was too rocky to farm. Today the Maine woods were owned by big, international timber companies that worked it in huge tracts. New Hampshire belonged mostly to small private owners who contracted with local loggers to cull their woods. During the eighteenth and nineteenth centuries, New England was heavily farmed, and hillsides like ours were all cleared for pasture. But as agriculture moved to the richer lands of Ohio, Illinois, and Minnesota, the Yankee forest started growing back. Today the old hill farms are all thick woods, and small-scale, intensive forestry is the norm. Local mills pay top dollar for good red oak, and because many people heat with wood, we could sell off the tops and much of the slash as well. A well-planned cut would yield much cash and little waste.

Moreover, the state tax laws had been written to encourage this sort of forestry. In New Hampshire standing timber is not factored into your tax assessment. You pay only when you cut. Until then, provided you don't build, farm, or otherwise "improve" your land, you can designate it as undeveloped and pay at the lowest rate. These policies encourage small landowners to let their woods grow big and old. They would seem to favor wilderness. However, the law also preserves your right to cut how, when, and where you please; it gives no consideration to other creatures or to the watershed as a whole. In short, it supports the dominion model and the ideal of private property. There is no ecological consideration at all.

Clean logging and selective cuts seemed like a good compromise at first. Rick had explained that a harvest every fifteen to twenty years would provide a sustainable yield of timber while improving the overall health and diversity of the forest. It would benefit wildlife by increasing the food supply, chiefly the buds and berries that are so sparse in old-growth woods. Using environmentally sensitive methods, such as horses, would reduce damage to soil, saplings, and perennial wildflowers. On the other hand, such a harvest would yield much less cash than a clear cut, perhaps as much as 80 percent less. Plus, it would ruin the sense of wildness, even if done with care. Just try communing with a stump.

So much for economics, I thought. What about ecological and emotional factors? What about wildness? I had already given up on rare or endangered species, and the property had no scenic vistas or picturesque rock formations. All it had, so far as I could tell, was the undeniable feeling of old growth, as palpable as anything I had felt in the Boundary Waters or the Sierra. The difference was that this old growth stood on ancestral land; it was a tangible link not only to aboriginal New England but to my ancestors. Surely it was worth protecting on these grounds alone.

But here again research complicated the picture. I discovered that the land in this part of New Hampshire had gone through drastic ecological changes over the past 350 years. According to historian William Cronon, the first European settlers found the landscape a rich ecological mosaic that had been created largely by natural circumstances such as topography and climate but was also materially affected by human culture. North of the Kennebec River, in Maine, the Indians lived by hunting and gathering. South of the river, they practiced small-scale agriculture, supplementing their crops by fishing, hunting, and foraging. They maintained small communities that migrated seasonally, following their sources of food. They cleared small fields by burning large standing trees and returned to these plots for eight or ten years. They also set fires in the woods twice a year to clear the underbrush for hunting and increase browse for game. To ensure their mobility, they amassed few possessions. Their nomadic lifestyle matched the ecological variety of the landscape. Although they went hungry at certain times of the year, they felt rich and prosperous overall, something the settlers could not understand.

Shortly after European contact, epidemics of smallpox, measles, and influenza began raging across New England. These were the first alien species introduced, and they brought sweeping ecological change. Even before large-scale European settlement began in the mid-1600s, 85 to 90 percent of the Indians had perished. The plagues shocked native cultures to their roots, devastating their wisdom and traditions while shattering established patterns of land use. Without burning and planting in the woods, sprout species such as birch, aspen, and maple began to grow up, and game increased accordingly. The first English settlers found a landscape thickly forested with old and young trees, abundant with game, and sparsely populated. They had no idea of the holocaust that had just occurred.

European culture brought large, permanent settlements and intensive agriculture to New England. The settlers stayed put and used the woods for timber, fuel, and game. They rapidly consumed the region's storied abundance. Deer, the principal source of wild meat, were soon decimated, forcing the passage of our first game laws in 1694. By 1800 the forest composition had changed completely. Few large oaks, white pine, hickory, or cedar remained; the woods consisted mainly of birch, aspen, and maple. Large areas had been cleared for planting or grazing. The deer, wild turkeys, beavers, bears, and wolves had all but disappeared; in their place the land supported thousands of sheep and cattle. These conditions persisted well into the nineteenth century, when coal power, railroads, and mechanized agriculture drew farming and industry away from New England.

By the time Nathan Whitney, my great-great-grandfather, bought the old homestead in Bennington, a new forest was springing up all over southern New Hampshire. Logging and sugaring had replaced grazing and cash crops on the old hill farms. People were leaving for better land in the Midwest or better jobs in the cities. The Great Depression killed what was left of New England's rural economy, leaving the land to absentee ownership and recreational use. By midcentury, when my father purchased the old Steele pasture, forests covered 80 percent of New England, and fifty years later the big animals had begun to return.

But this forest, I now realized, is quite different from what the Indians and settlers would have known. It presents a mosaic, but one that is due neither to seasonal migration nor European-style farming. The forest contains many large trees, even oak and pine, but also a thick understory that results from the absence of fire. Ecologically the land is wilder than ever before. Despite the presence of large human populations, there are sizable areas where few people go. Today New England presents a tissue of wilderness spread over a settled landscape, a mosaic of many small pieces of land that, like ours, have largely been let alone. Culturally speaking, this private land is a kind of new frontier. We are just becoming aware of it. What riches it may contain, we can scarcely imagine.

Nevertheless, it was also clear that our land was no fragment of aboriginal New England. There was nothing primeval about its wildness. I could have guessed as much from a crown of oak trunks, but somehow I had resisted that thought. I had wanted to believe that we owned a slice of original nature that was somehow beyond history, pristine and therefore sacred. I had wanted to think that our land could become a shrine.

Most distressing of all was the realization that whatever we did with our property would have little effect on the watershed as a whole. The property lines had been drawn for a long-vanished pastoral economy, yet the tax books had made them indelible. The laws had been written to favor an owner's discretion with no thought for the landscape as a whole. Ecological regional planning was all but impossible under such conditions. Wild things would just have to fend for themselves, depending for their survival on simple human neglect. I realized with a sinking heart that the difference between Cincinnati and New Hampshire was largely a matter of scale. A 0.4-acre city lot and a 40-acre woodlot could both be sold tomorrow, and the new owners could do whatever they liked. The biological clock could be reset at will, with no concern for long-term or dispersed ecological impacts. Both locations were enmeshed in the placeless geometry of urban space and the story-corroding currents of urban time. Impersonal ecology governed my relations to both.

All winter I brooded over these findings as logging began to seem more and more attractive. Our family was dispersed and settled in faraway parts of the country. It was not likely that we would ever visit, camp, or build on the New Hampshire land. We would always be absentee owners. If we cut, at least we would be using the land. The wood would most likely go into veneer or furniture, finding its way into people's homes, where it would bring comfort and delight. I had built furniture myself, and I loved the look of fine, straight-grained oak, the honeyed radiance of a hand-rubbed finish. More people would encounter our trees in that form than they ever would in the wild. And yet wildness was precisely what would be lost, obscured by the glossy surface of human design.

If we did not cut, the woods would keep growing wilder, but to what end? I suppose you could say that wildness is an infinite game, like marriage, evolution, or life itself. Does it have to have an end? Maybe not. But I needed something more solid to cling to. In the end I came back to our pioneer roots. Apart from sheer revulsion, that was the best argument I could muster.

It was late spring by the time I worked up the courage to share all this with my father. He listened quietly, watching me with close attention. His face was still radiant and alert, even though his days of canoeing and fishing were long past. As I came to the end, I felt his gaze settle on me like a big, warm hand.

"I guess you never did hear the full story," he said. "As a matter of fact, our family came from Massachusetts. Nathan Whitney worked in the mills, in Lynn, and then went up to Burlington, where he ran another mill. That's what brought him to Bennington."

"You mean, he wasn't a farmer?"

"No. He bought the paper mill. He was an industrialist."

"But what about the land? What about the homestead?"

"Oh, the big house had only five acres with it. He bought the Steele lot for sugaring. It was more of a hobby than a business, as I understand."

"Must have been pretty good syrup," I said, lamely.

"Wouldn't know," Dad replied. "A blight killed the maples the year I was born. Actually, I never even went up there when I was a kid. I just ran in the woods and fished in the river."

So there was no homestead, no farm, no pioneer past. My ancestors were industrialists! My father had never even set foot on the land. It took a moment for all this to sink in. But then a more disquieting thought occurred.

"Dad," I asked, "on your trips into Canada, when you went with Indian guides, did you see any evidence of logging?"

"Good heavens, yes!" he replied. "We went up on the railroad, and they were logging all up and down the line. When we got onto the river, we passed places where they were clear-cutting."

"So it was a working forest. Did you see many old trees?"

"I suppose we must have seen some," he said. "You have to remember it was sixty-five years ago."

"One more thing," I said. "When you went on those trips, did you and your friends ever think about getting into real wilderness, beyond any trace of people at all?"

"I don't think we had any idea of wilderness," he said. "We went for the fishing, and all the fish were way up north. You had to go by canoe and camp out to get to them. I didn't particularly enjoy roughing it. But I did enjoy being so far from Montclair, New Jersey." He paused. "You know, I only regret one thing. In all those trips, I never saw a bear in the wild. Still haven't."

There is a poem by Borges that begins, "There's a line of Verlaine's that I'm not going to remember again." It came to me then with a heart-piercing clarity. For I had seen many bears in the wild, in the California Sierra, the Boundary Waters of Minnesota, Alaska's Glacier Bay, and even the White Mountains of New Hampshire. Incredibly, the world was wilder now than it was in my father's day. I did not share his regret. Somehow his desire had passed to me for fulfillment. In history as in nature, it takes more than one generation for some things to mature.

Our conversation had destroyed family myths that I had cherished for years. It had exposed my naiveté about owning land. It was troubling, embarrassing, yet also clarifying. It did not decide the question of what we should do. Perhaps it merely confirmed what I had long known but had tried to dodge: what we do with the land always matters, even if we merely let it alone. We cannot escape playing a part in the story. All we can do is try to understand our choices and then choose as wisely and as responsibly as we can.

Meanwhile the land waits for us to become worthy of it. New England's greatest poet wrote, "The land was ours before we were the land's." It waits still, for becoming worthy is a life's work. We had ignored our New Hampshire land for fifty years, and it had grown whole, harmonious, and radiant. Unwittingly we had allowed a redemptive process to work, and the land had responded with its whole being. It had made us, unbeknownst to ourselves, vessels of grace.

DANTE'S RIVER

The Water Pilgrim

    To reach my house from the Gulf of Mexico, swim due north till you begin gasping for air. You'll need more than gills to cross the deoxygenated zone that spreads from the Mississippi Delta in an arc as wide as New Jersey. Persist until you smell the continent and follow its spoor of clay, rot, solvents, urine, detergents, and manure upstream, keeping always to the richest, most concentrated flow. Swing in great lazy arcs past oxbow lakes and bayous as the climate cools. Great tributaries will enter from your left—the Red, the Arkansas bearing feldspar and mica from the Rockies—but just ignore them and press on. After seven hundred miles, the Ohio enters from the right; you will know it by the scent of hardwood forests, coal dust, steel mills, and metamorphic rock. A quick fifty miles brings the Tennessee and the Cumberland, also on the right. Ignore these, too, but feel the current build. Press on toward the Great Falls at Louisville; you may have to leap them like a salmon. In fifty miles, the Kentucky enters from the south; if you're alert, you can catch the flavor of limestone and Appalachian hemlock, perhaps even feel the flickering ghosts of trout.

    In another fifty miles, the river bends south as the Great Miami enters from the left; it smells inviting, but it is not your path. Go up another ten miles; you'll know Cincinnati by the tang of sewage, dish soap, and hydrocarbons. Turn left at the cofferdam and enter Mill Creek. Where Indians camped for centuries on level sand, the stream now idles among rail yards and sewage plants after debouching from a concrete trough installed by the Army Corps of Engineers. Continue on past soccer fields, warehouses, and factories that produce everything from peach liqueur to skin creams and jet engines. Keep watch for a stand of old-growth forest nodding darkly on the left, then take the next left-hand fork and thread your way through the flood-control dam that holds back Winton Lake. This is a good place to come up for air; the lake may look like coffee, but I would not advise a drink. Proceed along the south shore to the second bay, where clearer water enters from Daly Creek. You are now 250 feet above the Ohio and more than 700 above the Gulf.

From here on you need a trout's body and a carp's gills. Slip among limestone slabs, past wooded yards, through culverts for about two miles, then dive into the sewer that runs beneath the subdivisions. This is the dark night of your journey, the longest buried stretch. When you emerge, the creek will be no more than finger deep. Turn fins, if you have them, into legs. Stand up, regain your balance, and ascend the first swale on your right until it disappears into the level woods. See the straw-colored house beyond the trees? That's mine. Come in and have a drink.

I have never made this journey but often dream of it. When Pam and I moved here, I insisted on living at the top of the watershed, as far as possible from the pollution and flooding that plague low-lying neigh-borhoods. Growing up in urban New Jersey had accustomed me to filthy surface water. Every time it rained, our driveway ran like a braided stream, turbid with mud and cinders from the parking lot above. My friends and I liked to play in the runoff, watching it pour into the street and swirl along the curb until it vanished into a grate, feeding an underground river that eventually spilled into New York Harbor. Hours later I could still hear it churning beneath the pavement as I walked to school, holding my nose against the dark, dank smell that wafted up through the manhole covers. And whenever we took the ferry to Man-hattan, the same odor rose all around, stale, fetid, sickeningly familiar. I tried not to look down at the gray water strewn with clots of soft, un-speakable debris, but fixed my gaze on the famous skyline that stood out as sharp and pure as crystal.

In those days, gray city water become a symbol of everything to be loathed and shunned. I yearned for clean, wild water, the streams and lakes of the Connecticut hills, where deer drank and fish swam, visible six feet down. I wanted water that smelled transparent, sharp as ice, as if it had been scoured by granite sand. I wanted to be able to bend down, like one of Gideon's soldiers, and drink from a cupped hand, then get up and move on without fear. Water become a prime field mark of wilder-ness for me, along with remoteness, old growth, and godlike summit views. I learned to climb for it, fighting the spirit of gravity. The best water was always the highest, pooled among boulders at the edges of snowfields in the Winds or broken to spray in thread cascades that poured out of glacial cirques high in the Sierra Nevada. I found it, too, in shallow basins weathered from slickrock on the Colorado Plateau, or in deep lakes in the Boundary Waters, where the whole country was as shaggy and rugged as the White Mountain forests of New Hampshire. These were the places where streams began, where heaven touched earth and bestowed the water of life. I became a water pilgrim, searching for sources and origins, taking inspiration from the trout that held themselves poised in the swiftest current, always facing upstream.

Call it romantic fancy if you like, but there was more to it than mere escapism. Coming of age in the 1960s had sensitized my generation to the blandishments and addictions of a market culture driven by greed and envy. The good things in life all came at a psychic price; the comfort and luxury of material blessings made people soft, covetous, and dependent. Water, which had once been nature's free and gracious gift, was now sold out of a pipe. How ironic that we should have to pay double, once for the blessing of consumer "goods" and again for the curse of pollution. Civilization had many ways of protecting business as usual. To young people restless for challenge and self-discovery, this realization brought only nausea and suffocation. Wilderness, with its clean water, beckoned us toward a life that seemed authentic, natural, and free.

The city's treatment of water seemed only a sign of its aspiration for total control. It dirtied the streams, then imprisoned them in sewers. It locked up the treated water in pipes. The only time we saw water moving, it was coming out of a spigot, disappearing down the drain, or rushing through some culvert or gutter. The sounds it made were harsh and mechanical, like the growl of engines. On wilderness trips, I loved to camp by moving water, by a lakeshore where waves clattered softly against rocks, or alongside streams with their white noise that seemed to be braided from many voices. The sound of mountain water was always incredibly soothing, its chaotic patterns as satisfying as the dance of flames in a campfire, the slow swirl of clouds, or the intricate, woven cadences of baroque music. So many nights, I would lie awake, trying to catch the message that always seemed just out of reach, like the voices of people laughing and talking behind closed doors. It seemed like an intimation of some other reality, but I knew it was only the sound of this world, the real voice of the lifeblood of nature.

New Englanders speak of "dead water" whenever a stream pools above rapids or behind a dam. That's what came to mind when I thought of city water: it was dead, poisoned by germs or toxic waste, sterilized by chlorine, suffocated by pipes and faucets. Dead water! It was all we drank. No wonder a strange, obscure numbness had crept into our bones. Such water might slake a momentary physical thirst but never the smoldering therophilia that drove me to the mountains. I wanted to drink from water that still held light, sky water, as Thoreau had called it. That's what I wanted in my tissues. On long backpacking trips, I could almost feel the toxins leaching out of my body as, drop by drop, the city water in my veins was replaced by mountain water. Weeks of hiking brought my mind to a poised alertness where it seemed coextensive, not only with the organism, but with the land itself. Truly embodied, I felt the water cycle passing through my cells. There were days when, striding along the trail, I would suddenly become aware of myself as a moving shape of water, coherent yet fluid, like a standing wave. On such days, every plant or animal seemed an exquisite, spun droplet, each stream a gesture of affirmation. I remembered Frost's poem "West-Running Brook," where the small waves beckon upstream toward their source. And I remembered the trout whose behavior matched the waves' dance.

I thought, too, of the long evolutionary journey whereby organisms like us—the plants, the trout, the marmots, even the other hikers—had carried salt and water upstream from the oceans until we reached these altitudes where the elements ruled. Imagine what skill, learned over eons, it had taken for life to survive in such extremes of temperature and exposure. The marks of violence were everywhere, in frost-shattered rock, wind-twisted limbs, or the raised grain of snow-scoured lodgepoles bleached to a glowing amber. These were places never settled by human beings. There were days above tree line when I felt the true heaviness of my organism, burdened with blood and plasma. I was no more than a sac of fluids hardly distinguishable, chemically, from seawater.

If life had indeed begun in the oceans, near thermal vents, as self-stoking autocatalytic loops of chemical reactions that, eons later, began clustering into protoplasmic blobs and thence learned, somehow, to grow the vital, semipermeable membrane—if all this did occur, then it was not hard to imagine the whole immense journey as life's urge to seek out and persist in the most severe environments, as if driven to contemplate its elemental origins. Where had sea salt come from but the mountains, washed down by the very streams I loved to climb? Sometimes, sweating over a pass or stepping off the trail to take a leak, I felt as if I were carrying my body's minerals back to their source. Once, hiking the John Muir Trail, my companion and I had even brought vials of sea salt collected from Pacific tide pools to sow in the headwaters of every stream we crossed. Perhaps it was no more than a whim, yet it moved us. Every time I felt like a compass needle swinging into accord with some unseen line of force. It was exhilarating to feel mind and body attuned to the thrust of evolution.

Spigot and Drain

But all that was far away and long ago, before I moved to the city and settled down to raise children and keep a house. Now I encounter water more often as a resource or a problem than as an emblem of spiritual aspiration. Any homeowner will tell you that the primary challenge in domestic engineering is keeping water out or getting it in.

Water falls from the sky onto my roof, whence it flows over the eaves and into gutters that carry it into the sewer. It falls on my lawn and woods, then runs over or percolates into the ground, where it flows downhill until it hits an impervious layer of rock, clay, or concrete. Where such layers surface, the water emerges as a spring. This can occur just as easily in your basement as in the swale out back; hence the importance of a well-graded yard. Sewers can back up; hence the virtue of living at the top of the watershed. Wood rots easily when wet, and toxic molds love damp wallboard; hence the necessity of a tight roof and well-caulked windows. In fact, rogue water can destroy almost everything we value in the house, from food, to furniture, to clothing, books, or papers. Thoreau may have dreamt of books written out in the open air, but most require a dry desk and closed windows. The dewdrop glistening on my true love's brow would smudge the sonnet written in her praise.

As a homeowner, then, I expend great effort caulking, puttying, painting, shingling, or otherwise trying to keep water out. But I also have to let it in for cooking, drinking, washing, and sanitation. In the house, it performs the same functions as it does in the body or in the ecosystem, providing a medium for life's chemistry and carrying off the waste. It enters from the spigot and exits through the drain.

In the wilderness, animals and people all use surface water, but in the city, people all use pipes. Their water comes from treatment plants that remove harmful microbes, chemicals, and sediment. Cincinnati operates two plants because it draws water from two sources, the Ohio River, which supplies over 80 percent, and the Great Miami Aquifer, which provides the rest. My neighborhood sits on the border between the two service areas and so may receive from either, depending on the day's demand. Cincinnati also sells water to outlying communities in three adjacent counties, a service area of more than 250 square miles.

When we moved here, I was worried about the water. I could not imagine drinking from the Ohio. Just think about what's upstream: the steel mills of Pittsburgh, Wheeling, and Steubenville; the Ashland Oil refinery; DuPont's huge chemical works along the Kanawha up at Charleston, West Virginia; not to mention thousands of square miles of farmland soaked with fertilizers and pesticides, or, indeed, the hundreds of small towns that dump raw sewage directly into the river or its tributaries. And let's not forget those Kentucky coal mines, sour as vinegar and salted with heavy metals. The Indians and the pioneers may have fished and drunk from the Ohio when it ran free, clear, and wild, but only a fool would do so today. Even after living here for fifteen years, I can't turn on the tap without a shudder. And yet our engineers assure us that Cincinnati's state-of-the-art treatment provides some of the best drinking water in the nation.

Although the Ohio presents quite a challenge, the great thing about water is that anything put in it can somehow be taken out. Moreover, most of the really awful pollutants such as heavy metals, aromatic solvents, or industrial organics like PCBs either bond with sediments or evaporate long before they reach Cincinnati. Therefore, according to my chemist friends, our waterworks treat mainly for pathogens, turbidity, and halogenated organics that form, ironically, from the chlorine used for disinfection. It is these smelly compounds that give tap water its stale, faintly metallic taste. Many are known carcinogens as well. Hence the continued popularity of home filtration and bottled water.

Soon after moving here, I looked into the treatment process because, after all, bottled water is expensive and unregulated. It is not subject to the government standards for municipal water. It may taste good, but who knows what's really in it? As for home filtration, it removes smelly organics but also the fluorine that protects your teeth. We want clean, health-inducing water that tastes good and costs next to nothing—quite a challenge for the engineers!

Down at the waterworks, I heard about the intricate path that Ohio or Great Miami water follows to reach my spigot. A huge station near the upstream edge of town pumps from the Ohio at a rate of 120 million gallons per day. All the way across town another plant pumps 16 million gallons per day from ten artesian wells that tap the aquifer, a bed of glacial sand and gravel two miles wide and 120–200 feet deep that runs from Dayton all the way to the Ohio. In round numbers, this means that greater Cincinnati consumes about 417 acre-feet of water per day. Thoreau, who drank straight from Walden Pond, took a jaundiced view of municipal water projects: "Now the villagers, who scarcely know where it lies, instead of going to the pond to bathe or drink, are thinking to bring its water, which should be as sacred as the Ganges at least, to the village in a pipe to wash their dishes with!—to earn their Walden by the turning of a cock or drawing of a plug!" If Walden supplied Cincinnati at today's rate, it would be sucked dry in less than a week.

Still, one must admire the Concord villagers; they knew the taste of purity. At Walden they could rely on nature to provide it, but here in the Rust Belt, we use engineering. Water from the Ohio is pumped first into settling basins where aeration and gravity cause larger particles to sink; coagulants, such as aluminum hydroxide, cause smaller particles to clump and settle out. After a sojourn in one of several reservoirs, the water flows through a sand and gravel bed that filters out even smaller particles, just like a natural aquifer; it then flows through a bed of activated charcoal granules that absorb organic compounds. Chlorine and fluorine are added to disinfect, the pH is adjusted toward the alkaline range to prevent copper and lead from leaching off your pipes, and the water flows into reservoirs and tanks to await distribution. Water from the Great Miami Aquifer follows a similar path, minus carbon filtration, which probably accounts for its higher levels of organics and radioactivity, twice as much in some cases. The water works performs three hundred tests per day keyed to 148 contaminants, of which 21 have been found in measurable amounts. Many of these are chlorinated organics that are not regulated by law but similar enough to known toxins such as DDT that they are cause for concern. Most are byproducts of the disinfection process.

All the water that comes from my tap has been treated in this way. It's all rated as high quality and fit to drink. I hate to use it for hosing down the driveway or washing the car or even watering the lawn, but what choice do I have? I suppose I could set up a rain barrel, but that would breed mosquitoes, and besides, it's too much of a hassle. Here in the East, water is plentiful and cheap. Even in times of drought, the Ohio runs brimming full. Unlike our compatriots out West, we flush without putting a brick in the tank; we shower without a bucket on the floor to catch the runoff. No one has heard of the Bureau of Reclamation, dry farming, xeriscapes, or water wars. Indeed, there's a general feeling that water is some sort of natural right, as limitless and inalienable as air. We don't worry much about where it comes from or where it goes.

I am told that the average American household consumes fifty gallons of water per person per day. That seemed like a lot until I became a parent. When you're a parent, you do a lot of cleaning. You wash dishes; you wash clothes; you wash faces; you wash bottoms; you wash the floor; you wash the dog; you wash your hands, sometimes six or eight times a day; you wash the sheets—and let me tell you, there is nothing like throw-up on the sheets at night to make you appreciate running water. Thoreau might have moderated his view of pipes if he had had kids to raise. Most of the time, you don't have time to think about where the water comes from or where it goes (carrying throw-up or whatever). You just want it running and the drain unclogged.

As for pollution, it's the last thing on your mind. You *need* detergents and cleansers. You *love* the fact that they cut grease and bleach out stains. I'll even admit to moments of whimsical affection for the sprawling Procter and Gamble works along Mill Creek, thinking, "They make the stuff that leaves my wash looking whiter and brighter." I love the fact that I can fill and rinse at the flick of a wrist or, even better, flush away so much household waste, whether human, animal, vegetable, or mineral, and the more odious the better. A swirl, a gurgle, and down it goes—out of sight, off-site, out of mind. The drain is a black hole, into which it is perilous to look. But who would want to? The sink empties, ready for more. The bowl refills, limpid as a spring. Cleanliness and serenity return, as if by magic, to the house.

It's only on days of exceptional honesty or resolve that I admit to a nagging worry about where all this stuff goes. My house pours all sorts of things into the watershed, from bodily waste to soapsuds to latex paint. It is, in fact, a "point source" of pollution. When the kids were young and making lots of messes, I repressed such thoughts. They gnawed at my environmental conscience; it was much easier to dream of wilderness with its pristine streams and lakes. But at some point I began to realize that the urge to roam and the urge to flush were closely linked. It may have been the day I was crossing Mill Creek after a heavy rain and saw a mallard skimming upstream over waves the color of peanut butter. So much beauty set against so much filth! Mill Creek represented everything I had ever wanted to escape. Yet what made it that way but waste from my very own house? The backpacker, imitating a bear in the woods, simply drops a scat and moves on. The urban householder, who must stay put, expels the waste and has it carried off. Flee or flush, it amounts to the same thing. My quest for purity in the wilderness simply mirrored the city's desire to slough its own waste downstream.

Of course, escape merely relocates the problem instead of dealing with it. Wendell Berry was right to observe that our environmental crisis stems from defects in character as well as in culture. For to deny one's history and refuse responsibility for one's acts is to live in bad faith. Tycoons and dictators may find it expedient to export evil or scapegoat the weak, but history shows that there is no future in such behavior. It can't work for long in a closed system like a watershed or a world community. Nature's method is to turn one creature's waste into another's resource. That's how it works in the wilderness, where evolution has developed elegant and complex pathways of transformation. But nature has all the time in the world.

On the day I saw the mallard, I had no idea how nature's method could ever work in the city, where there's so much pollution and the ecosystem has been so deeply abused. Everyone spoke of Mill Creek as an open sewer. It had always been that way; it was the price of prosperity. They wrote it off. But the mallard had not, even though humans had done the damage. I realized it was time to begin exploring downstream.

The Mill Creek

For a water pilgrim, the first step downstream is the hardest. It goes against every instinct, not to mention three thousand years of myth and poetry that associate holiness and inspiration with mountain springs. When Thoreau sang of Walden's purity, he was not thinking chemically but metaphysically. His scorn for the ignorant farmers who had polluted Concord's ponds was fueled by the wrath of a true believer in the spiritual character of place. For Thoreau every human act left its signature. You could read the character of people and civilizations on the face of their land.

Considering Mill Creek, I expected the downward path to yield only horror and depression. If pollution signified character, this would be a descent into hell. Dante had given water a big role in his underworld: he and Virgil encounter rivers of boiling blood, roaring cataracts, and putrid swamps. The deeper they go, the worse it gets; the rivers become more violent, smelly, and lethal by degrees until, at the bottom of the universe, they coalesce into a frozen lake where the souls of traitors are trapped like straws in glass. Dante envisions a moral absolute zero, where love's motion ceases under the immense weight of all the sin washed down from above. He and Virgil escape by climbing a small stream that has cut a tunnel through the rock on the other side. Its source, we learn, is the earthly paradise at the top of the mountain of Purgatory. There, repentant sinners who have completed the mountain's therapeutic program undergo a second baptism that removes original sin, leaving them lighthearted and free to mount up to the stars.

Dante's guide through Hell was a Roman poet. Mine, it turned out, was a biologist named Stan Hedeen who had spent two decades studying the Mill Creek with students from Xavier University. I met him, not in a dark wood, but in a mall parking lot where members of the Sierra Club had gathered for a tour sponsored by the Mill Creek Restoration Project. Stan was a wiry, intense man with sharp features and a gray goatee. He looked a bit like Trotsky, except for a mobile grin that flashed at odd moments. He wore rumpled khaki pants and a T-shirt that read "Mill Creek Yacht Club." I could tell he was used to dealing with incredulity, even in a friendly crowd like this. He had the wry wit and granite patience of a maverick.

Robin Corathers, director of the Mill Creek Restoration Project, briefed us on the itinerary and herded us onto a bus, explaining that her group's goal was to turn Mill Creek into a greenway suitable for wildlife and recreation. Today's tour would showcase the challenges and opportunities they faced. Robin was a small, soft-eyed women with brown hair and a teacher's earnest manner. I asked her how she had gotten involved with Mill Creek, and she said she had come to Cincinnati seventeen years ago, thinking to stay for five at most. She had always wanted to live by the Pacific and even tried looking in the early 1990s, but it didn't feel right. She stayed here and researched the creek, developing a blueprint for its restoration. Her motive, it turned out, was simple: "This has become home."

As we cruised past "Mount Rumpke," a huge landfill that is the highest point in Hamilton County, Stan gave a brief history of Mill Creek since the Pleistocene, when glaciers changed the drainages and the Ohio captured the lower Licking River, leaving only this small south-flowing creek to occupy its broad valley. When Indians lived here, Mill Creek was pure, dark, and verdant (its Shawnee name, Maketewah, means "he is black"). They fished its pools and hunted its banks, as did the early white settlers until burgeoning industry found it more useful as a sewer. Tanneries, slaughterhouses, and factories all dumped runoff into the creek throughout the nineteenth century. Though much cleaner now, it is still heavily polluted by household sewage and leachate from buried industrial waste. Nevertheless, Stan assured us with a grin, there were still some reasons not to abandon hope.

Our first stop was a covered bridge high up on one of the western tributaries. It looked like a small barn that someone had plunked down over the creek, which was only about thirty feet wide. Stan said it was the oldest bridge in Hamilton County. Beneath it the creek chuckled along over limestone slabs that were studded with brachiopods as big as Ritz crackers; Stan said they were *Rafinesquina*, 450 million years old. Algae grew on the edges of the rocks, waving in the current like green hair, but the water looked surprisingly fresh and clean. Huge trees crowded the shore, chiefly cottonwoods and sycamores, suggesting the thick woods that had once covered the entire county and made the creek safe for shade-loving fish and invertebrates.

Stan began turning over rocks, pointing out caddis-fly larvae and water pennies, which are good indicators of cleanliness because they have sensitive gills. "You wouldn't want to do this after a rain," he said. "It's best to wear rubber gloves, especially lower down. However, the great thing about streams like this is that they are self-cleaning. If we would just stop dumping all that bad stuff in, these critters would wash down and recolonize. Our studies have shown that it happens surprisingly fast, a matter of two to three years."

We scrambled among the slabs, exclaiming whenever someone found a caddis case, which looked like a matchstick dipped in shredded coconut, or the black thumbnail disk of a water penny stuck to the underside of a rock. It felt like hunting for treasure. Under the dense boughs yellow with autumn, where the bridge cast its dark shadow over sparkling riffles, I could imagine what the whole stream must have looked like two centuries ago. I caught a glimpse of the vision that had inspired Robin and her activist colleagues. A stray foam cup or foil snack packet snagged on a rock looked shockingly out of place.

Back in the bus, we headed downstream toward Winton Lake, which had been built by the Corps of Engineers to protect homes and businesses in the lower valley. Robin explained that the creek was dangerous during rains, not just because of all the bacteria and viruses it carried, but because of flash floods, which are as common here as they are in the Utah desert. I thought of rain falling on roofs, sidewalks, or parking lots like the one we had started from; the water would run right into the sewers and overflow into the creek just as quickly as if it had fallen on slickrock. Someone asked how much of the watershed was impervious surface, and Stan replied that in the lower stretches it was about 35 percent. The broad, shallow valley was easy to build on but vulnerable to floods, so the corps had installed containment dams and channelized the bed, with mixed results, as we would soon discover.

We crossed Winton Road, a north-south artery, and caught a glimpse of the lake. It looked like mud flats ringed with flood debris, driftwood, plastic jugs, old tires, that sort of thing. "Water's low," someone remarked. Stan explained that the corps was dredging the lake, which had silted up much faster than expected. We turned down an unmarked dirt road, branches scraping the bus like fingernails, and stopped in a brushy field where a path led through thickets of aster and poison ivy to the lake. We stepped from the woods into a desert scene: acres of dried mud cracked into thick, irregular scales with knee-high weeds and saplings poking up everywhere. "All this year's growth," Stan said, pushing through. "The lake was drained about a year ago."

Out on the flats, it was windy and exposed. On one side crouched the tangled woods; on the other, a rampart of crushed rock and compacted earth rose fifty feet or more. Stan pointed out the gauging station, a concrete tower that was plugged into the dam by a catwalk; it looked like a big staple holding everything together. A bathtub ring showed the lake's high-water mark. It was a pretty shallow lake. But Stan explained that you always build the dam across the deepest part of the valley; in fact, we were standing on fifty to sixty feet of mud! Tracks of heron, deer, and raccoon were pressed into the mud like cuneiform. Poking around, Stan found a mussel shell as big as a mitten. He kicked a scat. "Coyote. This would be a good place to see one. Around 5:00 a.m.!"

We climbed back into the bus and drove down the steep slopes below the dam into the valley, where we stopped at Putt-Putt Golf and Games on Reading Road for our first look at the main stem of the creek. Crumbling asphalt gave way to ragged meadow as we headed for the tree line that marked the bank. A four-foot black snake slithered away, sleek as a garden hose; no doubt he was amply nourished by field mice and birds' eggs.

We found the creek running in a deep trough cut through soil banks; it was a bit cloudy here, but pebbles were still visible on the bottom. Stan said we were near the site of the first white settlement above Cincinnati; the first mill had been built here, on Gorman Farm, which was now being run by the Cincinnati Nature Center. (There was one other working farm in town.) Stan pointed out fish in the stream, alien carp, native white suckers, perhaps a bass. He drew our attention to the banks, a tangle of roots and soil topped by shrubs, weeds, and small trees. This point marked the last "natural" stretch of the creek that we would see until we got almost to the river. Most of the lower reaches had been channelized. I was amazed at how fresh and natural the creek looked even here, deep in the industrial zone. What wild companions did the black snake have?

We pulled out box lunches and ate at picnic tables in a small city park nearby. Birds flitted past, house finches, house sparrows, and starlings checking us out. A woman got up, and the birds zoomed in, pecking for sandwich crumbs. Her blue sweatshirt read, "A Good Planet Is Hard to Find." Many people, I noticed, were drinking bottled water. I sat with a colleague of Stan's and his wife, who taught at-risk kids in the public schools. They spent part of each summer cooking for Sierra Club service trips. They had raised their family in Cincinnati, but as soon as they retired, they were moving to Colorado.

Stan herded us back to bus. "Miles to go!" he grinned. "It gets pretty nasty from here on. Lots of cool stuff to see, though." What did he relish more, our discomfort or his local knowledge? Robin explained that we were going to the "GE/Pristine Superfund Site," where PCBs had been dumped when General Electric was making insulation and rocket parts during the Cold War. The soil was contaminated by leaking drums and storage tanks. On rainy days, you could see leachate oozing from the banks. It was a big problem.

We drove along the edge of the huge GE plant, where they now made aircraft engines. It seemed to fill the valley, over a thousand acres of factories, warehouses, laboratories, and office buildings interspersed with tank farms, rail yards, and parking lots. We turned off on a narrow, unmarked road that led toward a paving plant where piles of old concrete and asphalt stood waiting to be turned into more impervious surface. At least, someone remarked, they were recycling! The road crossed a rusty bridge and ended in a dirt lot paved with cinders, where someone had set out orange trash barrels, as if it were a park. Maybe the truckers had lunch here after dumping their loads at the plant. Nearby hundreds of rusty barrels were stacked in a fenced yard with a gatehouse. Overhead high-tension lines buzzed against the blue. A huge steel pipe rose from the cinders, topped by a manhole cover. Stan said it was an overflow port for a combined sewer line. In a big storm, it would spout raw sewage like a gusher.

We poked around the edges of the lot—gingerly, as if probing a sore. Robin pointed out several leachate zones, where her group had planted saplings of willow and other shrubs with an appetite for heavy metals and other industrial pollutants, a process known as "phytoremediation." She talked about laws, liabilities, all the reasons why no one wants to buy contaminated property. The city of Reading used to get its water from the aquifer underlying Mill Creek, but when contamination reached their wells five years ago, they had to start buying water from Cincinnati. All this industry had been built on rich bottom land, prime agricultural soil, but you wouldn't want to grow crops here now. It would take years of phytoremediation to bring it back, once the dumping stopped. Robin's group was certainly taking the long view, much more than a single lifetime.

Meanwhile, Stan had been off talking with the guard at the gatehouse. He came back, grinning at our glum faces. "Cheer up," he said. "It's actually quite secluded here. The guard says he's seen a lot of wildlife along the creek. Critters are more resourceful than we think."

We climbed into the bus, grateful to escape this blighted landscape for the wide-open spaces of I-75, which, Stan observed, had been built in the bed of an old canal. Though the highway followed the valley, we caught only fleeting glimpses of the creek between factory walls or bridge abutments. We passed Jim Beam with its odor of rotting fruit, and the bus stopped at a bridge below the Elda Landfill, Cincinnati's principal dump. I could hear the roar of sanitation trucks and bulldozers as pepper black flocks of starlings soared over acres of garbage. Stan said there was some leaching from the dump, but it was impossible to say how much or how long it would continue—decades for certain, more likely centuries. But that's not why he had brought us here.

"Notice the channelization," he said, pointing downstream from the bridge. "When the corps does a project like this, they broaden the streambed two or three times, tear out all the trees, and line the banks with riprap, using broken rock or old pavement bonded with concrete. The result is 'physical pollution' in the form of sunlight and heat, which the original native species can't tolerate because they're used to cool shade. So, even if we stop dumping, we still have a habitat problem. However," he added, "if you look downstream, you'll notice that Mother Nature has been quietly putting in gravel bars and meanders to rebuild the bed. You can already see a few willows and cottonwoods taking root."

Below the bridge, steel girders had been driven into the bed, interlocking to form a low dam behind which green water pooled, clear to five feet. Below the dam, a school of foot-long bass darted across the plunge pool, ignoring an old tire hung up on one of the girders. Behind us cars zoomed across the bridge, oblivious. A freight train rumbled past, horn blaring and bells clanging, hauling a string of tank cars and boxcars toward P&G. Upstream the bank was strewn with slabs of old pavement, among which young trees had grown up; some were almost a foot in diameter. White butterflies danced over the green water. Swallows darted and wheeled beneath the bridge.

Downstream afternoon sunlight sparkled on the meanders between the gravel bars. For a moment, Mill Creek looked as beautiful as any western river. If I raised my eyes, I saw lines of tank cars worming their way toward a black clot of factories. If I dropped them to the creek, I saw willows, gravel bars, a mallard paddling through a splash of sunfire. I saw wildness and beauty returning. At that moment, Mill Creek appeared as a corridor of serenity. This, I realized, was what Stan and Robin were fighting for.

But the vision lasted only a moment. Our next stop was inside the P&G complex, where the creek flowed in a deep concrete trough through a fantastic maze of piping, tanks, steel strutwork, and factory buildings. There was no one around on a Saturday afternoon, and the place looked as if it had been swept clean. Stan pointed out the vertical concrete walls and flat, paved creek bed strewn with pebbles, tree limbs, and odd bits of litter—a plastic milk jug, a running shoe. The creek itself was a thin trickle near the center. Green beards of algae trailed downstream from islands of sand and gravel topped with chunks of driftwood. Even here the creek was rebuilding its bed. Stan surveyed the algae with approval. "Plenty of nutrients," he said. "Given a summer or two, these islands would be stabilized by weeds and saplings. They build up fast. P&G has to call in bulldozers twice a year to clear out the channel. You can imagine what a big flood would do to their investment!"

We continued down the west side of the creek through old industrial neighborhoods, passing through Salway Park, where kids played soccer right up to the edge of the channel. Robin's group had planted eight hundred trees and two butterfly gardens here. On the far side, cars and semis roared down the interstate. Robin said the creek was a migration corridor; she had seen mallards and a great blue heron here; Stan had logged seven kinds of ducks, including black ducks and gadwalls. We were now four and a half miles from the Ohio, and the neighborhoods seemed to grow older and dingier with every bend. We crossed the West Fork tributary, which was dumping a lot of sediment, and passed under the I-74 viaduct. Across the creek, huge rail yards spread into view. A black plume of oil washed downstream from a pipe sticking out of the bank.

At the Cincinnati Sanitation Department garage, we turned down a private road that had once been a railroad bed and stopped just before the Western Hills viaduct. Stan said we had reached the Ohio River Pool, where Mill Creek drops its sediment. The sloping concrete walls of the channel looked serene and impenetrable, though we knew that in time they would be covered in silt. They ended, surprisingly, just beyond the viaduct, where trees and shrubs crowded the bank once more. Stan laughed. "The corps ran out of money right about here. It's original shoreline all the way to the Ohio, most of it on the grounds of the sewage plant." Someone exclaimed and pointed as a kingfisher broke from the bank and flew upstream.

We walked down the old rail bed, which was lined with honeysuckle, locust, and young sycamores. It ran right above the creek, and the air had a moist, stale odor that was disturbingly familiar. I finally recognized it as the smell of New York Harbor! Stan led us down a ramp to a huge, open concrete tank. The smell billowed out of it, nauseous and overpowering. We edged closer and peered over the rail. On one side, a dark tunnel opened into the bank like a mine shaft, out of which gray water trickled over slimy black rocks before disappearing into a grate. This was another combined sewer overflow, much bigger than the one we had seen near GE. Stan explained that the neighborhood sewers fed into a trunk line that ran beneath the creek all the way to the sewage plant. But the line could handle only so much storm water; without these overflows, it would simply explode. Now, he explained, when the water rises toward the top of the tank, it pushes open the heavy steel doors hanging from the rim and pours directly into the creek, saving the trunk line and the sewage plant at the expense of the Ohio River. You wouldn't want to be standing here during a storm, not without goggles and a surgical mask. There are 158 combined overflow ports in the Mill Creek watershed. They open whenever it rains more than a tenth of an inch per hour.

A tenth of an inch—that meant every time it rained! I gripped the rail, momentarily faint, though it may have just been the smell. I tried to imagine gray water surging into the chamber and swirling higher and higher until it burst through the gates in a disgusting flood. Mill Creek would then truly be an open sewer. It happened all the time.

Robin and Stan explained how the problem of combined sewers had arisen long ago, when the city was smaller and homes were converting to flush toilets from backyard privies. At the time, it seemed sensible to dilute household waste with storm water. No one was thinking seven generations ahead, and pollution was not yet a household word. Now we would have to pay dearly for any solution. Laying parallel lines and reconnecting the gutters would disrupt households, business, and traffic for at least a decade, besides costing untold millions. It would be cheaper to build small treatment plants on tributaries higher up the watershed, but land was expensive, and who would want one in their backyard? At present the planners favored a fantastic scheme to blast an immense cavern into the bedrock one hundred feet or more below the creek bed. The runoff would all go there and be pumped to the treatment plant. I tried to imagine the whole dark labyrinth of the sewer system gathering water from every quarter, all the filth, disease, and waste of human life, and pouring it into the ultimate black hole. Suppose the pumps broke or the intakes clogged? Who would go down to fix them? This was displacement and escape carried to Dantean extremes.

Dazed, I stepped back from the rail and turned toward the creek. Three mallards were paddling upstream, their green heads and gray brown plumage accented handsomely against the buff concrete. Farther down, framed by the immense parabolic truss that supported the viaduct, a small gray and black bird with a long slender bill stood hunched on a rock. It was just beyond the channelized stretch, and I asked Stan what it was.

He smiled. "That's a black-crowned night heron. Two years ago some workers at the sewage plant noticed one and called the Audubon Society. They had never seen anything like it. We discovered a nesting colony on the plant grounds, which are fenced in and free of coyotes besides being generally quiet and secluded. These birds are wild and secretive; there's only one other known colony in Ohio, out on an island in Lake Erie. Here they fly up along the creek at night, feeding on fish, sometimes all the way to the covered bridge. The fact that they're here means the Mill Creek is starting to clean itself, while we still try to figure things out." He sighed and glanced at his watch. "It'll be dark soon. Let's go. We have seen everything."

The Baby and the Heron

In the days that followed, my mind kept coming back to that image of the heron perched above soiled water on the edge of wildness framed by a concrete arch. How could a place so foul and lethal to us prove tolerable, even inviting to such a beautiful wild creature? No organism can live in an excess of its own waste products, but Mill Creek had been soiled by our waste, not the heron's. The viruses and bacteria so deadly to us were clearly innocuous to it and to the bass and suckers on which it fed. I recalled that many of our worst diseases arose first in domestic livestock that had lived for centuries in close contact with humans. Swine Flu, chicken pox, smallpox, tuberculosis, and measles are some of the better-known examples. Ecological dependency and physical intimacy foster coevolution, creating loopholes in the interspecies barrier that opportunistic pathogens can exploit. Human viruses and bacteria are often benign to other organisms because to infect, they must be intimate with their hosts. They have to get past the immune system, and that means they have to coevolve. Therefore, it is the heron's very wildness that protects it from Mill Creek's human waste.

In biological terms, pollution depends on the organism. One creature's poison is another's meat. To Earth's original organisms—thermococcal bacteria that swarmed in hot acids and fed on hydrogen sulfide—oxygen gas was deadly. When photosynthesis evolved and began pumping it into the atmosphere, the thermococci retreated to hot springs and deep ocean vents. Eventually forms emerged that could use the oxygen for metabolism, and the deep symbiosis between plants and animals was born. Because the earth is a closed system, no waste can ever be fully expelled. Whenever an excess appears in the environment, nature's method is to develop an organism that can use it. Thus, energy, nutrients, and information are kept constantly moving through the millions of loops that make up the ecosystem. Whatever is cast off gets received, accepted, and transformed. The result is abundant life. And water, even the water of Mill Creek, is the primary vessel for this alchemy of grace. To the heron, the creek is not foul but productive and inviting. The sparkle of sunlight on its surface is true.

When we pollute, we think only of water's ability to dissolve, suspend, or carry away. We don't think of its power to receive or to foster transformation. The word "pollution" first arose in a religious context; its Latin root meant "impure, unfit for ritual or sacrifice, corrupt." In English usage, the physical and moral senses of the word did not begin to separate until the time of Shakespeare, and even today they remain closely linked. Hence the righteous zeal of so many grass-roots environmental groups and the fervor of activists like Robin Corathers and Stan Hedeen. If there is sin in pollution, I am sure that it arises not only from the violence it does to our home places but also from our desire to avoid responsibility. It is so much easier simply to flush and forget. But a watershed is no bottomless pit. Everything we do leaves a mark or a trace, and eventually it returns. In Dante's poem, the souls of the damned do not disappear; they persist, and they suffer the consequences of the acts brought on by their self-serving habits of mind. Just so today, in the closed system of the watershed or the planet, we will reap only suffering if we keep on trying to escape our own waste. It's not good enough anymore to live at the top of the watershed or to dump manufacturing residues into the common stream, hoping that they will surface far from the bottom line. For pollution is nothing more than the history we would like to deny, indelibly written in the flesh of the world. It is what remains when we dissolve nature in money.

Despair comes easily after long days of exposure to rail yards, roaring interstates, the rainbow smears of leachate, and the stench of combined sewer overflows. The problem feels overwhelming, the whole system too vast and sick ever to be repaired. It's hopeless. But then I remember the heron, the wildness that always returns with even the smallest opportunity, the aerial plankton seeding rooftop pools, the Mill Creek patiently rebuilding its bed in the midst of a concrete channel. I think of Stan and Robin, people of contrary but capable imagination who, by paying attention, have caught the spoor of a redemptive dream. Somehow, somewhere they made the choice to embrace rather than shun Mill Creek. Perhaps, like Dante, they knew that the downward path, though fraught with horror, would lead to the light if only they followed it all the way through. So they became water pilgrims of another kind, and at the lowest point, they met the heron.

Three years after Pam and I moved to the city, our second daughter was born. She came right on time. Pam's water broke as she was getting up from the kitchen table after a late evening cup of tea. She staggered against the counter, seized by a powerful contraction as a dark stain spread down her leg. It was the water of life bursting out as primeval wildness took her once more, but this time we were ready. I bundled her into the car and drove through dark streets down a steep ravine into the valley. We crossed Mill Creek, invisible in its dark trough. No doubt bass were idling along the gravel bars while herons, gifted with keener sight, cruised upstream in search of them. Our hospital was at the top of the hill. Four hours later, Elizabeth leapt into the world all moist and pink and bawling for life. Water was flowing all around us, in the blood and wetness of birth, Pam's soaked brow, my tears, even the damp, warm washcloth that the nurse was dabbing ever so gently on the faces of mother and child. Later, when we were left alone, Pam sucked ice chips and sipped spring water before teaching Elizabeth how to nurse. I could feel the water cycle, old as life, flowing through us.

Several weeks later, we presented Elizabeth for baptism. Standing before the congregation, Pam held her up to the marble font while the minister dipped in his hand and dribbled some water onto her tiny brow, intoning the familiar words. This ceremony was supposed to be about washing away original sin, a sort of manufacturer's defect in our nature, but Elizabeth didn't seem to have any defects. She seemed to have a gift for enjoying herself, a confidence and delight that I was struggling every day to attain. If anyone needed cleansing, it was not Elizabeth but me.

Perhaps, I thought, it would make more sense to think of baptism as a reminder of how much original grace we inherit from the water that runs through our cells. From the oceans to the clouds to the intimate meshwork of tissues and capillaries, it permeates and sustains the world of life. So Jesus spoke literally of living water, but the ancients had long recognized its spiritual value. No matter how divided or scattered, it always gathers together, centering to a stillness that mirrors the sky. In this way, it connects heaven and earth. Because it is pure at heart, it can forgive any indignity; it can bear all uncleanness without being changed. Humbly it takes the shape of whatever it fills, yet its tendency is always to flow. In this way, by not resisting, it overcomes all things.

Elizabeth gazed out with d word "Gehenna," which was actually the name of a
smiling up from the congrega usalem where refuse was dumped and burned. Far
stained glass, the sparkling b hen, people imagined hell as a place of chaos and
drawn from a city pipe, even burning, where things were taken to be destroyed
bending over her and looking of hopelessness and anonymity from which there
silhouette of a heron.   hether or not you believe in an afterlife, it is still
                             your body coming to such an end, along with all
                             red. Surely the book of life was not written simply
                             lump says otherwise. It's a sneer flung in the face of
                             ok at it, and yet I can't turn away.
                             d carries me past the dump toward the cemetery,
                             es soon open on the right. The whole place
                             ven hundred acres, extending from Mill Creek all
                             he hill, but only the lower two-thirds have been
                             still wild woods, one of the largest such tracts in
                             y to the creek, a stone wall marks the original
                             4, after cholera epidemics had clogged the many
                             ds near the city center. Spring Grove was designed
                             the living as well as honor the dead. Its parklike
                             ndreds of people on sunny days. I often like to turn
                             take one of the cemetery roads downhill, winding
                             es and ornate nineteenth-century monuments
                             od plain with its artificial ponds, where swans and
                             year round and turtles bask in the sun. Especially
                             , when the flowering trees are out—yellow for-
                             cherry, purple redbud, flowering crab—you'll find
                             lling, jogging, bicycling, or just relaxing: lovers
                             ing strollers, art students sketching, kids tossing
                             lucks, mourners laying flowers, even the occasional
                             runing or raking furtively, as if reluctant to be
                             the natural world is flapping, buzzing, warbling,
                             ry side. Spring Grove has over nine hundred
                             shrubs from all over the world. It's a veritable
                             ies. And between the snowdrops in February and

the witch hazel in November, you can find flowers at almost any time of year. If exuberance is beauty, nature is nowhere more beautiful than here.

Nevertheless, despite all the movement and activity, Spring Grove's prevailing mood is peace. No doubt this emanates, in part, from the monuments themselves. Like statues they invite contemplation and project repose. Some, made of sandstone or marble, are weathering gently under the combined effects of frost wedging and acid rain. Their carved decorations and epitaphs have blurred like faces seen through a misted pane. The granite monuments, in contrast, look as crisp and sharp as if they were cut yesterday. They stand out handsomely against the intricate textures of grass, bark, and shrubbery. Each one lifts up a name above the green tide, like a raised fist waving a banner as the ship goes down. We don't see or think about the buried body sinking into decay. We see the name, but what does it tell us? Only that someone cared enough to honor the dead. But, just as the dead tell no tales—at least not in this life—so their monuments provide no stories. The only meaning here is carried by the mourners themselves. It's their memories that invest the monuments with meaning. To the rest of us, the stones are mute, like quotation marks around a blank space on the page. Assertive and public in appearance, the stones remain private and secretive when questioned. In the graveyard, history is not recorded but hidden.

Why, then, does the place have such appeal? Why does it feel so peaceful? Well, for one thing, it helps us believe that the dead are at rest, quiet and secure. The dead have been cataloged, labeled, and filed away, like last year's tax returns. They are done with; their stories are finished. The rest of us can now get on with the business of living. And that, of course, means continuing our own life stories. We don't like stories that never come to an end, but at the same time, we all want a second chance. We may want the other guy's story to conclude, preferably in a satisfying way, but we want our own to go on as long as possible. So if the monuments make us think of death, they also make us dream of what lies beyond.

For thousands of years, people in many cultures have imagined the afterlife in terms of perfected nature, where it's always spring and nothing dies or decays, where the earth produces food in abundance and the animals all get along—no predators, no parasites, no disease, no crime, no war, no human evil. The word "paradise" has come down virtually unchanged in meaning or pronunciation from ancient Persia, where it meant a walled garden cultivated for beauty and pleasure, a place where the noble householder could escape the squalor of the streets or the harshness of the desert. By making paradise into God's pleasure ground, the Hebrews merely eternalized the garden's beauty and harmony, imagining a nature perfectly contoured to human needs. A nature, that is, completely purged of wildness.

This vision is attractive, I admit. Perhaps that is why it has been the dominant image for heaven in Western mythology and art. But the more I think about it, the more it gives me the creeps. Life there might be fun for a while, like a resort vacation, but boredom would inevitably set in. What would there be to learn? Without the challenge of wildness, how would you grow? Therophilia would soon drive you forth, like Adam and Eve (who, I imagine, might have welcomed a few thorns and thistles after all that tropical fruit). As Emerson said, it's not comfort and pleasure we crave but vivid life.

That's why I like Spring Grove in small doses—say, about once a month in the spring or fall. It's a place of respite and repose, but it's only for passing through. There's no future there. I savor its imagery of sweetness and harmony, but I realize that its air of timelessness is only a false eternity. It's a simulacrum of perfected nature created by constant husbandry, as much an artifact of culture as the factories and streets outside. I always feel a twinge of relief when I drive out the gate onto Gray Road, heading uphill past the dump and into the forest. I see how the landfill and the cemetery represent two sides of a coin that we, like our Greek forebears, use to seal the eyes of the dead. Perhaps we need to think of the dead at rest in order to feel at peace ourselves. I just know that I want to die with eyes wide open. I don't want to miss a thing.

Gray Road climbs through the forest, switching back beneath overhanging boughs until it tops out on the glacial plain of College Hill, my neighborhood, and the sky spreads into view once more. I've made this trip hundreds of times, and it always gives me a thrill to see big, silver-bellied cumuli sailing over the houses, or cirrus unfurled like Arabic script against the blue. The sky! I tend to forget about it in the city, where I'm always looking down at a desk or out toward oncoming traffic, clamped to the level surface of the earth. How seldom I ever look up, and yet there is the sky extending over me, pouring down light and fresh air and sweet distilled water, enough to replenish the earth and all its creatures free of charge forever.

Especially on clear winter nights when the moon is down, the trip up Gray Road brings me face to face with the sky. Near the top, where trees still screen out the city lights, I can see stars burning in the dark slot above the road. If it is very cold and dry, I can sometimes make out the pale foam of the Milky Way strewn in a faint arc above the snug brick houses. Then it's time for a walk in the park with the dog, no matter how late it is. We might catch a glimpse of a shooting star or a spacecraft drifting across the zenith. I always marvel that more people aren't out to catch the show. They're inside the glowing cubicles of their houses, entranced by the flickering phosphor of TV or computer screens or swathed in dim reading light. From outside, their rooms look warm and cozy, yet how pale their radiance is compared to daylight. I know the momentary blindness that comes when you step into the dark yard from a lighted room. It takes a while for your eyes to open wide enough for starlight. Moreover, the scattering of city light by dust and haze creates a glow that can obscure all but the brightest stars. Driving toward Cincinnati out of the countryside, I can see this dome of "light pollution" from thirty miles away. Photographs taken from space at night show the cities of the industrial world splattered like foxfire along the rims of continents. In 2001 a group of astronomers matched these photographs with demographic data and discovered, shockingly, that one out of five people worldwide live in places where they can no longer see the Milky Way.

How far we have come since ancient times, when people saw the full sky every night, unobscured by their own pale fire or sooty exhalations. In those days, philosophers paid careful attention to the heavens, which were deemed to be the abode of gods. They noted the alignments and progressions of all heavenly bodies, reading in them the character and destiny of nations. In our age of exact science, we tend to dismiss such views as mythic or superstitious, but at least those people were keeping watch. They were not sitting indoors hypnotized by TV; they were outside looking up, entranced by primeval wildness shining across the light-years. We may be the richest nation on earth, the most advanced in technology, with the mightiest army, the most atomic bombs, and the most recognized brand names, but as a people we seem to be afraid of the dark. It may be a side effect of luxury and the indoor life that has made us soft, dependent, and infatuated with our own imagery. Or maybe it's because we are nervous about what we might find if we start poking around in the dark. To walk out at night means to enter the planet's shadow, losing your own shadow in the process, so that your inner demons are projected onto nature. It takes a great effort to step across the threshold. You have to shade your eyes against the glare of culture long enough for them to shift over into night vision.

Gazing into the shadow evokes a contrarian path, the path of invisibility that runs down among the oppressed and despised and forsaken. But this is also the path of holiness, the path of ascetics and mystics, of hermits and wanderers, of voyagers, artists, and madmen, of Eve reaching for the apple or Jesus healing on the Sabbath. It is the renegade path of John Muir rejecting industry for the wild or Gary Snyder taking the poet's way out into horrors and angels. The contrarian path is also the path of practice—necessarily, for it means resisting the flow of custom and the spirit of gravity. It requires abnegation and anonymity, and yet it opens the mind.

Entering the shadow, you find that things begin to glow with their own light. What Teilhard called the "within" of things begins to shine through. After a while, you experience strange reversals of perception. The indoor light begins to seem like darkness. The enlightenment promised by culture begins to seem like blindness. The luminosity of abstract thought becomes a blinding glare that exposes you, like jack-light, to hazards from the bush. And yet, gazing into that outer darkness, you hear no wailing or gnashing of teeth but only the whine of locusts on hot summer nights, the whir and click of small things pursuing their own ultimate concerns.

The gifts of darkness can be strange and wonderful. Several weeks after Elizabeth was born, Pam woke me at midnight. She had been nursing, walking the baby through the dark house to comfort her, when she happened to look out the window. The backyard trees were full of fireflies floating like sparks up to the topmost branches where they merged with the glitter of the stars. I told this story all over town, and no one had ever seen anything like it. Yet it's a common occurrence in early July. Now Pam and I never miss it, though our children are long since weaned and grown.

On other nights, we have seen Mars drifting like a ruby across the housetops, or Leonid meteors streaking like tracer bullets into the trees beyond the soccer field. We watched Comet Hale-Bopp from our front doorstep as it appeared like a plumed star over our neighbor's house. Although the ancients feared comets as portents of evil, we greeted the sight with wonder, as if an angel had chosen to step down and dance on our roof. We sat outside for more than an hour, chatting quietly with the neighbors as they drove in one by one. We did not go indoors until a cloud bank moved in and hid the comet from view.

Now, on my night walks, I think of comets, meteors, and galaxies even when the sky is obscured by smog or light pollution. I know the constellations are there, along with myriads of lesser, unnamed stars. I know, because I have been to the wilderness and seen what the night sky looks like at ten thousand feet in the High Sierra. I have floated in a canoe, perfectly still, at the center of a big lake in the Boundary Waters with a clear sky overhead and no city lights for a hundred miles. The whole visible universe seemed to be mirrored in the waters of earth. It felt as if we were sailing through the sky. Experiences like these, more than any sign or portent, remind me that deep heaven always shines for us, even when hidden by mists of our own making. That's one reason I still need the wilderness: it helps me to live by faith.

The people of old had two images for heaven: one was the walled garden of paradise, and the other was the sky. Just as they envisioned epic heroes sailing to the Hesperides or the Fortunate Isles, so too they imagined voyages to the moon, the planets, or the stars. Dante, whom Yeats called "the chief imagination of Christendom," lifted his pilgrim through the nine vast planetary spheres of the Ptolemaic universe, which, astronomers tell us, is still the most accurate model for what can be seen with the naked eye. The ancients had precise measurements for the sizes and distances of the heavenly bodies, just as we do. In the poem, when Dante enters the sphere of the fixed stars, he is 65 million miles from Earth and moving at 4,700 miles per second. He gazes back wonderingly at the home planet. From this distance, it's small enough for the Greek cosmologists to treat as a mathematical point, yet Dante sees it as a "little threshing floor" where souls are sifted and redeemed. With the clairvoyance of beatitude, his gaze wanders lovingly across the Mediterranean along the coasts of Italy and Spain. Then he turns once more to the stars.

Now even Dante's stupendous universe seems quaint, as we peer with orbiting telescopes into the farthest, most original depths of space and time. We have walked on the moon but found no paradise. We have sent robot probes to Mars, Jupiter, and beyond. We dream of following them with manned spacecraft. Humans, it seems, must always reach out toward heaven. Maybe it's just our drive for exploration and discovery, or some deep, genetic restlessness that spurs us, likewise, to creativity and art. Maybe it's simply a yearning to start over, to escape history, to rise above our own squalid limitations. Maybe we imagined heaven in the sky because we were awed by its wildness and splendor and believed we would never get there, even though now, of course, we do.

Astronauts report that space flight infuses them with a deep, religious awe. It is an extraordinary feeling to soar above the sky, beyond sunset and dawn, to cross the horizon at last and touch, with a tingling heart, the velvet, depthless immensity of space. You would think that the astronauts would spend every moment gazing out the portholes toward the most distant lights, those stars at the far end of imagination that have lured voyagers since the beginning of history. But they report that the most compelling sight of all is the earth itself, our own blue planet aswirl with clouds, rusty with deserts and smudged with rain forests—tiny, intricate, unique, and unmistakably alive.

Dante flung his imagination into the sky like a net of gems, hoping to catch the gleam of eternity. I often wonder what he would have thought of those first images sent back by Apollo. For all its aspiration, his great poem ends with the view from Earth, with the pilgrim gazing upward at the revolving stars. It's the view of a mortal man at the end of his time, worn out by his life's work and about to say good-bye. Dante's life had been marked by devastating loss: his love, his political career, his home, his country, his hopes for peace and justice in the world. He had to give up every attachment one by one, even nature and his own body, every-thing except the great story of learning and longing in which he had depicted heaven using simple, homely images from the earth: a coal glowing inside its coat of flame, dust motes dancing in a shaft of light, a white rose opening to the sun. If Dante had flown with Apollo, I am sure that he, too, would have looked back toward the earth, for everything he knew and loved was there.

I admit, it will be hard to leave. I love this green world alive with mysteries. What comes after nature? Yeats wrote that once out of nature, he would never take his bodily form from any natural thing. But I prefer John Muir, who confessed, "I only went out for a walk, but decided to stay out till sundown, for going out, I realized, was really going in." What is life but a walk between sunrise and sunset? I love morning work, but more and more I look forward to sundown, for it's then that the stars begin to appear, and they are always worth waiting for. They remind me that heaven consists of wildness: incomparable abundance, infinite play, continual creation. To Aquinas the variety of created beings merely testified to the infinite plenitude of God. What would eternity be, after all, without the productions of time?

Maybe that's why imagination always swings in a great parabolic arc back to our place of origin. The sky may be our focus of aspiration, but the earth is the focus of our love. Our bodies belong there. We have to leave them behind, wherever it is we go. Besides, no one really knows what heaven looks like. Even Jesus refused to describe it: how could he expect the disciples to believe what he said about heaven if they did not believe what he said about earth? I once asked my mother, who ponders these sorts of things, what she thought about heaven and earth, and she said that the older she got, the more this life seemed to her like that of a baby in the womb. Nine months, nine decades. At first you're all comfortable and protected; all your needs are met. But as time goes by, you grow bigger, stronger, more complicated. You start moving around, trying to stretch your limbs, pushing against the tough membranes that hold you in. You become aware of your mother's body. You start responding to sounds and light, dim signals from a vast, mysterious realm outside. Near the end, you begin to kick and squirm; you're ready to come out into the world your body has been prepared for. The womb, stretched tight by your own growth, feels stifling. You turn upside down; you feel tremendous pressure, strangling, painful, a surge of fear. And then, suddenly, you're out, gasping for breath, feeling air—spirit!—for the first time. It's terrifying, and yet it feels so right. Meanwhile, strong, loving hands take you up, wipe you off, wrap you in soft, warm blankets. You feel sweet, silky skin against your cheek. You close your eyes against the dazzling light.

They say that as death approaches, the veil between the worlds starts to grow thin. People report seeing old friends, parents, or grandparents gathering round. Sometimes these figures appear dim and shadowy, sometimes clothed in brightness, but people always know who they are. They talk to the dying, sometimes about whether it's time to leave. Some people also report the presence of angels, guardians who have stood by them all along without ever being noticed or acknowledged. It's hard to know what to make of such stories, but whenever I hear them, my mother's imagery rings true. Whatever heaven may be, I know that it must grow out of our earthly life.

I suspect, actually, that heaven is not a place at all, but a state of mind. We won't get there by sailing beyond the horizon or climbing a stair of fire on titanium wings. We will get there only by living this earthly life as best we can. We can't know what heaven looks like, but we already know what it feels like. We experience it in the wholeness, harmony, and radiance of old-growth forests, in marriages that have endured for five decades or more, in the shining faces of beautiful old people who have weathered catastrophe and betrayal without losing their capacity to love. One day we may wake up to discover that we have been living in heaven all along, at times when we felt completely playful, when we loved un-

conditionally, when we accepted a gift wholeheartedly, without calcula-
tion, when we noticed that streak of sunlight on a maple twig where,
incredibly, the first robin of spring was sitting.

Meanwhile time flows. Everything grows. The seasons arrive and de-
part. The trees succeed one another in the forest. Outside my window, a
white-throated sparrow pauses in one of my oaks on his way to the
Boundary Waters. Deep in my loins, a carbon and a nitrogen atom from
different stars clasp to form part of a protein that grows into part of my
daughter's body. One day she's romping through head-high grass; the
next day she says to me, "Dad, after college I want to live someplace
beautiful, like Colorado, not this crummy old city." How can I blame
her? I never wanted to live here either. In fact, I'm still trying to learn
how. But if Pam and I ever do leave, I hope it will be for as good a reason
as we came.

I never wanted to die in Cincinnati, Ohio. But what difference would it
make? The important thing is not where we die but how we live. Becoming native to a place is a labor of love and a life's work. It means stitching
your life to that of a place with a thread spun from mindfulness, attentiveness, husbandry, pilgrimage, and witness. Stories knit these compo-
nents of practice together. Flung outward, they clothe our relationships;
flung inward, they map the soul. Stories enable us to enter and dwell
attentively in a place; they enable us to travel and return, then eventually
to leave for good. We need stories to stay alive spiritually: without them
we would all turn into hungry ghosts. Stories are the only things we can
take with us out of this world. They are the wings that bear us up or the
chains that drag us down. In the end, it is stories that enable us to die.

I watch my children poised on the threshold of adventure, ready to
leap off into their own stories. I open my hands. My children shoot into
the sky like birds. I reach for my wife's hand, feeling the strong palm, the
delicate bones. I squeeze it gently, and its warmth runs up my arm. My
heart breaks, scatters, then slowly gathers together. I realize that it has
broken before, and that if it breaks often enough, it will someday become as fluid and clear as water. Some nights I lie awake remembering
my father's stories or listening to my mother's dreams. I rise and step out
the back door, into the planet's shadow where fireflies and comets wait.

Some nights the air is so fresh and clear that I can almost smell the sweetness of alpine meadows borne more than a thousand miles on the western wind. Then I dream of being able to walk anywhere in America without losing the spoor of wildness. I dream of a black-crowned night heron that drinks from the same creek as the human child. I dream of a sky unstained by the haze of enterprise and a night as dark and clear as the mind of God, where anyone on earth can glimpse the love that burns in the heart of the sun and the other stars.

NOTES

Seventh and Vine

Page 14, Gary Snyder develops the metaphor of the city as a sea anemone in his poem "Walking the New York Bedrock Alive in the Sea of Information," from *Mountains and Rivers without End* (Washington, DC: Counterpoint, 1996).

Page 17, Joseph Meeker develops the connection between biological time, robust ecological systems, and human redemption in *The Comedy of Survival* (Tucson: University of Arizona Press, 1997).

Page 17, I am indebted to Renée Roberts of the Union Institute and University Graduate College for information on the Benedictines and the invention of the mechanical clock (see her 1998 dissertation, "The Clock and the Rose: Time and Self-Transformation in *The Romance of the Rose* and *The Divine Comedy*," chap. 1).

Page 18, Erving Goffman explains his concept of the total institution in *Asylums: Essays on the Social Situation of Mental Patients and Other Inmates* (New York: Anchor Books, 1961), 4–5.

Page 22, For discussions of pastoralism and its effect on American culture, see Lawrence Buell, "Pastoral Ideology," in *The Environmental Imagination: Thoreau, Nature Writing, and the Formation of American Culture* (Cambridge, MA: Harvard University Press, 1993), 31–52; Leo Marx, *The Machine in the Garden: Technology and the Pastoral Ideal in America* (New York: Oxford Uni-versity Press, 1964); and Don Scheese, *Nature Writing: The Pastoral Impulse in America* (New York: Twayne Publishers, 1996), 1–38.

Page 22, George Williams argues that the design of New England colleges also reflects Edenic and military imagery from classical tradition: "It is within the Paradise Cycle that the college or university has at its center a *green*, symbol of paradise restored amidst the wilderness, [and] its *campus* for the training of the spiritual militia of Christ"; see *Wilderness and Paradise in Christian Thought* (New York: Harper, 1962), 211.

The Wild Within

Page 25, For discussions of the arms race as an addictive process, see Kurt Vonnegut, *Fates Worse Than Death* (New York: Putnam, 1991), 132–38; Gregory

Bateson, *Steps to an Ecology of Mind* (New York: Ballantine Books, 1973), 324; and John Tallmadge, "Therefore Choose Life: The Spiritual Challenge of the Nuclear Age," Pendle Hill Pamphlet 300 (Wallingford, PA: Pendle Hill Publications, 1991).

Page 25, The Inuit winter depression known as *perlerorneq* ("the weight of life") is described by Barry Lopez in *Arctic Dreams* (New York: Scribner's, 1986), 243.

Page 32, Loren Eiseley describes the "lime habit" behind our bone chemistry in *The Immense Journey* (New York: Random House, 1957), 6.

Page 32, Regarding the similarities between chlorophyll and hemoglobin, scientists have deduced that the parent pigment is probably cytochrome c, which occurs in the mitochondria of most organisms; all are involved in electron transfer and cellular energetics. For details, see Michael Onken (Washington University), "Re: Chlorophyll/hemoglobin," at http://www.madsci.org/posts/archives/dec96/846475225.Mb.r.html; see also "Chemical of the Week: Chlorophyll," at http://scifun.chem.wisc.edu/chemweek/CHLRPHYL/Chlrphyl.html.

Page 32, I am indebted to Dainin Katagiri Roshi of the Minneapolis Zen center for the image of a flower blooming with the whole spring behind it.

Invisible Landscapes

Page 38, Lopez describes a native hunter glassing a hillside in *Arctic Dreams*, 260–61.

Page 38, Richard Nelson's account of Koyukon hunting practices and natural history can be found in his book *Make Prayers to the Raven: A Koyukon View of the Northern Forest* (Chicago: University of Chicago Press, 1983).

Page 40, For information on the spread of domesticated food plants in North America, see Jared Diamond, *Guns, Germs, and Steel: The Fates of Human Societies* (New York: Norton, 1999), 151 and passim.

Page 40, For accounts of Native American use of fire as a land management tool, see William Cronon, *Changes in the Land: Indians, Colonists, and the Ecology of New England* (New York: Hill & Wang, 1983), 48; and Miron Heinselman, *The Boundary Waters Wilderness Ecosystem* (Minneapolis: University of Minnesota Press, 1996), 71.

Page 41, For conceptions of Paradise, see George H. Williams, *Wilderness and Paradise in Christian Thought* (New York: Harper, 1962); A. Bartlett Giamatti, *The Earthly Paradise and the Renaissance Epic* (Princeton, NJ: Princeton

University Press, 1966); Clarence J. Glacken, *Traces on the Rhodian Shore* (Berkeley, CA: University of California Press, 1967), chaps. 3, 5, and 7; and Mircea Eliade, *The Sacred and the Profane* (New York: Harper, 1961).

Starting from Home

Page 52, The fifth-century BC Roman general Lucius Quinctius Cincinnatus was renowned in antiquity as an epitome of civic virtue. He was working on his farm when the Senate, hearing that the Roman army was surrounded by invaders, appealed to him to assume dictatorial powers. He did so and defeated the invaders, but after sixteen days he gave up his powers to return to his farm. The story is told by Livy in his *History of Rome (Ab Urbe Condita)*, bk. 3, chaps. 26–29.

Page 52, For a vivid account of the frontier wars in Ohio, see Allan W. Eckert, *The Frontiersmen* (New York: Bantam Books, 1967).

Page 59, Bill McKibben's analysis of television can be found in *The Age of Missing Information* (New York: Random House, 1992).

Page 66, The word "therophilia," meaning "love of wildness," derives from the Greek *therion*, "wild animal," as in "theriomorph," "theropod," "uintathere"; the Greek shares the same Indo-European root with Latin *ferus*, "wild animal," from which we get "ferocious," "ferity," and "fierce," and the Old English *wilde* and *wildeor*, from which, of course, we get "wilderness." It cannot be mere coincidence that the woodchopper Thoreau describes in *Walden* was named Alex Therien.

A Matter of Scale

Page 71, The famous Jeffrey pine on Sentinel Dome in Yosemite was photographed several times by Ansel Adams and subsequently by many other amateur and professional photographers. It finally perished during the severe drought of 1976–77, but even in death its gaunt, skeletal form still compelled photographers until severe storms brought it to the ground in August 2003.

Alien Species

Page 94, Jared Diamond provides a lucid and wide-ranging analysis of the role of domesticated plants and animals in the evolution and spread of human cultures in *Guns, Germs, and Steel*; for additional authoritative discussion of alien species and the Columbian exchange, see Alfred W. Crosby, *Ecological Imperialism: The Biological Expansion of Europe, 900–1900* (Cambridge: Cambridge University Press, 1986); and George W. Cox, *Alien Species in North America and Hawaii: Impacts on Natural Ecosystems* (Washington, DC: Island Press, 1999).

Page 98, Michael Pollan's critique of lawns occurs in the chapter titled "Why Mow?" from his witty and illuminating book *Second Nature: A Gardener's Education* (New York: Atlantic Monthly Press, 1991).

Page 99, For information on Amur honeysuckle and its ecological history in North America, see J. O. Luken and J. W. Thieret, "Amur Honeysuckle: Its Fall from Grace," *Bioscience* 46 (1) (1996): 18–24; also Todd F. Hutchinson and John L. Vankat, "Invasibility and Effects of Amur Honeysuckle in Southwestern Ohio Forests," *Conservation Biology* 11 (5) (October 1997): 117–24.

Page 102, E. O. Wilson describes his biogeography experiments in *Naturalist* (Washington, DC: Island Press, 1994), 238–81.

Page 103, For the diffusion of corn, see Diamond, *Guns, Germs, and Steel*, 109, 151.

Page 103, For the "tens rule," see Cox, *Alien Species in North America and Hawaii*, 22.

Page 104, I am indebted to Stacy Alaimo for drawing my attention to grotesque cinematic representations of nature; see her essay "Discomforting Creatures: Monstrous Natures in Recent Films," in *Beyond Nature Writing: Expanding the Boundaries of Ecocriticism*, ed. Karla Armbruster and Kathleen Wallace (Charlottesville: University of Virginia Press, 2001), 279–96.

Page 108, The concept of nature has a long and problematic history; for details, see R. G. Collingwood, *The Idea of Nature* (Oxford: Clarendon Press, 1949); Clarence J. Glacken, *Traces on the Rhodian Shore*; and Michel Foucault's chapter on natural history, "Classifying," in *The Order of Things: An Archaeology of the Human Sciences* (New York: Vintage, 1973).

Old Growth

Page 114, Barry Lopez's reflections on stories and storytelling occur in his essay "Landscape and Narrative" in *Crossing Open Ground* (New York: Vintage, 1989).

Page 115, Forest scientist and explorer Robert Marshall was a founder of the

Wilderness Society, and his ideas were catalytic in the early days of the preservation movement; see his essay "The Problem of the Wilderness" in *The Scientific Monthly*, February 1930, 141–48.

Page 115, Saint Thomas Aquinas (1225–74) sought to build a systematic and universal philosophy by combining Christian doctrine with the ideas of Aristotle. His theological system provided the intellectual foundation for Dante's *Divine Comedy* as well as for most subsequent Catholic theology. Like many people, I first learned of his famous criteria for beauty from Stephen Dedalus, hero of James Joyce's novel *A Portrait of the Artist as a Young Man* (1916); in original form, they can be found in Thomas's *Summa Theologiae* 1.39.8c. For a thorough explanation of these ideas, see Umberto Eco, *The Aesthetics of Thomas Aquinas*, trans. Hugh Bredin (Cambridge, MA: Harvard University Press, 1988), 65 et seq. Thomas's Platonic conception of the world as a vast organism has interesting affinities with certain aspects of modern ecological thought (see Eco, *Aesthetics*, 89–93).

Page 117, With respect to changing views of succession and species distribution within ecosystems, see Donald Worster's history of ecological thought, *The Wealth of Nature: Environmental History and the Ecological Imagination* (New York: Oxford University Press, 1993), especially chap. 13, which recounts the struggle between the climax theory of Frederic Clements and the ecosystem model of Eugene Odum, on the one hand, and the individualistic, disturbance-based, and "chaotic" models of Henry Gleason, William Drury, and Ian Nisbet, on the other; the former posit a final state of equilibrium toward which all ecosystems naturally and inevitably tend, while the latter treat succession as a Darwinian process of chance and circumstance with no goal or direction.

Page 118, The pioneering fire-ecology studies conducted in northern Minnesota by Miron Heinselman and his colleagues are described in his *Boundary Waters Wilderness Ecosystem*.

Page 119, The notion of a "conversation of death" between predator and prey is elaborated by Barry Lopez in *Of Wolves and Men* (New York: Scribners, 1978), 94–95.

Page 121, For Zen wisdom and the beginner's mind, see Shunryu Suzuki, *Zen Mind, Beginner's Mind* (New York: Weatherhill, 1980), 46–48; for the artless art, see Eugen Herrigel, *Zen in the Art of Archery*, trans. R. F. C. Hull (New York: Vintage, 1971), 69–74.

Page 125, James P. Carse's ideas on play are elaborated in *Finite and Infinite Games* (New York: Ballantine, 1986).

Page 126, Thomas Berry's beautiful image of mutually enhancing presence occurs in *The Great Work: Our Way into the Future* (New York: Bell Tower, 1999).

Page 127, For Gary Paul Nabhan's observations on biodiversity in desert oases, see *The Desert Smells like Rain: A Naturalist in Papago Indian Country* (San Francisco: North Point Press, 1982), chap. 7.

Page 127, For Darrell Addison Posey's account of sustainable indigenous horticulture in Amazonia, see "The Science of the Mebêngôkre" in *Finding Home: Writing on Nature and Culture from* Orion *Magazine*, ed. Peter Sauer (Boston: Beacon Press, 1991), 135–48.

Escalante

Page 134, Ed Abbey's depiction of the Escalante, with photographs by Philip Hyde, can be found in *Slickrock: Endangered Canyons of the Southwest* (San Francisco: Sierra Club; New York: Scribners, 1971).

Page 135, For a comprehensive and lyrical account of the Escalante's human and natural history with information on current ecological, political, and recreational issues, see Thomas Lowe Fleischner, *Singing Stone: A Natural History of the Escalante Canyons* (Salt Lake City: University of Utah Press, 1999).

Page 135, Historian, photographer, and activist Thomas H. Watkins was for many years editor of *The Living Wilderness*, quarterly journal of the Wilderness Society; a prolific author, he wrote movingly about the canyon country on numerous occasions, for example, in *Stone Time, Southern Utah: A Portrait and a Meditation* (Santa Fe, NM: Clear Light Publishers, 1994) and *The Redrock Chronicles: Saving Wild Utah* (Baltimore: Johns Hopkins University Press, 2000).

Page 153, The classic study of the origin of the natural sublime and the effect of seventeenth-century technology on the imagination is Marjorie Hope Nicholson's *Mountain Gloom and Mountain Glory: The Development of the Aesthetics of the Infinite* (New York: Norton, 1963); for the aesthetics and social importance of nineteenth-century American landscape painting, see Barbara Novak, *Nature and Culture: American Landscape and Painting, 1825–1875* (New York: Oxford University Press, 1980).

Page 162, Gary Snyder's interview comment about Cincinnati appeared in *The Ohio Review* (Fall 1977), 75.

A Small Piece of Land

Page 177, My information on the ecological history of New England is drawn from William Cronon's *Changes in the Land*.

Page 181, The line from Jorge Luis Borges's poem "Limits (or Goodbyes)" as translated by Alan Dugan is quoted from *Selected Poems, 1923–1967* (New York: Delacorte Press, 1972), 237.

Dante's River

Page 189, Information about Cincinnati's municipal water supply is publicly available from the Greater Cincinnati Water Works Web site (http://www.cincinnati-oh.gov/water/pages/-3026-/); my facts and figures were drawn from their "Water Quality Report" for 2000.

Page 189, For hydrologic information on Walden Pond, see John A. Coleman and Paul J. Friesz, *Geohydrology and Limnology of Walden Pond, Concord, Massachusetts* (us Geological Survey: Water-Resources Investigations Report 01-4137, available: http://water.usgs.gov/pubs/wri/wri014137/).

Page 193, For a lively and detailed account of the human and natural history of the Mill Creek watershed, see Stanley Hedeen, *The Mill Creek: An Unnatural History of an Urban Stream* (Cincinnati: Blue Heron Press, 1994). Information on the Mill Creek Restoration Project is available from its Web site, http://www.millcreekrestoration.org.

Staying till Sundown

Page 209, For the history of the word "paradise," see Giamatti, *Earthly Paradise and the Renaissance Epic*, 11–15.

Page 210, Images of the earth at night are available on the NASA Web site:http://earthobservatory.nasa.gov/Newsroom/NewImages/images.php3?img_id=4333.

Page 210, For sobering figures on worldwide light pollution and the obscuring of the Milky Way, see P. Cinzano, F. Falchi, and C. Elvidge, "The First World Atlas of the Artificial Night Sky Brightness," *Monthly Notices of the Royal Astronomical Society* 328 (2001), 689–707 (available at http://www.lightpollution.it/worldatlas/pages/fig1.htm).

Page 211, Pierre Teilhard de Chardin argued that evolution and its productions revealed a dimension of reality that he called the "within" of things; this capacity, which gave rise to the emergent properties observed in systems of increasing complexity, was not directly observable as were the phenomena studied by empirical science; see *The Phenomenon of Man* (New York: Harper & Row, 1965), 53–66.

Page 213, I am indebted to Professor Noel Swerdlow of the University of Chicago for introducing me to the Ptolemaic figures for distances to the planets and dramatizing their implications for Dante's poem; see also O. Neugebauer, *The Exact Sciences in Antiquity* (New York: Dover Books, 1969), 191–207.